FIRST EDITION

SOCIAL JUSTICE MOVEMENTS

LA DELLA L. LEVY M.A., M.ED.

COLLEGE OF SOUTHERN NEVADA

cognella® | ACADEMIC PUBLISHING

Bassim Hamadeh, CEO and Publisher
Mark Nagy, Custom Project Editor
Gem Rabanera, Project Editor
Christian Berk, Associate Production Editor
Miguel Macias, Senior Graphic Designer
Stephanie Kohl, Licensing Coordinator
Natalie Piccotti, Senior Marketing Manager
Kassie Graves, Director of Acquisitions
Jamie Giganti, Senior Managing Editor

Cover image Copyright © 2015 iStockphoto LP/funky-data.

Printed in the United States of America.

ISBN: 978-1-5165-2394-8 (pbk) / 978-1-5165-2395-5 (br)

SOCIAL JUSTICE MOVEMENTS

CONTENTS

INTRODUCTION

The role of the artist in social justice protest is immeasurable. Historically, artists of various forms have pushed the envelope and moved society in a direction of political and social change. Music has been the most significant vehicle for revolution. Visual art and poetic art form have provided the road map for social directional shifts, causing society to examine its structural norms and pathways for justice. According to civil rights activist and artist Harry Belafonte, "artists are the gatekeepers of truth. We are civilization's anchor. We are the compass for humanity's conscious." Belafonte also states a universal truth that "art in its highest form is art that serves and instructs society and human development."

This anthology is largely inspired by historical events and protest movements that have transcended human consciousness and moved society in a global directional shift that has changed our humanity and evolution as a species. The readings have been carefully selected to enhance the discussion and knowledge of the reader toward their understanding of how artists have shaped and inspired social justice protests movements. The text examines various political movements for social, political, economic justice, and subsequent impact on existing political and social structures. This text serves to enhance the discussion concerning the theoretical framework of governance and the reality experienced by those who exist on the periphery of society: women, ethnic minorities, people of color, and those who have been historically marginalized. Their experience in the process of governance has been uniquely disrupted by systemic oppression socially, economically, and politically. Institutional mechanisms manifested in the form of institutionalized racism have hindered citizens' pursuit of justice in this nation. However uniquely impactful there have been social justice protest movements that have also served to change American Public Policy and subsequent laws in order to fully protect democratic ideals. This is the subject of discourse in this anthology / reader. This text can be used in any political science or interdisciplinary postsecondary course.

The corresponding course that I created for the first edition of this anthology is titled: The Role of the Artist in Social Justice Movements. The text and the course examine the role of artists who have used various instruments of justice to help advance political and social change by utilizing the tools of transformation of consciousness, either through their music, film, poetry or other visual art forms. These tools were the artist instruments of justice. The anthology also shows the impact of everyday citizen activists in social justice protest movements. This anthology is designed to analyze historical social justice protest movements from the 1960s birth of the free-speech movement, the civil rights movement, the women's liberation feminist movement, to the recent economic inequality protest movements. The anthology makes a close study of the impact each movement has had on the evolution of human consciousness, resultant social structures, cultural norms, and subsequent public policy creation. This text also provides a framework analysis of even more recent social justice protest movements, such as the occupy Wall Street social justice protest movement and the women's rights protest that preceded the election of our forty-fifth President, Donald Trump.

This anthology is organized around three integral time frames of social justice protest movements covering the twentieth and twenty-first century social justice protests. I have selected movements centered on economic inequality, social and racial inequality, to a further examination of gender and political inequality. The first set of readings is centered around a theme titled, Historical Narratives. These readings address the historical context of systematically marginalized groups and significantly impactful social justice protest movements. These protest movements are ongoing and include the civil rights movement, the women's feminist liberation movement, the black liberation movement and other social conscious transformation, political and economic justice protest movements.

The second set of readings is centered around a theme titled, Transitional

Narratives—Twenty-First Century Protest Agenda. These readings address social justice protest movements that have been ushered in by previous movements and have become our twenty-first century human rights initiative. In this global diasporic protest initiative, there is a transference of knowledge, power, and activism through the instantaneous exchange of information via the World Wide Web. Activism and organizing for political transformation and power redistribution often historically took years or decades; however, it would in the twenty-first century age of technology take months or even weeks to organize activists across the globe to organize movements for social justice, economic reform and political equality. Fragmented groups and activists saw a unifying moment with the newfound ease of organizing and disseminating knowledge provided by the World Wide Web. Knowledge became the source of power, unifying groups and creating a source of coalition building. This transitional moment has produced a unifying and universal element of human rights protest advanced by these new millennium social protest activists.

The third set of readings deals with the theme titled Revolutionary Narratives—The Seeds of Change: The Personal is Political. This last set of readings is inspired by prominent feminist activist Betty Friedan whose impactful text, *The Feminine Mystique* revealed that the personal is political and conveys the significant impact that we as individual citizens have on the timeline of social and revolutionary change. What we do in our private lives has significant political implications and consequences. These readings are designed to convey our ability to navigate civil society and actively embrace our role as citizen activists. This is at the very core of our democracy, and it is the essence of our ability as citizens to be empowered for social change. The term revolutionary is often applied to disruptive moments in history that have proven to be destabilizing to governments and systems of organization. However, in this revolutionary moment that has changed the role of social movements and defined what it means to be a citizen a new narrative is emerging. Governments are being held accountable for ensuring governance to all its citizens. An engaged, fully conscious electorate is demanding that accountability. The occupy movement demonstrated this conscious raising citizen activism, demanding of our government to be legitimate and equitable to all its citizens.

In each movement for social justice and political transformation, artists, community activists, and ordinary citizens have been integral in their role in facilitating changes in our democracy and advancing the cause of economic, political, and social equality. The artist's impact in these protest movements through his or her musical lyricism, visual film, and poetic rhyme is undeniable. A close study of various artists and protest movements that have been impactful and contributed to the American pursuit of justice by using their unique art form as a tool for social change will be conducted in this reader. This book is dedicated to my students with whom I have had the privilege of teaching over the past sixteen years. You have inspired me, awakened my consciousness, and quickened my spirit to the impact of artists and their significance in incubating protest movements. From Maya Angelou and James Baldwin to Nina Simone, Tupac and Marvin Gaye each have shaped, awakened, and inspired our consciousness by stirring and birthing a protest agenda.

Civil rights activist and artist Paul Robeson summarizes most accurately the role of artist and protest movements—"Artists are the gate keepers of truth. We are civilization's radical voice."

Professor La Della L. Levy M.A, M.Ed—Political Science Professor College of
Southern Nevada

PRE-UNIT REFLECTION QUESTIONS

After each unit, the reader should be able to critically analyze and engage these three core points (Note: Base your answers strictly on the reading and current events related to the readings in the text.):

1. Based on the readings, please provide and analyze in detail three ways in which policy changes need to occur in order to break up concentrated wealth in the United States, thus reducing economic inequality and class based economic stratification.

2. Based on the readings, please explain how social protest movements change American public policy. How does transformation of consciousness initiate social, political, and subsequent economic change. How and why does culture inaugurate and yet resist social justice policy implementation?

3. Explain how the concept of intersectionality is demonstrated in the readings from this section. Think about how this intersectionality impacts women of color, participants in the women's liberation movement, oppressed people, and other marginalized groups who exist at the periphery of society seeking economic, political, and social justice. How do institutions provide the seeds of change and also the tools of systematic oppression? Refer back to the reading "Intersecting Oppressions: Rethinking Women's Movements in the United States," and revisit this quote of "how individuals are socially located in the middle of crosscutting systems of oppression that form mutually constructing features of social organization."

HISTORICAL NARRATIVES: VOICES OF THE OPPRESSED

Bold Rule Changes to Break Up Concentrated Wealth

In a world of increasing in equality, the legitimacy of institutions that give precedence to the property rights of "the Haves" over the human rights of "the Have Nots" is inevitably called into serious question.

—David Korten (1937)

We must change the rules of the economy so that they serve and lift up the 100 percent, not just the 1 percent. Starting in the mid-1970s, the rules were changed to reorient the economy toward the short-term interests of the 1 percent. We can shift and reverse the rules to work for everyone.

THREE TYPES OF RULE CHANGES

There are three categories of policy changes that we need: rules and policies that raise the floor, those that level the playing field, and those that break up overconcentrations of wealth and corporate power. These are not hard-and-fast categories, but a useful framework for grouping different rule changes.

1. Rule changes that raise the floor
   - Ensure the minimum wage is a living wage
   - Provide universal health care
   - Enforce basic labor standards and protections
2. Rule changes that level the playing field
   - Invest in education
   - Reduce the influence of money in politics
   - Implement fair trade rules
3. Rule changes that break up wealth and power
   - Tax the 1 percent
   - Rein in CEO pay
   - Stop corporate tax dodging
   - Reclaim our financial system
   - Reengineer the corporation
   - Redesign the tax revenue system

Figure 1.1

Three types of rule changes to reduce in equality.

RULE CHANGES THAT RAISE THE FLOOR

Policies that raise the floor reduce poverty and establish a fundamental minimum standard of decency that no one will fall below. The Nordic countries—Norway, Sweden, Denmark, and Finland—have very low levels of in equality, and they are also societies with strong social safety nets and policies that raise the floor.

One-third of people in the United States have no paid sick days, and one-half have no paid vacation days. Everyone deserves the right to take time off when sick and have a few weeks of vacation each year. In the rest of the developed world, these are considered basic human rights.

Examples of rule changes include:

Ensure the Minimum Wage Is a Living Wage. The minimum wage has lagged behind rising basic living expenses in housing, health care, transportation, and child care.

Provide Universal Health Care. Expand health coverage so that every child and adult has a minimum level of decent health care. No one should become sick or destitute because of lack of access to health care.

Enforce Basic Labor Standards and Protections. Ensuring basic worker rights and standards can lift up the bottom 20 percent of workers who are particularly exploited and disadvantaged in the current system. These rule changes include the forty-hour workweek, minimum vacation and family medical leave, sick leave, and protections against wage theft. Such rules contribute to a more humane society for everyone.

RULE CHANGES THAT LEVEL THE PLAYING FIELD

Policies and rule changes that level the playing field eliminate the unfair wealth and power advantages that flow to the 1 percent. Examples include:

Invest in Education. In the current global economy, disparities in education reinforce and contribute to in equality trends. Public investment in education is one of the most important interventions we can make to reduce in equality over time. "Widespread education has become the secret to growth," writes World Bank economist Branko Milanovic. "And broadly accessible education is difficult to achieve unless a society has a relatively even income distribution."[1]

Reduce the Influence of Money in Politics. Through various campaign finance reforms—including public financing of elections—we can reduce the nexus between gigantic wealth and political influence. Reforms include limits to campaign contributions, a ban on corporate contributions and influence, and a requirement for timely disclosure of donations.

Implement Fair Trade Rules. Most international free trade treaties have boosted the wealth of the 1 percent, whose members are the largest shareholders of global companies. Free trade rules often pit countries against one another in a race to lower standards addressing child labor, environmental protection, workers' rights to organize, and corporate regulation. Countries with the weakest standards are rewarded in this system. Fair trade rules would raise environmental and labor standards, so companies compete on the basis of other efficiencies.

RULE CHANGES THAT BREAK UP WEALTH AND POWER

We can raise the floor and work toward a level playing field, but we cannot stop the perverse effects of extreme in equality without boldly advocating for policies that break up excessive concentrations of wealth and corporate power.

None of the raise-the-floor and level-the-playing-field rule changes and policy adjustments described above will succeed unless we directly tackle the great imbalance of wealth and power.

For example, we cannot pass campaign finance laws that seek clever ways to limit the influence of the 1 percent, as they will always find ways to subvert the law. Concentrated wealth is like water flowing downhill: it cannot stop itself from influencing the political system. The only way to fix the system is to not have such high levels of concentrated wealth. We need to level the hill!

This section examines several far-reaching policy initiatives, the tough changes that have to be considered if we're going to reverse extreme in equality. Some of these proposals have been off the public agenda for de cades or have never been seriously considered.

Tax the 1 Percent. Historically, taxing the 1 percent is one of the most important rule changes that have reduced the concentration of wealth. In 1915, Congress passed laws instituting federal income taxes and inheritance taxes (estate taxes). Over the subsequent decades, these taxes helped reduce the concentrations of income and wealth and even encouraged Gilded Age mansions to be turned over to civic groups and charities.[2]

Taxes on higher income and wealth reached their zenith in the mid-1950s. At the time, the incomes of millionaires were taxed at rates over 91 percent. Today, the percentage of income paid by millionaires in taxes has plummeted to 21 percent. Back then, corporations contributed a third of the nation's revenue. Today, corporations pay less than one-tenth of the nation's revenue. The corporate 1 percent pays an average of 11.1 percent of income in taxes, down from 47.4 percent in 1961.[3]

Taxes on the wealthy have steadily declined over the last fifty years. If the 1 percent paid taxes at the same actual effective rate as they did in 1961, the U.S. Treasury would receive an additional $231 billion a year.[4] In 2009, the most recent year for which data are available, 1,500 millionaires paid no income taxes, largely because they dodged taxes through offshore tax schemes, according to the IRS.[5]

As with in equality, the higher up the income ladder people are, the lower the percentage of income they pay in taxes. This is why Warren Buffett's disclosure about his own low taxes was so important. Buffett revealed that in 2010, he paid only 14 percent of his income in federal taxes, lower than the 25 or 30 percent rate that his co-workers paid. Buffett wrote:

> While the poor and middle class fight for us in Afghanistan, and while most Americans struggle to make ends meet, we mega-rich continue to get our extraordinary tax breaks. Some of us are investment managers who earn billions from our daily labors but are allowed to classify our income as "carried interest," thereby getting a bargain 15 percent tax rate. Others own stock index futures for 10 minutes and have 60 percent of their gain taxed at 15 percent, as if they'd been long-term investors.
>
> These and other blessings are showered upon us by legislators in Washington who feel compelled to protect us, much as if we were spotted owls or some other endangered species. It's nice to have friends in high places.

The richest 400 taxpayers have seen their effective rate decline from over 40 percent in 1961 to 18.1 percent in 2010.[6]

Between 2001 and 2010, the United States borrowed almost $1 trillion to give tax breaks to the 1 percent. The 2001 and 2003 tax cuts passed under President George W. Bush were highly targeted to the top 1 and 2 percent of taxpayers. They included reducing the top income tax rate, cutting capital gains and dividend taxes, and eliminating the estate tax, our nation's only levy on inherited wealth.

Are we focusing too much on taxing millionaires, given the magnitude of our fiscal and in equality problems? Won't we have to raise taxes more broadly?[7] It is true that taxing the 1 percent won't entirely solve our nation's short-term deficit problems or dramatically reduce in equality in the short run. But it will have a meaningful impact on both problems over time. Thirty years of tax cuts for the 1 percent have shifted taxes onto middle-income taxpayers; they have also added to the national debt, which simply postpones additional tax increases on the middle class. Progressive taxes, as were seen in the United States after World War I and during the Great Depression, do chip away at inequalities. These extreme inequalities weren't built in a day, and the process of reversing them will not be instant, either. But when there is less concentrated income and wealth, there will be less money available for the 1 percent to use to undermine the political rule-making process.

Rein in CEO Pay. The CEOs of the corporate 1 percent are among the main drivers of the Wall Street in equality machine. They both push for rule changes to enrich the 1 percent and extract huge amounts of money for themselves in the process. But they are responding to a framework of rules that provide incentives to such short-term thinking. An early generation of CEOs operated within different rules and values—and they had a longer-term orientation.[8]

There is a wide range of policies and rule changes that could address the skewed incentive system that results in reckless corporate behavior and excessive executive pay. What follows are several principles and examples of reforms that will reduce concentrated wealth among the 1 percent and also reform corporate practices:

- *Encourage narrower CEO-worker pay gaps.* Extreme pay gaps—situations where top executives regularly take home hundreds of times more in compensation than average employees—run counter to basic principles of fairness. These gaps also endanger enterprise effectiveness. Management guru Peter Drucker, echoing the view of Gilded Age financier J. P. Morgan, believed that the ratio of pay between worker and executive could run no higher than twenty to one without damaging company morale and productivity.[9] Researchers have documented that Information Age enterprises operate more effectively when they tap into and reward the creative contributions of employees at *all* levels.[10]

An effective policy would mandate reporting on CEO-worker pay gaps. The 2010 Dodd-Frank financial reform legislation included a provision that would require companies to report the ratio between CEO pay and the median pay for the rest of their employees. This simple reporting provision is under attack, but should be defended, and the pay ratio should become a key benchmark for evaluating corporate performance.[11]

- *Eliminate taxpayer subsidies for excessive executive pay.* Ordinary taxpayers should not have to foot the bill for excessive executive compensation. And yet they do—through a variety of tax and accounting loopholes that encourage executive pay excess. These perverse incentives add up to more than $20 billion per year in forgone revenue.[12] One example: no meaningful regulations currently limit how much companies can deduct from their taxes for the expense of executive compensation. Therefore, the more firms pay their CEO, the more they can deduct off their federal taxes.

An effective policy would limit the deductibility of excessive compensation. The Income-Equity Act (HR 382) would deny all firms tax deductions on any executive pay that runs over twenty-five times the pay of the firm's lowest-paid employee or $500,000, whichever is higher. Companies can pay what ever they want, but over a certain amount, taxpayers shouldn't have to subsidize it. Such deductibility caps were applied to financial bailout recipient firms and will be applied to health insurance companies under the health care reform legislation.

- *Encourage reasonable limits on total compensation.* The greater the annual reward an executive can receive, the greater the temptation to make reckless executive decisions that generate short-term earnings at the expense of long-term corporate health. Outsized CEO paychecks have also become a major drain on corporate revenues, amounting, in one recent period, to nearly 10 percent of total corporate earnings.[13] Government can encourage more reasonable compensation levels without having to micromanage pay levels at individual firms.

An effective policy would raise top marginal tax rates. As discussed earlier, taxing high incomes at higher rates might be the most effective way to deflate bloated pay levels. In the 1950s and 1960s, compensation stayed within more reasonable bounds, in part because of the progressive tax system.

- *Force accountability to shareholders.* On paper, the corporate boards that determine executive pay levels must answer to shareholders. In practice, shareholders have had virtually no say in corporate executive pay decisions. Recent reforms have made some progress toward forcing corporate boards to defend before shareholders the rewards they extend to corporate officials.

An effective policy would give shareholders a binding voice on compensation packages. The Dodd-Frank reform includes a provision for a nonbinding resolution on compensation and retirement packages.

- *Accountability to broader stakeholders.* Executive pay practices, we have learned from the run-up to the 2008 financial crisis, impact far more than just shareholders. Effective pay reforms need to encourage management decisions that take into account the interests of all corporate stakeholders, not just shareholders but also consumers, employees, and the communities where corporations operate.

An effective policy would ensure wider disclosure by government contractors. If a company is doing business with the government, it should be held to a higher standard of disclosure. Taxpayers, workers, and consumers should know the extent to which our tax dollars subsidize top management pay. One policy change would be to pass the Patriot Corporations Act to extend tax incentives and federal contracting preferences to companies that meet good-behavior benchmarks that include not compensating any executive at more than 100 times the income of the company's lowest-paid worker.[14]

Stop Corporate Tax Dodging. There are hundreds of large transnational corporations that pay no or very low corporate income taxes. These include Verizon, General Electric, Boeing, and Amazon. A common gimmick of the corporate 1 percent is to shift profits to subsidiaries in low-tax or no-tax countries such as the Cayman Islands. They pretend corporate profits pile up offshore while their losses accrue in the United States, reducing or eliminating their company's obligation to Uncle Sam.

These same companies, however, use our public infrastructure—they hire workers trained in our schools, they depend on the U.S. court system to protect their property, and our military defends their assets around the world—yet they're not paying their share of the bill. In a time of war, the unequal sacrifice and tax shenanigans of these companies are even more unseemly.

Corporate tax dodging hurts Main Street businesses, the 99 percent that are forced to compete on a playing field that isn't level. "Small businesses are the lifeblood of local economies," said Frank Knapp, CEO of the South Carolina Small Business Chamber of Commerce. "We pay our fair share of taxes and generate most of the new jobs. Why should we be subsidizing U.S. transnationals that use offshore tax havens to avoid paying taxes?"[15]

This same offshore system facilitates criminal activity, from the laundering of drug money to the financing of terrorist networks. Smugglers, drug cartels, and even terrorist networks such as al-Qaeda thrive in secret offshore jurisdictions where individuals can hide or obscure the ownership of bank accounts and corporations to avoid any reporting or government oversight.[16]

The offshore system has spawned a massive tax-dodging industry. Teams of tax lawyers and accountants add nothing to the efficiency of markets or products. Instead of making a better widget, companies invest in designing a better tax scam. Reports about General Electric's storied tax dodging dramatize how modern transnationals view their tax accounting departments as profit centers.[17]

The combination of federal bud get concerns and a growing public awareness of corporate tax avoidance will lead to greater focus on legislative solutions. One strategic rule change would be for Congress to pass the Stop Tax Haven Abuse Act, which would end costly tax games that are harmful to domestic U.S. businesses and workers and blatantly unfair to those who pay their fair share of taxes.

One provision of the act would treat foreign subsidiaries of U.S. corporations whose management and control are primarily in the United States as U.S. domestic corporations for income tax purposes. Another provision would require country-by-country reporting so that transnational corporations would have to disclose tax payments in all jurisdictions and not easily be able to pit countries against one another.[18]

The act would generate an estimated $100 billion in revenues a year, or $1 trillion over the next decade.

Reclaim Our Financial System. Wall Street and the top 1 percent have conducted a danger-ous experiment on our lives. They have destroyed the livelihoods of billions of people around the planet in a bid to control the financial flows of the world and funnel money to the global 1 percent.

We sometimes forget that our financial sector is a human-created system that should serve the public interest and be subordinate to the credit needs of the real economy. Instead, we have a system where the planet is ruled by a tiny 1 percent of financial capital.

As quoted earlier, David Korten writes in "How to Liberate America from Wall Street Rule" that the "priority of the money system shifted from funding real investment for building com-munity wealth to funding financial games designed solely to enrich Wall Street without the burden of producing anything of value."[19]

Communities across the country, as discussed earlier, are shifting funds out of the specu-lative banking sector and into community banks and lending institutions that are constructive lenders in the real economy.

More than 650,000 individuals have closed accounts at institutions such as Bank of America and moved their money. A number of religious congregations, unions, and civic organizations have followed suit. Now local governments are beginning to shift their funds. In the City of Boston, the City Council has voted to link deposits of public funds to institutions with strong commitments to community investments.[20]

Here are some interventions to break Wall Street's hold on our banking and money system.[21]

- *Break up the big banks.* Reverse the thirty-year process of banking concentration and support a system of decentralized, community-accountable financial institutions com-mitted to meeting the real credit needs of local communities. Limit the size of financial institutions to several billion dollars, and eliminate government preferences and subsidies to Wall Street's too-big-to-fail banks in favor of the 15,000 community banks and credit unions that are already serving local markets.

- *Create a network of state-level banks.* Each state should have a partnership bank, similar to what's been in place in North Dakota since 1919. These banks would hold government funds and private deposits and partner with community-based banks and other financial institutions to provide credit to enterprises and projects that contribute to the health of the local economy. The North Dakota experience has shown how a state bank can provide stability and curb speculative trends. North Dakota has more local banks than any other state and the lowest bank default rate in the nation.

- *Create a national infrastructure and reconstruction bank.* Instead of channeling Federal Reserve funds into private Wall Street banks, Congress should establish a federal bank to invest in public infrastructure and partner with other financial institutions to invest in reconstruction projects. The focus should be on investments that help make a transition to a green, sustainable economy.

- *Provide rigorous oversight of the financial sector.* The 2010 reforms to the financial sector failed to curtail some of the most destructive, gambling-oriented practices in the economy. The shadow banking system—including unregulated hedge funds—should be brought under greater oversight, like other utilities, and Congress should levy a financial speculation tax on transactions to pay for the oversight system.

- *Restructure the federal reserve.* The Federal Reserve has been creating money and channeling it to beneficiaries within the economy with no public accountability. The Fed contributed to the economic meltdown by failing to provide proper oversight for financial institutions under its jurisdiction, keeping easy credit flowing during an asset bubble, ignoring community banks, and then propping up bad financial actors. The Fed must be reorganized to be an in de pen dent federal agency with proper oversight and accountability. Its regulatory functions should be separated from its central bank functions, the new regulator given teeth to enforce rules, and individuals who work for the regulatory agency prevented from subsequently going to work for banks.

Reengineer the Corporation. The concentration of power in the corporate 1 percent has endangered our economy, our democracy, and the health of our planet. There is no alternative but to end corporate rule. This will require not only reining in and regulating the excesses of the corporate 1 percent but also rewiring the corporation as we know it.

Unfortunately, the Supreme Court's *Citizens United* (2010) decision moves things in the wrong direction, giving corporations greater "free speech" rights to use their wealth and power to change the rules of the economy. An essential first step in shifting the balance back to the 99 percent is reversing the *Citizens United* decision through congressional action.

There are good and ethical human beings working in corporations and in the 1 percent. But the hardwiring of these companies is toward the maximization of profits for absentee shareholders and toward reducing and shifting the cost of employees, taxes, and environmental rules that shrink profits. The current design of large global corporations enables them to dodge responsibilities and obligations to stakeholders, including employees, localities, and the ecological commons. The corporate 1 percent may pledge loyalty to the rule of law, but they spend an inordinate amount of resources lobbying to reshape or circumvent these laws, often by moving operations to other countries and to secrecy jurisdictions.

At the root of the problem is a power imbalance. Concentrated corporate power is unaccountable—and there is little countervailing force in the form of government oversight or organized consumer power.

Looking at corporate scandals such as those of Enron and AIG, or at the roots of the 2008 economic meltdown, we find case studies of the rule riggers within the corporate 1 percent using political clout to rewrite government rules, dilute accounting standards, intimidate or co-opt government regulators, or outright lie, cheat, and steal.

Changing the rules for the corporate 1 percent is not anti-business and, by creating a level playing field and a framework of fair rules, will actually strengthen the 99 percent of businesses that most contribute to our healthy economy. A new alignment of business organizations reflects this. The American Sustainable Business Council is an alternative to the U.S. Chamber of Commerce and advocates for high-road policies that will build a durable economy with broad prosperity.[22]

Communities have used a wide range of strategies to assert rights and power in relation to corporations. In 2007, the Strategic Corporate Initiative published an overview of these strategies in a report called "Toward a Global Citizens Movement to Bring Corporations Back Under Control." Many strategies are incremental, but worth understanding as part of the lay of the land in rule changes.[23]

- *Engage in consumer action.* As stakeholders, consumers have leverage to change corporate behavior. Examples include consumer boycotts that changed Nestlé's unethical infant formula marketing campaigns around the world and softened the hardball anti-worker tactics of companies such as textile giant J. P. Stevens. New technologies are enabling consumers to be more sophisticated in leveraging their power to force companies to treat employees and the environment better.[24]

- *Promote socially responsible investing.* Shareholders can also exercise power by avoiding investments in socially injurious corporations. In 2010, over $3 trillion in investments were managed with ethical criteria.[25] Companies do change some behaviors when concerned about their reputations.

- *Use shareholder power for the common good.* For more than forty years, socially concerned religious and secular organizations have utilized the shareholder process to change corporate behavior and management practices. Shareholder resolutions, in conjunction with educational and consumer campaigns, have altered corporate behavior, such as the movement to pressure U.S. companies to stop doing business in South Africa during the apartheid era.

- *Change rules inside corporations to foster accountability.* There are internal changes in corporate governance that potentially could broaden accountability and corporate responsibility. These include:

  - *Shareholder power reforms.* Presently, there are many barriers to the exercise of real shareholder ownership power and oversight. Corporations should have real governance elections, not handpicked slates that rubber-stamp management decisions.
  - *Board independence.* Public corporations should have in de pendent boards free of cozy insider connections. This will enable them to hold management properly accountable.
  - *Community rights.* Communities should have greater power to require corporate disclosure about taxes, subsidies, treatment of workers, and environmental practices, including use of toxic chemicals.

- *Require federal corporate charters.* Most U.S. corporations are chartered at the state level, and a number of states, including Delaware, have such low accountability requirements that they are home to thousands of global companies. But corporations above a certain size that operate across state and international boundaries should be subject to a federal charter.

- *Define stakeholder governance.* A federal charter could define the governing board of a corporation to include representation of all major stakeholders, including consumers, employees, localities where the company operates, and organizations representing environmental interests. The German experience with co-determination includes boards with community and employee representation.

- *Ban corporate influence in our democracy.* Corporations should be prohibited from any participation in our democratic systems, including elections, funding of candidates, political parties, party conventions, and advertising aimed at influencing the outcome of elections and legislation. This would require legislation to reverse the impact of the Supreme Court's *Citizens United* decision.

CITIZENS UNITED AND CORPORATE POWER

In January 2010, the U.S. Supreme Court decided the case known as *Citizens United v. Federal Election Commission.* It gave new rights of free speech to corporations by saying that governments could not restrict independent spending by corporations and unions for political purposes. This opened the door for new election-related campaign spending and has given birth to super PACs that further erode the power of the 99 percent to influence national politics.

Senator Charles Schumer (D-N.Y.) sponsored legislation called the DISCLOSE Act to force better disclosure of campaign financiers, but it has been opposed by the U.S. Chamber of Commerce and other big business lobbies.

Other potential remedies include a push for an amendment to the Constitution to remove the free speech rights for corporations that *Citizens United* provides. Move to Amend is a coalition organizing such an amendment.

The reeingineered corporation will still employ thousands of people and be innovative and productive. But it will be much more accountable to shareholders, to the communities in which it operates, and to customers, employees, and the common good.

Redesign the Tax Revenue System. This final section of rule changes examines how far-sighted tax and revenue policies can aid in the transition to a new and sustainable economy. Present tax rules do not reflect the widely held values and priorities of the 99 percent. Rather, they reflect the designs and worldview of the powerful 1 percent of global corporations and wealthy individuals. The 1 percent devotes considerable lobbying clout to shaping and distorting our tax laws, which is one of the reasons those laws are so complex and porous.

Our tax revenue system should be simple, treat all fairly, and raise adequate revenue for the services we need. Tax rules and bud gets are moral documents; we should not pretend they are value neutral.

We've already discussed two ways that the tax code has been distorted. The first is how it privileges income from wealth over income from work by taxing capital gains at absurdly low rates.[26] Second, the offshore system gives advantages to the global tax dodgers in the corporate 1 percent who force domestic businesses in the 99 percent to compete on an uneven playing field.

Another example is the way our tax code offers larger incentives to mature extractive industries such as oil and natural gas instead of directing resources to communities and corporations that conserve resources, care for the Earth, and catalyze new green enterprises.

The present tax system not only fails to raise adequate revenue from those most capable of paying but also serves as a huge impediment to progress. Current tax rules lock us into the economy of the past, rather than encouraging a transition to a new economy rooted in ecological sustainability, good jobs, and greater equality.

Conventional tax wisdom asserts that we should "tax the bads" by placing a higher price on harmful activities. Hence the notion of "sin taxes" levied on liquor, tobacco, and now, with increasing ferocity, junk food. Taxing these items raises revenue to offset the societal costs of alcoholism, cancer, and obesity. But sin taxes, like any sales tax, are regressive, requiring lower-income households to pay a higher percentage of their income than the wealthy pay.

There are three major "bads" that our tax code should be revised to address:

1. Extreme concentrations of income, wealth, and power that undermine social cohesion and a healthy democracy

2. Financial speculation, such as the activities that destabilized our economy in 2008

3. Pollution and profligate consumption that deplete our ecosystems

There are several bold interventions that focus on "taxing the bads" of our contemporary era and reversing two generations of tax shifts away from the 1 percent. They cluster around three foci: taxing concentrated wealth, taxing financial speculation, and taxing the destruction of nature.

- *Tax inheritances.* Levy a progressive estate tax on the fortunes of the 1 percent. At the end of 2010, Congress reinstated the estate tax on estates over $5 million ($10 million for a couple) at a 35 percent rate. Congress could close loopholes and raise additional revenue from the 1 percent with the greatest capacity to pay. The Responsible Estate Tax Act establishes graduated tax rates, with no tax on estates worth under $3.5 million, or $7 million for a couple, and includes a 10 percent surtax on the value of an estate above $500 million, or $1 billion for a couple. Estimated annual revenue: $35 billion.[27]

- *Institute a wealth tax on the 1 percent.* A "net worth tax" should be levied on individual or house hold assets, including real estate, cash, investment funds, savings in insurance and pension plans, and personal trusts. The law can be structured to tax wealth only above a certain threshold. For example, France's solidarity tax on wealth is for those who have assets in excess of $1.1 million.

- *Establish new tax brackets for the 1 percent.* Under our current tax rate structure, households with incomes over $350,000 pay the same top income tax rate as households with incomes over $10 million. In the 1950s, there were sixteen additional tax rates over the highest rate (35 percent) that we have today. A 50 percent rate on incomes over $2 million would generate an additional $60 billion a year.

- *Eliminate the cap on social security withholding taxes.* Extend the payroll tax to cover all wages, not just wage income up to $110,100. Today, some in the 1 percent are done paying their withholding taxes in January, while people in the 99 percent pay all year.

- *Institute a financial speculation tax.* A tax on financial transactions could generate significant funds for reinvesting in the transition to a financial system that works for everyone. Speculative trading now accounts for up to 70 percent of the trades in some markets. Commodity speculation unnecessarily bids up the cost of food, gasoline, and other basic necessities for the 99 percent. A modest federal tax on every transaction that involves the buying and selling of stocks and other financial products would both generate substantial revenue and dampen reckless risk taking. For ordinary investors, the cost would be negligible, like a tiny insurance fee to protect against financial instability. Estimated revenue: $150 billion a year.[28]

- *Tax income from wealth at higher rates.* Giving tax advantages to income from wealth also encourages speculation. As described by Warren Buffett and others, we can end this preferential treatment for capital gains and dividends and at the same time encourage average families to engage in long-term investing. Estimated revenue: $88 billion per year.

- *Tax carbon.* Instead of taxpayers paying indirectly for the expensive social costs associated with climate change, taxes could build some of these real costs into purchases and products. Perhaps the most critical tax intervention to slow climate change would be to put a price on dumping carbon into the atmosphere from the transportation, energy, and other sectors. For example, the real ecological and societal costs of private jet travel would greatly increase the cost of owning or using private jets.[29] A gradually phased-in tax on carbon would create tremendous incentives to invest in energy conservation and regional green infrastructure. Proposals include a straight carbon tax or a cap-and-dividend proposal that would rebate 50 percent of revenue to consumers to offset the increased costs of some products and still generate $75–100 billion per year.[30] We could also explore similar taxes on other pollutants, such as nitrates that are destroying our water supplies.

- *Tax excessive consumption.* Consumption of unnecessary stuff, especially by the 1 percent, is filling our landfills and destroying our environment. A tax on certain nonessential goods, such as expensive jewelry and technological gadgets, would reflect the real ecological cost of such items. It could apply only to purchases that exceed a certain amount, such as cars that cost more than $100,000. Some states currently charge a luxury tax on high-end real estate transactions.

Objections by some in the 1 percent to these proposals will be strong, along with howls of "class warfare" and "job killing." Some will argue that government shouldn't be in the business of picking winners in the economy. But the reality is that our current tax policy is picking winners every day, and they're usually in the 1 percent.

For several generations after the introduction of a federal income tax at the end of the nineteenth century, our progressive federal tax system was moderately effective in reducing concentrations of wealth. As we briefly described, during the 1950s wealthy individuals paid significantly more taxes than they do today. Since 1980, however, we've lived through a great tax shift as lawmakers moved tax obligations off the wealthy and onto low-and middle-income taxpayers, off corporations and onto individuals, and off today's taxpayers and onto our children and grandchildren.

This program would reverse these tax shifts and set up signposts to help with the transition to the new economy.

NOTES

1 David Lynch, "How Inequality Hurts the Economy," *Business Week Insider,* November 16, 2011, www.businessweek.com/magazine/how-inequality-hurts-the-economy-11162011.html?campaign_id=rss_topStories (accessed January 3, 2012).

2 See Bill Gates Sr. and Chuck Collins, *Wealth and Our Commonwealth: Why American Should Tax Accumulated Fortunes* (Boston: Beacon Press, 2003).

3 Alison Goldberg, Chuck Collins, Sam Pizzigati, and Scott Klinger, "Unnecessary Austerity: U.S. Deficits Worsened by Failure to Tax Millionaires and Tax Dodging Corporations," Institute for Policy Studies, Program on Inequality and the Common Good, April 2011, www.ips-dc.org/reports/unnecessary_austerity_unnecessary_government_shutdown (accessed February 6, 2012).

4 Ibid.

5 Amy Bingham, "Almost 1,500 Millionaires Do Not Pay Income Tax," ABC News, August 6, 2011, http://abcnews.go.com/Politics/1500-millionaires-pay-income-tax/story?id=14242254#.TrwQYWDdLwN (accessed January 3, 2012).

6 Sam Pizzigati, "The New Forbes 400—and Their $1.5 Trillion," Inequality.org, September 25, 2011, http://inequality.org/forbes-400-15-trillion (accessed January 3, 2012).

7 Adam Davidson, "It's Not Just About the Millionaires," *New York Times*, November 9, 2011, www.nytimes.com/2011/11/13/magazine/adam-davidson-tax-middle-class.html (accessed January 3, 2012).

8   See David Callahan, *Kindred Spirits: Harvard Business School's Extraordinary Class of 1949 and How They Transformed American Business* (Hoboken, NJ: Wiley, 2002).

9   Rick Wartzman, "Put a Cap on CEO Pay," *Business Week*, September 12, 2008, www.businessweek.com/managing/content/sep2008/ca20080912_186533.htm (accessed January 3, 2012).

10 For a review of the literature, see "The Ineffective Enterprise," a discussion that appears in Pizzigati, *Greed and Good*.

11 Sam Pizzigati, "The Paycheck Data CEOs Don't Want Us to See," *Too Much*, January 8, 2011, http://toomuchonline.org/the-paycheck-data-ceos-dont-want-us-to-see (accessed January 3, 2012).

12 Sarah Anderson, John Cavanagh, Chuck Collins, Mike Lapham, and Sam Pizzigati, "Executive Excess 2008: How Average Taxpayers Subsidize Runaway Pay," Institute for Policy Studies, August 25, 2008, www.ips-dc.org/reports/executive_excess_2008_how_average_taxpayers_subsidize_runaway_pay (accessed January 3, 2012).

13 Lucian A. Bebchuk and Yaniv Grinstein, "The Growth of Executive Pay," *Oxford Review of Economic Policy*, Summer 2005.

14 Introduced by Rep. Jan Schakowsky (D-Ill.), the Patriot Corporations Act (HR 1163 in the 112th Congress). See: www.opencongress.org/bill/112-h1163/show; and a background article by Sam Pizzigati, "Can We Cut CEO Pay Down to Size?" *Yes*, September 1, 2010, www.yesmagazine.org/new-economy/can-we-cut-ceo-pay-down-to-size.

15 Frank Knapp, "Statement at Press Conference," Business and Investors Against Tax Haven Abuse, October 11, 2011, http://businessagainsttaxhavens.org/press-release-small-businesses-agree-with-new-senate-study-don%E2%80%99t-reward-job-destroyers-with-another-tax-holiday (accessed January 3, 2012).

16 Nicholas Shaxson, *Trea sure Islands: Uncovering the Damage of Offshore Banking and Tax Havens* (Basingstroke, Hampshire: Palgrave Macmillan, 2011).

17 David Kocieniewski, "G.E.'s Strategies Let It Avoid Taxes Altogether," *New York Times*, March 24, 2010, www.nytimes.com/2011/03/25/business/economy/25tax.html?_r=2 (accessed January 3, 2012).

18 The Stop Tax Haven Abuse Act was introduced in the 112th Congress by Senator Carl Levin (D-Mich.) in the Senate as S 2669, and by Representative Lloyd Doggett (D-Tex.) in the House, as HR 2669. For a summary of the legislation, see Senator Carl Levin's website, "Summary of the Stop Tax Haven Abuse Act of 2011," July 12, 2011, http://levin.senate.gov/newsroom/press/release/summary-of-the-stop-tax-haven-abuse-act-of-2011/?section=alltypes.

19 David Korten, "How to Liberate America from Wall Street Rule," New Economy Working Group, July 2011, 6, http://neweconomyworking group.org/report/how-liberate-america-wall-street-rule.

20 See www.moveourmoneyusa.org, http://moveyourmoneyproject.org, and the New Bottom Line Campaign to move $1 billion, www.newbottomline.com/new_bottom_line_money_movers_pull_nearly_50_million_from_big_banks.

21 Korten, "How to Liberate America."

22 The range of emerging business organizations that support high-road and healthy economic policies includes the American Sustainable Business Council (www.asbcouncil.org), Main Street Alliance (www.mainstreetal liance.org), Business for Shared Prosperity (www.businessforshared-prosperity.org), and Small Business Majority (www.smallbusinessmajority.org).

23 Strategic Corporate Initiative, "Toward a Global Citizens Movement to Bring Corporations Back Under Control," Corporate Ethics International, 2007, http://corpethics.org/section.php?id=17 (accessed January 3, 2012).

24 For inspiring examples about the impact of shareholder activism, see the website of the Interfaith Center on Corporate Responsibility, www.iccr.org.

25 Forum for Sustainable and Responsible Investment, "2010 Report on Socially Responsible Investing Trends in the United States," 2010, http://ussif.org/resources/research/documents/2010TrendsES.pdf (accessed January 3, 2012).

26 Someone like Warren Buffett gets preferential tax treatment and is taxed at only 15 percent. Meanwhile, the earned wages of a doctor, teacher, or a scientist in a top income tax bracket will be taxed at a 35 percent rate.

27 Figures represent an annualized average of cuts recommended over a five-year time period in Andrew Fieldhouse, "The People's Budget: A Technical Analysis," Economic Policy Institute, http://grijalva.house.gov/uploads/The%20People%27s%20Budget%20-%20A%20Technical%20Analysis.pdf.

28 Dean Baker, "The Deficit-Reducing Potential of a Financial Speculation Tax," Center for Economic and Policy Research, January 2011, www.cepr.net/documents/publications/fst-2011-01.pdf (accessed January 3, 2012). Note: In November 2011, Rep. Peter DeFazio (D.-Ore.) and Senator Tom Harkin (D-Iowa) introduced bills to create a U.S. financial transaction tax at a lower tax rate than that calculated by CEPR. At a rate of 0.03 percent on each transaction, the Joint Committee on Taxation estimated that these bills would generate $353 billion in revenues over ten years.

29 Sarah Anderson et al., "High Flyers: How Private Jet Travel Is Straining the System, Warming the Planet, and Costing You Money," Institute for Policy Studies, June 2008, www.ips-dc.org/reports/high_flyers (accessed January 3, 2012).

30 Gilbert E. Metcalf and David Weisbach, "The Design of a Carbon Tax," Harvard Environmental Law Review, January 2009, www.law.harvard.edu/students/orgs/elr/vol33_2/Metcalf%20 Weisbach.pdf (accessed January 3, 2012).

From North to South in the 1960s

A BLACK ACTIVIST'S RECOLLECTIONS[1]

JOHN BROWN CHILDS

> *Being a Negro American involves a willed ... affirmation of self as against all outside pressures—an identification with the group as extended through the individual self which rejects all possibilities of escape that do not involve a basic resuscitation of the original American ideals of social and political justice.*
> —Ralph Ellison, *Shadow and Act* (1964, 137)

MARCH 7, 1965, "BLOODY SUNDAY": THE SELMA-TO-MONTGOMERY MARCHES

In early 1965, Alabama was the scene of intensive action by the Alabama Voting Rights Project, an ongoing program of the Student Nonviolent Coordinating Committee (SNCC) and the Dallas County Voters League. Their goal was the dismantling of the system suppressing African American voting through both legal and violent means in segregated Alabama (and throughout the South). On February 16, an unarmed young voting rights activist named Jimmie Lee Jackson was shot in the stomach by a state policeman while participating in a demonstration on behalf of yet another activist, James Orange, who was being held in jail in the city of Marion, Alabama. Jackson died a few days later. His death sparked a call by Martin Luther King Jr.'s Southern Christian Leadership Conference (SCLC) for a major march from Selma to the Alabama state capital of Montgomery to confront

Governor George Wallace. On what became known as "Bloody Sunday," March 7, the first march attempted to cross the Edmund Pettus Bridge in Selma on the route to Montgomery. The marchers were met by a wall of state police wielding long batons and tear gas. The police violently beat and forced back the marchers, including King, along with John Lewis and Amelia Boyton of SNCC, among many others. One thousand of the bloodied demonstrators were arrested. Two days later a second attempted march turned back instead of crossing the bridge.[2] On the night following that aborted march, three white ministers, who had come to give their support, were attacked with clubs by the Ku Klux Klan (KKK). One of them, Rev. James Reeb, a minister from Boston, died of his injuries soon afterward. Finally, the Lyndon B. Johnson administration, responding to the uncomfortable national and worldwide attention now focused on the suppression of the civil rights activists in Alabama, provided the protection of a force of two thousand US Army troops, a federalized Alabama National Guard unit of nineteen hundred, and federal marshals, all supported by a court order. With international and national media present, a third march on March 21 of about eight thousand people from around the country made it to Montgomery. This massive show of nationwide support from some unions, religious organizations, community groups, and celebrities, including Harry Belafonte, Marlon Brando, Pete Seeger, and Joan Baez, produced some of the iconic images of the civil rights struggle.

In the wake of the Selma-to-Montgomery marches, and with much of the media departed, follow-up and less visible SNCC voting rights demonstrations in Montgomery were violently suppressed, prompting that organization, through a key figure, James Forman, to ask for support from around the country. At the time of the nationwide call, I was a member of Friends of SNCC at the University of Massachusetts (UMass) in the town of Amherst. Friends of SNCC was a national support network for fundraising media work and other assistance in aid of that organization. At the University of Massachusetts, for all practical purposes, it was mostly composed of members of another organization, Students for a Democratic Society (SDS), founded nationally in 1962. I went with this group to Alabama in response to the call for assistance.

Before we continue further, I must beg the reader's indulgence for my ragged-time recollaborations with the past, as memories juggle among themselves, flowing along many curving, spiraling trails and mystifying crossroads, propelled by diverse familial-ancestral inspirations, friendships, societal impacts, cultural resources, and global stirrings of freedom, pushing, pulling, and sometimes hinting, through cryptic Delphic signs, at the why, where, when, and how I should take part in civil rights, antiwar, and community activism.[3] As I express these thoughts, I must humbly speak herein the names of the many brave women and men whose contributions to social justice are of a magnitude deeper than any depth-plumbing measurement I could ever take of myself.

1963/1965: CULTURE FOR ACTIVISM AND ACTIVISM FOR CULTURE

So in Macon County, Alabama, I read Marx, Freud, T. S. Elliot, Pound, Gertrude Stein and Hemmingway. Books which seldom, if ever, mentioned Negroes were to release me from whatever "segregated" idea I might have had of my human possibilities. ... Reading had become a conscious process of growth and discovery, a method of reordering the world.

—Ralph Ellison, *Shadow and Act* (1964, 116)

I was one of a small number of students who created the SDS chapter at the University of Massachusetts in 1963. Most of us had originally been in the organization that we called Young Independents to distinguish ourselves from the mainstream parties' youth groups, the Young Democrats and the Young Republicans, as well as from the extreme right-wing Young Americans for Freedom. Nationwide SDS chapters were highly autonomous and self-created (at least the ones I knew were). Our membership at UMass (reflecting the demographics of the state itself) was largely interethnic working-class—Irish American, Italian American, Eastern European Jewish, Latino, and African American. A few came from leftist union families with roots in what had been the progressive Congress of Industrial Organizations, before it affiliated with the American Federation of Labor to form the umbrella AFL-CIO. But we saw ourselves as a "new left," free from the dictatorial hierarchical forms of the "old left." Along with other SDS chapters, we organized ourselves around analysis, principles, and strategies detailed in the 1962 Port Huron Statement manifesto. Named for that Michigan industrial city, it called for "a participatory democracy" of "alternatives to the present." These alternatives would be distinct from "the dreams of the older left" that had been perverted by Stalinism into a heavy-handed "centralized bureaucracy" that totally suppressed "organized opposition." SDS would also rise above the alienating materialism of capitalism by establishing "a democracy of individual participation" in "social decisions" in ways that encouraged both "independence ... [and] common participation" by all (Port Huron Statement 1964, 7). SDS's manifesto also emphasized a struggle against racism worldwide as a pivotal part of its objectives. Much to the astonishment and anger of most students and residents of Amherst, our SDS chapter (all twelve of us) organized demonstrations in 1964 and 1965 against the first stirrings of US military involvement in Vietnam with the sending of military "advisers" to that country. Our little local peace marches were met with threats, insults, and a few thrown bottles. We raised funds for SNCC and organized supporting talks, meetings, and demonstrations. We felt very much a part of a world in positive eruption of liberation and self-development (both individual and collective). The young women and men I knew were all very aware of the world and of being part of a postwar "new generation" and "new left" infused with a kindred spirit sweeping the globe.

Several of my friends in the UMass SDS were interested in Leon Trotsky, seeing in him an alternative to the official Communist Party of the United States, but probably more importantly, constructing a sense of him as a righteous rebel against top-down hierarchical organization. In that light we read Isaac Deutscher's tragically infused work about Trotsky (e.g., *The Prophet Armed* [1954] and *The Prophet Unarmed* [1959]). Some of my SDS friends would later go on to join the Trotskyite Socialist Worker's Party. But for me, it was also necessary to read André Malraux's *Man's Fate* (1934) (*La condtion humaine* [1933]) and to delve into George Orwell's *Homage to Catalonia* (1952), *1984* (1949), and *Animal Farm* (1945). Some found these readings "counterproductive"; I benefited from Orwell's antidogmatism and his instinct for egalitarian justice. For the same reason I found sustenance in Albert Camus's antitotalitarian *The Rebel* (1951). Ralph Ellison's *Invisible Man* (1947) challenged the society around me and spoke directly to my developing sense of self. Lorraine Hansberry's eye-opening play *A Raisin in the Sun* (1959) (the title inspired, of course, by Langston Hughes's 1951 poem "A Dream Deferred")[4] strengthened me through its provocations, as did Richard Wright's autobiography, *Black Boy* (1945) and James Baldwin's prescient urban essays in *The Fire Next Time* (1963). Also striking was Herman Melville's powerful 1850 novella *Benito Cereno* about a shipboard slave revolt that almost succeeds due both to the intelligence and planning of the revolt's leader and to the naïve sense of false superiority held by a white captain from another ship. John Steinbeck's trenchant novel about workers during the Great Depression, *The Grapes of Wrath* (1939) (and the Henry Fonda movie version of the same title), illuminated one of the dark sides of American history. Mariano Azuela's gripping novel of the Mexican revolution, *The Underdogs* (1963) (*Los de abajo* [1915]), provided a complex picture of both the strengths and limitations of struggle. I read as well Rachel Carson's stirring early warnings about the degradation of the environment in *Silent Spring* (1962) and Herbert Marcuse's acute libertarian-socialist analysis of alienation and criticism of orthodox Leninist practices in *One Dimensional Man* (1964)—a group of us SDS members went to hear him speak in Boston at the Massachusetts Institute of Technology. Also distinctive was Buckminster Fuller's hopeful global outlook in *Operating Manual for Spaceship Earth* (1963) and Frantz Fanon's muscular cry of pain in *The Wretched of the Earth* (1963).

The black social psychologist Kenneth Clark's anatomy of ghettoization, *Dark Ghetto: Dilemmas of Social Power* (1965), with its analysis of Harlem, was a valuable framework for both urban analysis and action, while Claude Brown's *Manchild in the Promised Land* (1965) provided the gritty details of growing up on the streets of that New York City enclave. I was prodded by the writings of LeRoi Jones (later Amiri Baraka), with his indictments of racism in novels, poetry, and plays such as *The System of Dante's Hell* (1965), set in the ghetto of Newark, New Jersey, and *The Dutchman and the Slave* (1964). St. Clair Drake and Horace Cayton's epic social analysis *Black Metropolis* (1945) illustrated the positive dimensionality of African American parallel society with all its richly complex dimensions in the segregated South Side of Chicago. In 1962, Charles Kay Smith, an English literature professor at UMass generously gave me thought-invigorating books, including Arthur Lovejoy's classic history of ideas, *The Great Chain of Being* (1936), and Leslie White's anthropological counterpart, *The Science of Culture* (1949). I also drew from Mahatma Gandhi and Henry David Thoreau (especially Thoreau's impassioned antislavery, antiauthoritarian essay "On Civil Disobedience" [1849]). The great African American scholar and activist W. E. B. Du Bois was a model in terms of politically directed intellectual work, such as *The Souls of Black Folk* (1903) and *The Suppression of the African Slave Trade* (1904). The Senegalese writer and filmmaker Ousman Sembene's novel Les bouts de bois de Dieu (1960) (*God's Bits of Wood*), about a militant railroad workers' strike, struck home for me. So did C. L. R. James's *World Revolution, 1917–1936: The Rise and Fall of the Communist International* (1937), with its dynamic theory and analysis of race, class, and empire, and also his *The Black Jacobins: Toussaint L'Overture and the San Domingo Revolution* (1963). Jawaharlal Nehru's *The Discovery of India* (1946) and Kwame Nkrumah's writings informed me about the wider world. Also, of course, I read Karl Marx, then Vladimir Lenin, whose thoughts I tempered with the insightful warnings of Orwell's works and Arthur Koestler's *The Darkness at Noon* (1940).

I read Alan Ginsberg's epic poem *Howl* (1956), with its elongated scream against the materialism of America. Also insightful was Ken Kesey's *One Flew over the Cuckoo's Nest* (1962) about the rebellion of those held by a brutal mental institution director. Meanwhile, all around were the sounds of emergent cultural/political democratic revitalization. I think for example of pianist-composer Thelonious Monk, with his jagged-edged compositions, strung together for a revolution. One now classic album cover, that for *Underground* (1958), shows Monk playing, wearing a beret, a Sten gun slung round his shoulder, with a German officer tied to a chair being forced to listen to what would have been declared "decadent Negro music" in Nazi Germany. The great bassist Charles Mingus struck out with his wonderfully acrid *"Fables of Faubus"* (1959), which dissolves the image of Arkansas governor Orville Faubus, who tried to prevent integration at Little Rock High School. The Mingus suite "Oh Lord, Don't Let Them Drop That Atom Bomb on Me" spoke to other concerns with equal effectiveness. Always haunting was Billie Holiday's powerful 1939 performance of "Strange Fruit" growing on Southern trees, with its eerie and compelling musical images of lynchings of black men. I also listened over and over again to the great Nina Simone's trenchant antisegregation song, "Mississippi Goddamn" (1963), about the killing of the civil rights activist Medgar Evers. Inspiring political "folk music" poured out from Sonny Terry and Brownie McGee, Leadbelly, and the Indigenous Cree composer/singer Buffy St. Marie from Canada, who had herself been a student at the University of Massachusetts. Bob Dylan, with "Masters of War" (1963), "Hard Rain's A-Gonna Fall" (1962), and "Blowin' in the Wind" (1963), spoke directly to the young generation about the perils of nuclear war and the importance of the civil rights struggles, as well as early pushing back against the war in Vietnam. I remember also the soul-filling impact of the powerful voices of Joan Baez, Pete Seeger, and Odetta, with their songs of justice.

Also challenging the status quo was the politically infused, but never simply didactic, work of African American artists, such as Romare Bearden, with his vibrant paintings and collages. His friend Jacob Lawrence's historical saga series of paintings, such as *The Great Migration* and *The Life of John Brown*, and African-American-turned-Mexican-citizen Elizabeth Catlett's drawings, paintings, and sculptures also spoke to an intertwined view of culture and political consciousness. The parallel sympathetic images (which influenced the black artists named here) of the Mexican muralistas, such as Diego Rivera and David Alfaro Siqueiros, struck me, as did the work the great Spanish artist Francisco Goya, with his nightmarish reminders of war's horrors. Many movies, viewed at the university, flung open global windows for me—such as Roberto Rosellini's tragic movie of the Italian resistance, Open City (1945); Akira Kurosawa's *The Bad Sleep Well* (1960), about corruption of politics and the soul; Jean Luc Goddard's antiwar *Le petit soldat* (1958) and *Les carabiniers* (1963); and Orson *Wells's Citizen Kane* (1941), which Goddard admired, to name but a few that flashed in front of me. Ingmar Bergman's stark and sometimes humorous meditations on life transported me from New England to other times and places and so added to the ferment of liberation in the air.

1950s: SCHOOL DAYS AS A "SAVAGE"

I went to public high school in Amherst from 1956 to 1960. During that time I joined with friends, including the son of the local printer, to create (what we thought was) a satirical newspaper. We wrote it, printed it, and distributed it. I learned to operate the hot-lead linotype machine that set the type. We delivered our paper at night to peoples' houses, hoping for their surprise at finding it alongside their local newspapers in the morning. I suppose it was a kind of "underground news-paper" before that term came into general use. My buddies were mostly third- and fourth-gener-ation white, ethnic Irish, Italian, French Canadian, Ukrainian, and Polish—and they, along with the "colored" children of the town, were primarily working-class. The other part of the high school was mostly "Anglo" children of the professional class, many of them the sons and daughters of college professors at one of the two main institutions of higher learning in Amherst, the University of Massachusetts and Amherst College. The high school was quite rigidly divided between these two populations. From these experiences I learned a lot about the importance of economic class and about the existence of white ethnicity that paralleled, but was separated in degrees from, race. I experienced being called "nigger"—none of my white ethnic friends faced that. But all of us—the working-class students—faced automatic channeling into zones of society that were dif-ferent from those of our middle-class counterparts. My mother and father fought with the school to have me put into college preparatory classes. They largely succeeded. But it was a fight.

My mother, father, and I had moved from my birthplace—an urban housing project in the inner-city Roxbury section of Boston—in the early 1950s to Amherst (hometown of Emily

Dickinson), where my mother's family had lived since the 1880s. As young women, my mother and her sisters worked as cooks and housekeepers for the local upper class, including the descendants of Dickinson's family, among others. My mother once told me about doing her high school homework in the kitchen of the house in which she worked as a teenager. The teenage son of that household did not do well in high school. My mother, by contrast, was on the honor roll, despite long hours of housecleaning and cooking. One day she heard the father criticizing his son for not surpassing my mother, despite his advantages. My mother was determined to get out of that kind of work and went on to be a young teacher in Alabama. During World War II, opportunities in the defense industry opened up the lives of my aunts and uncles. My aunt Helen, for example, went from doing domestic housework to working as a welder building ships. My father's brother, Arthur Childs, was an Army Corps of Engineers lieutenant, serving in Burma. Three of my mother's brothers, Maxwell, John, and Chesley, served in the segregated army. They were part of what "Negro America" called the "Double-V Campaign," for victory against fascism in Europe and racism in the United States. One of those uncles was a military policeman. I have their photographs—they were proud, handsome young men who fought the Nazis in Europe, despite the inequalities and discrimination leveled against them within both the military and the wider American society.

As a young boy, I soon grew to love reading and writing, which became a means of geographic and historical world travel while wandering no more than a few physical miles. Books offered expansive routes and welcoming, quiet backrooms, or *arrière boutiques*, as Montaigne called his own such work space, all of them somehow touching a broader, more open world of a much richer spirit than the narrow compressions of racial and class barriers encountered during my youth. Even before high school, as an eleven-year-old in the early 1950s, I developed a neighborhood newspaper (my mother typed it and copied it using inked mimeograph rolls). Writing, printing, and publishing are the iron of ink in my spirit's blood. The corrosiveness of degrading racial insults aided and abetted by some teachers required that iron. For example, in seventh grade, we were asked one day to tell where our (immigrant) families had come from. When it was my turn, I said Africa and also "American Indian." There was silence in the room, then laughter among some of my classmates, encouraged by the teacher. I was descended, someone said, "from savages." As an even younger boy, in the predominately white church's summer "Bible class" that I attended one year, the teacher, looking at me pointedly, said that "slavery was good because it got your people out of savagery." I walked out and persuaded two of my white friends to walk out with me. I never went back. But I could find support in books to counteract these small but sharp cuts that were so common. By way of illustration, one such book was Basil Davidson's *Lost Cities of Africa* (1959), which I found when I was in high school. It provided a reinforcing revelation about civilizations in Africa that helped to buttress me against the isolating corrosion of prejudice. In 1959, when the "guidance counselor" at my high school told me that I was "not college material" and should just go into the military, I said, "No, I know that I can do things differently."

AUGUST 28, 1963: THE MARCH ON WASHINGTON FOR JOBS AND FREEDOM

In August 1963, in my third year as a student at the University of Massachusetts, I joined with thousands of people responding to a call to attend the March on Washington for Jobs and Freedom. Only a few weeks before, Medgar Evers, the noted African American social-justice activist with the National Association for the Advancement of Colored People (NAACP), who was also a World War II US Army veteran with combat experience in France, was shot in the back and killed outside his home in Jackson, Mississippi. The assassin, one Byron De La Beckwith, was a member of the local white supremacist group, the White Citizens Council. Evers had survived previous assassination attempts. De La Beckwith was not convicted of the murder until 1994, after two previous all-white juries had failed to find him guilty. Evers was buried at Arlington National Cemetery with full military honors.[5]

In the shadow of that recent terrible killing, I went to the nearby town of Greenfield, Massachusetts, where several buses were assembled to take people to Washington, DC. When we got on the highway, I had my first experience of a mass—or should I say massive—out-pouring of people's will to engage in social-justice change. The highway from Massachusetts to Washington (about 450 miles) was clogged with buses all headed for the same destination. Over two hundred thousand people poured in from around the country. At every entrance to the highway, more buses appeared, festooned with signs demanding "Equal Rights!" and "Voting Rights." And everywhere the US flag was to be seen as people also demonstrated their belief in the need to make fully real the founding words of the republic about equality and "unalienable rights" to "Life, Liberty, and the pursuit of Happiness." Our bus caravan was organized by local labor unions, the NAACP, churches, and synagogues. In Washington, I was fortunate to stand (far) behind the podium at the Lincoln Memorial, thanks to a press pass. From that vantage, I could see the thousands gathered there. I heard King's uplifting vision of a future equality. But I was especially attracted by what was, for me, the more political, militant speech of SNCC's John Lewis,[6] who criticized the federal government for failing to uphold the Constitution and having bowed to local state authority in Alabama, Mississippi, Louisiana, and elsewhere. He highlighted poverty and overall economic inequality. He emphasized the necessary protections of human rights and the power of more universalistic ideals. He said in part, "We march today for jobs and freedom, but we have nothing to be proud of, for hundreds and thousands … are not here, for they have no money for their transportation, for they are receiving starvation wages … or no wages at all." Until such equality was achieved, he said, SNCC and its supporters "[could not] support the administration's civil rights bill." He added toward the end of his speech, "I want to know which side the federal government is on? The revolution is a serious one. Mr. Kennedy is trying to take the revolution out of the streets and put it in the courts. Listen Mr. Kennedy, the black masses are on the march for jobs and freedom." The words "revolution" and "black masses" stood out for me. It is no wonder that despite King's eloquence, John Lewis and SNCC were, for many of us, vibrant emblems of the deep changes necessary for progress.

Less than four weeks after the March on Washington, four young African American girls—Addie Mae Collins, Cynthia Wesley, Carole Robertson, and Denise McNair—were killed when white pro-segregationists bombed the Birmingham, Alabama, Sixteenth Street Baptist Church, a central location for intense activism by the SCLC and the Congress of Racial Equality. Twenty-two other people were injured. There had been previous bombings in the city as part of a campaign by white supremacists aimed at derailing school integration in Birmingham (also widely known as "Bombingham"). Under Police Commissioner Eugene "Bull" Connor, a staunch pro-segregation supporter, the main immediate police response to that attack on the church was not investigation of who had committed the act but rather a violent repressive action against black citizens protesting it. The triptych of Evers's assassination, followed by the March on Washington, followed by the Birmingham church bombing—all within the space of a few months—spoke both to the stark brutality of racism and to the growing potential for expanding mobilization to dismantle segregation.

1800s–1900s: RED CLAY ANCESTORS, LINCOLN NORMAL SCHOOL, THE CITY OF MARION, AND PERRY COUNTY, ALABAMA

Out of respect for the living influence of my ancestors and relatives upon my life, I must at this point offer some reflections about ancestral echoes resonating for me. I think of my father's family in the red clay farming country around Marion, Alabama. In the 1930s, my mother, Dorothy Pettijohn (born in Amherst in 1908), went south to teach at a church-run Alabama school for impoverished African American sharecroppers' children in Cotton Valley, not far from Selma and Montgomery. The school was part of an educational network organized by the Congregational Church's American Missionary Society working in the United States. The Congregationalists had been active in the antislavery movement and after the Civil War sought to provide basic educational support to those newly freed from enslavement as well as their descendants. Given the intentionally corrosive lack of support from Southern state governments for African American education, such schools were of great importance. Because she was a "colored" woman—Native American/African American—she had no real access to teaching jobs "up north." In nearby Perry County, Alabama, she met my father, John Brown Childs, in 1938 (they were married in Birmingham). Cotton Valley and my father's hometown of Marion are not far from the famous and influential African American college Tuskegee Institute, founded by Booker T. Washington in 1881, (Tuskegee students would play a major role in civil rights actions of the 1960s). My mother knew one of Washington's daughters and also met the famous African American scientist, inventor, and educator George Washington Carver (born in slavery in 1864), who taught at Tuskegee. She once told me the following story about her experiences at the Cotton Valley school in the 1930s: "One year a new teacher, a white man, arrived. Not long after that arrival, a group of KKK men abducted him and beat him nearly to death. I think they left him for dead. A group of us, the teachers, found him and hid him in a field of corn. That night we got him out of there and helped him eventually to safety up north."

My father, John Brown Childs, was born in Marion, Alabama, in 1909. In Marion, the Childs family started and ran, for many years, a highly successful business known as Stephen Childs' Sons Bakers and Confectioners, Growers and Shippers of Plants and Vegetables; Agents for Jacob's Chocolates and Bon-Bons. The store and bakery provided skilled employment to several black workers. The business was itself an important positive African American development in that Deep South town. Two years after the end of the Civil War, in 1867, two of my father's forebears, James Childs and Alexander H. Curtis, along with eight other black men and their families, had founded the first high school for "colored" children in that area with an emphasis on producing teachers. Named the Lincoln Normal School (after Abraham Lincoln, a radical name, detested by whites in that KKK-dominated region), the school provided a vital and growing foundation for African American educational and community development beyond Perry County and Alabama. Lincoln Normal School's purpose, according to its African American founders, was "to afford the means of education to the largest practicable number of applicants."[7] As the great African American educator Horace Mann Bond pointed out, Lincoln Normal provided "a *complete* social and moral as well as educational community." Of the importance of the school, Bond observed, "When we note Perry County, Alabama ... from statistics of illiteracy of the population, of farm tenancy among the Negroes, and of abysmally low per capita public school expenditures for the Negro population ... the conclusion is inescapable, that doctorates emerged from such areas because of the intervention of [Lincoln and similar schools]" (1972, 40, 97–98).

Among those to attend Lincoln Normal was Roberta Childs, who became an influential civil rights activist in Washington, DC, in the 1930s and 1940s. Her son William Hastie, a Harvard graduate, became the first black federal judge in US history. Hastie joined President Franklin D. Roosevelt's "Black Cabinet" of African American civil rights advisors on New Deal socioeconomic issues. He served as an assistant to the secretary of war and resigned that position in 1943 to protest racial segregation in the US military during World War II. He later taught at the Howard University Law School in Washington, DC. One of his students at Howard was

Thurgood Marshall, the first African American Supreme Court justice and the major advocate in the landmark 1954 *Brown v. Board of Education* school-desegregation case. The Marion-born Coretta Scott, future wife of Rev. Martin Luther King Jr., was a student at Lincoln. Another Lincoln graduate was my paternal cousin Jean Childs (1933–1994), who later married the Rev. Andrew Young, one of King's key lieutenants. But Jean was an activist in her own right (her papers can be found at Emory University in Atlanta, Georgia). In the 1950s and 1960s, she participated in the voter rights organizing of Alabama. She codeveloped curricula for the Citizenship Schools that had originated with Septima Clark and Esau Jenkins in 1954, aiming to expand black literacy and so undermine the "literacy-test barriers erected as a major stone in the wall of segregation." In 1979, she chaired the "International Year of the Child" and was active in the Children's Defense Fund. I share my name with my father, John Brown Childs, who was named after the white abolitionist John Brown, hanged by the federal government for his 1859 twenty-one-man (black and white) raid on the Harper's Ferry, Virginia, federal arsenal to seize rifles for the fight against slavery. Although my parents did not know it when I was born and named, my birthday, December 2, is also the date of John Brown's hanging. My father later died on the anniversary of John Brown's birth. One of my mother's relatives helped John Brown's widow move to California after his death. She is buried in Los Gatos, not far from where I now live in Santa Cruz, California. I have visited John Brown's Connecticut birthplace; the "New Africa" farm, originally set up by him for free black farmers, which is the gravesite for John Brown and his sons in North Elba, deep in the Adirondack Mountains of New York State; the arsenal at Harper's Ferry, Virginia, where he was captured; and the place of his execution by hanging in Charlestown, Virginia. I feel a great affinity with this man, called by Thoreau a "determined foe" of slavery, who "had the courage to face his country herself when she was in the wrong" ([1859] 2000, 718–719).

BLUE HILLS ANCESTORS, 1600s–1800s: BROTHERTOWN/ EYAMQUITTOWAUCONNUCK, THE PLACE OF EQUAL PEOPLE—MASSACHUSETTS AND UP-COUNTRY NEW YORK[8]

I was born in 1942 in Boston, Massachusetts, where my mother and father were living in a housing project in the predominantly black working-class Roxbury section, or "ghetto." Malcolm Little—later to become famous as Malcolm X—was a young man living in Roxbury with his mother seven streets away from my family's apartment when I was born.[9] My Roxbury birthplace is only a few miles north of the Blue Hills. There, in the Blue Hills, is a body of water called Punkapoag, which means "the place of the fresh clear-water pond" in the Algonkian language of my maternal Indigenous ancestors, who lived there during (and long before) the 1600s. My ancestors were part of a large confederacy called the Massachusaug (*massa*, meaning "big"; *chusaug*, meaning "hill place")—the English colony of Massachusetts Bay took its name (and lands) from them. In 1774, responding to many decades of cultural erosion and land loss as English colonists expanded their grip on the land, a gathering of refugee Christian Native peoples, including some of my maternal ancestors, under the leadership of Rev. Samson Occom, a Mohegan man and Presbyterian minister, migrated northwest to the lands of the Oneida Nation, one of the Five Nations in the Haudenosaunee ("Iroquois") Great League of Peace. The approximately fourteenth-century founding of the league, through the development of a peace that ended wars among them, is the major source of my concept of transcommunality—the deep focus of my scholarly and community work.[10] The Oneidas generously gave them use of a place in their territory, where the refugee "Indians" from New England created a community they called Brothertown. In their Algonkian language it was named Eyamquittowauconnuck, meaning "the place of equal people." Eventually many Oneidas and their allied nations were forced out by relentless westward expansion of European settlers. Some Haudenosaunee moved north to Canada; others went to the western Great Lakes region, where they live today.[11] Others stayed on their original, but much reduced, lands in New York State. My Native American ancestors, whose family name had become Burr and who had intermarried with the Oneida, returned to their ancestral homeland of Massachusetts. Eli and Saloma Burr, my great, great, great-grandfather and -grandmother, settled in western Massachusetts, where my mother was later born. Both Eli and Saloma are listed in the 1868 Massachusetts State "Indian Census" as Oneida people. Eli Burr's grandfather is cited as an Oneida sachem, or chief.

Brothertown and Lincoln Normal School, one northern Native American, the other southern African American, were both places of strong, proud people seeking to sustain freedom and creative development among and for the marginalized and despised. My ancestors, from north to south, were among those building what they hoped would be sustaining sanctuaries that could buffer people from the forces of hatred while offering requickening frameworks for justice and dignity. Their spirit of freedom infused and guided me back in the 1960s and continues to do so today.

MARCH 15, 1965, MONTGOMERY, ALABAMA

Having now paid the respect that I owe to my ancestors and my family relations, I will return to my involvement in Alabama, following the original 1965 Selma-to-Montgomery marches. My SDS companions and I heeded the nationwide call from James Forman of SNCC to send allies to Montgomery. At no time did I have a sense of joining something called "the Movement."

Rather I was acting in support of a specific organization, SNCC, which emphasized a distinctive set of tactics and strategies. My feelings and, as I recall, the feelings of my friends, as we prepared for the journey by car from Massachusetts to Alabama, included exhilaration, an impatience to be there, and a resigned fear of being badly beaten or killed. We left Amherst, Massachusetts, in three old, beat-up cars. Mine was perhaps the most vulnerable. Sure enough, a few hours into our trip, just outside New York City, my brakes failed, with smoke pouring from them. I mention this very minor incident only because of something that struck me at that time (and still does). With my car on the side of the north-south Interstate 91 running from Maine to Florida, the brakes smoking, we called New York City SDS (from a pay phone—no cell phones of course). Within an hour someone from that chapter arrived and took charge of the car. It was to be towed and repaired and would be ready for me when, or if, I passed that way again. SDS was not a centralized, strongly hierarchical organization. Yet, despite such loose heterogeneity, or maybe because of it, the effectiveness of SDS in that small moment really struck home for me. They responded with great efficiency and, indeed, generosity. So we jammed ourselves into the reduced convoy of two cars and continued. Our first major stop was the SNCC organizational center in Atlanta, Georgia.

At the Atlanta SNCC offices, the level of organization was even greater. SNCC provided us with food and housing for the night. We received detailed instructions, maps, contacts in Montgomery, and instruction in methods of nonviolent resistance. We were told that SNCC would provide helmets for frontline demonstrators faced with baton-welding police. A SNCC worker, perhaps observing our eager and probably innocent-looking faces, asked, "Are you sure you want to keep going? They're crazy down there." I suspect he knew what our answer would be. The next day, we piled back into our two cars to drive down into the deeper South. Even as we drove, several thousands were also in motion, coming from around the country. It was a sustaining sensation, to be part of a literal movement of people, simultaneously focused on justice, moving down "freedom's road," as one inspirational song put it.

Importantly for us, and for all those going to support SNCC, that road from north to south was mostly along federal interstate highways, and it would have been less passable for later activists had it not been for those called the "Freedom Riders." In 1961, inspired by African American college students who had conducted sit-ins at segregated lunch counters, courageous groups of black and white Freedom Riders rode interstate highway buses into segregated states to push into social reality the legal framework of Supreme Court rulings desegregating transit on such highways.[12] Despite severe beatings by white mobs and the firebombing of one bus, which nearly burned one group to death, the Freedom Riders persisted and expanded, with more and more volunteers pouring in. Their persistence pushed John F. Kennedy's reluctant administration into actually supporting safe interracial travel on federal interstate highways.[13] The Freedom Riders' honorable bravery provided a tremendous tactical and logistical advantage to the accelerating nationwide civil rights mobilization.[14]

MARCH 1965: SOME SKETCHES FROM MONTGOMERY—"IF THEY WON'T LET US SIT AT THE JUSTICE TABLE, WE'LL KNOCK THE *** LEGS OFF THE TABLE!"

Almost immediately upon our arrival in Montgomery, we joined a large demonstration headed for the state capital. We were blocked by police from moving forward. The instructions came to us from the organizers: "We're doing a sit-down; everyone sit-down and lock arms." It was evening. I remember hearing a siren somewhere on the streets behind us. Someone said, "It's an ambulance," and it was coming at us from behind. At that moment a phalanx of mounted police began charging us from the front. So the siren was part of a setup to hem us in. Many of the police had heavy, skull-crunching batons, probably about three feet in length, which they began swinging from their horses. We were caught between that attack in front and the siren-blaring vehicle behind us. The fearful power of those poor, driven horses, their lethality as they came rushing toward us along with the flailing batons of their riders, could not be resisted. We broke, scrambling in small clusters to the sides of the street and up onto doorsteps and porches. I could hear people moaning in pain and the police cursing and threatening.

Somehow, in the midst of what seemed like abject confusion and retreat, we regrouped inside the nearby African American Beulah Baptist Church. I remember the heat of that night, the sweat from the fear and the temperature. It was not clear about what would happen next. Any kind of attack, such as a firebombing of the church, was possible, even expected. It was a deeply isolating moment as we waited together in a sanctuary, surrounded by hostile people and state authority. We rallied our spirits. People spoke from the pulpit of the church. A suggestion was made that (amid our apparent isolation) the United Nations be contacted. But what stands out so clearly to me is one of the SNCC leaders, James Forman, in his uniform of farmworker blue-denim coveralls saying (as I recall it now and omitting one expletive), "If they won't let us sit at the justice table, we'll knock the *** legs off the table!"[15] I felt a tremendous exhilaration at hearing such defiance in that moment of vulnerability. We were a room full of bruised, bloodied people forced to retreat and surrounded it seemed not just by KKK-supporting police outside the building but by the entire apparatus of the government of Alabama. Forman's statement fit with SNCC's ultimate banner of a black panther and the slogan "Move On Over or We'll Move On Over You."[16] Coming in the midst of so much violent death and injury from those racial fundamentalists, who would stop at nothing to uphold the system of racist inequality, Forman's militancy, which still held onto the tactic of nonviolence—but without an accompanying quiescent tonality—struck home with me and with many others in that compressed moment inside the church. There was no dejection in his words. Instead there was buoyant rejection of injustice.[17]

Another day, I was tasked with driving a car with food to demonstrators who were encircling the Alabama State Capitol Building. Before getting into the car, I thought about Viola Liuzzo, a thirty-nine-year-old white, Italian American mother of two from Detroit, who, horrified by the beatings at the Edmund Pettus Bridge on Bloody Sunday, had come to Alabama on her own. She had been involved in numerous political actions in the Detroit area. As she told her husband, the battle in Montgomery was "everybody's fight."[18] On March 25, she and an African American volunteer named Leroy Morton were driving to help local marchers get home. A car with four KKK members pulled up beside them and shot her twice in the head, killing her. With that and the other images of the many killed and beaten in mind, I got into the car with a companion from another contingent whom I did not know. It was evening. The demonstrators were ringed by state police, who were preventing people from joining them. As we approached the ring of state police, I slowed down, hesitating about the next step. What would I say to get us through their line? My companion was getting agitated. He began to yell, "Just run them over, run right through the cops, don't be chicken." To put it mildly, that would have been a dangerous decision, and getting shot for assaulting the police with a moving vehicle certainly would not have helped get the food to the demonstrators. I chose not to follow his demands. I stopped and negotiated for a few minutes, and for some reason we were allowed to bring the food in on foot. Thinking about my companion in later years, I have always wondered if his outburst came from an intensity of political passion or if he was a police-inserted agent provocateur, planted to harm SNCC.

During what seemed like constant marches through Montgomery in hot, humid Southern air, we faced the usual threats: "We're going to kill you niggers" and, alternatively, to the white activists, "We're going to kill you nigger-lovers." There were, of course, sound reasons to take such threats completely seriously. On one day as we marched through a neighborhood of houses with porches, a door opened. I remember a moment of apprehension. A white woman came out with a jug of ice water, which she offered to us on that humid day. In retrospect we were probably naïve in our acceptance, but accept the water we did. It tasted good. That woman had a lot of heart. Thinking about her over the years is a constant corrective for me about the basic limitations of predictability and prejudgment of others. As the Chuck Berry song puts it, "C'est la vie, say the old folks, just goes to show you never can tell." Of course, there were always some whites in the South, including newspaper editors, judges, and just "plain folks," who did not go along with the segregationist agenda. Maybe there were some others behind the closed doors of houses along that street who had views not dissimilar to hers but did not want to risk their lives—and I can certainly understand that. That moment of her public courage stays with me—indeed, one never knows.

Six months following the Selma-to-Montgomery marches and the demonstrations in Montgomery itself, the US Congress and President Johnson passed the 1965 Voting Rights Act into law, legally abolishing a webbing of fraudulent restrictions that had been used to disqualify African Americans from voting. Not long after the events in Montgomery, community protests against police brutality in Los Angeles erupted into six days of often violent unrest. Soon following those developments, Martin Luther King Jr. began an urban push with his Poor People's Campaign. On April 4, 1968, Reverend King was assassinated in Memphis, Tennessee, while supporting a strike by African American sanitation workers. In the midst of such terrible setbacks, we acted, I believe, not because we could predict the (hoped for) outcomes. Instead, there was a core ethical, "do the right thing" dimension to the civil rights struggles. Civil rights activists were certainly infused with an optimistic spirit of action. But there was no inevitable straight line of progress. Rather than a prepackaged process, we were engaged in a struggle with all the complexity implied by that word. The fierce and widely supported segregationist tactics of brutality, the many setbacks, defeats, and sad losses, and the assassinations, bombings, jailings, and beatings continued before, during, and after even the most successful of demonstrations and changes in federal law. Yet even those defeats and losses, we can now see, were steps toward a victory that completely dismantled the system of legal segregation. None of those brave-hearted women, men, and children who were killed died in vain.[19]

As a result of the freedom struggle in the South, much has indeed changed. The dismantling of segregation in turn opened important institutional doors and provided expanded political room for many other significant movements, such as the women's movement. But the lifting of legal barriers exposes ever more clearly the profound and growing economic inequalities experienced by those who cannot afford to walk through now open doors. John Lewis's 1963 March on Washington statement about economic crisis being a civil rights issue rings even more true today than when he made it. The multidecade deindustrialization and automation that is still hollowing out major cities, leaving residents with bleak job prospects, is a crisis not yet fully addressed.[20] The amazing advent and reelection of President Barack Obama highlights positive developments but does not alter the fact that, regarding economic inequality, the United States ranks today as "the worst nation" on the Internal Monetary Fund's list of countries with advanced economies, including France, Australia, Canada, Norway, and the Netherlands, among others. The United States has the highest infant mortality rate among this group of countries. It also has the highest incarceration rate in the world, with a rate of 743 imprisoned for every 100,000 people. The majority of those incarcerated are people "of color."[21] As Hurricane Katrina and other natural disasters have so tragically illustrated, there are high degrees of vulnerability within the US population. Meanwhile, a recalcitrant and increasingly right-wing Republican Party, which overtly swore to sabotage any and all of Obama's efforts, even before his first inauguration as president, remains fanatically strong. So today we still face the basic questions posed in 1969 by the redoubtable Ella Baker, whose wisdom and guidance helped to create SNCC. She said, "I think at this stage the big question is what is the American society? Is it the kind of society … that permits people to grow and develop according to their capacity that gives them a sense of value, not only for themselves, but a sense of value for other human beings?"[22]

MY WORK TODAY: TRANSCOMMUNAL PEACE EDUCATION IN CALIFORNIA PRISONS—JAILS AND COMMUNITIES, LEGACIES AND FUTURES

After 1965, I spent five years doing education-focused urban-community work in Massachusetts. I participated in the movement against the war in Vietnam as well as in the wider peace movement. I took part in organizing local contingents of two large demonstrations against the war, one in New York in 1966, involving about two hundred thousand people, including many military veterans,[23] and the other in Washington in 1968, where we joined one hundred thousand people. I worked with two underground newspapers (*Mother of Voices* and *the Carbuncle Review*).[24] In 1970, realizing that, given my personal ethical-political inclinations, I would be in the best position to combine activism with scholarship by becoming a university teacher, writer, and ally of progressive groups, I entered the graduate program in urban anthropology at the State University of New York in Buffalo. I received my PhD in 1975, with a dissertation that involved me in working with politically active black ministers in that city.[25] Over the several past decades, I have continued both to write about community activism and to participate in various organizations. My main focus for many years has been the making of "bridge-building" alliances among diverse communities. My core concept of transcommunality refers to modes of cooperation in which the heterogeneity of different communities and agendas is respected while becoming the basis for cooperation rather than conflict.

Currently, I am volunteer-teaching classes about transcommunal cooperation and peacemaking among interethnic groups of men in the Soledad state prison and in the Santa Cruz country jail. It is one of the positive developments, now occurring in the United States, that one finds transcommunal cooperation among African Americans, Latinos, whites, Native Americans, Asian Americans, and others inside prison walls. These classes, held in conjunction with the interethnic alliance-oriented community organization Barrios Unidos (United Neighborhoods)[26] in California, are only possible because there is an impulse toward transcommunal cooperation already alive among many key individuals inside prison. Despite the very real tendencies toward mistrust and conflict among different communities, this cooperative ethic is alive, well, and growing. This bodes well for the reduction of violence in many communities, especially when we have the support of prison veterans who are respected out on the street. Such reduction in violence is an important part of any positive community revitalization, which in turn is necessary for political strength and voice. At Barrios Unidos, we are fortunate to have support from the highly respected Harry Belafonte, Danny Glover, and Luis Rodriguez for our work. Simultaneously, there are thousands of organizations doing alliance-based social-justice activism around the United States, in places ranging from cities to reservations to farming towns. I believe that the legacy of many forward-looking political movements in the second half of the twentieth century, including the civil rights movement, created what has become a richly textured grassroots organizational environment with much greater breadth of multifaceted transcommunal complexity and progressive potential than what we had in the "1960s." Consequently, I fully concur with Ralph Ellison's still accurate assessment that "there is no way for one group to discover by itself the intrinsic forms of our democratic culture. This has to be a cooperative effort, and it is achieved through contact and communication across our divisions of race, class, religion, and region" (1986, 143).[27]

WORKS CITED

Alfred, Taiaike. 2005. *Wasase: Indigenous Pathways of Action and Freedom.* Peterborough, Ontario: Broadview Press.

Arsenault, Raymond. 2006. *Freedom Riders: 1961 and the Struggle for Social Justice.* Cambridge, MA: Oxford University Press.

Bond, Horace Mann. 1972. *Black American Scholars: A Study of Their Origins.* Detroit, MI: Belknap Publishing.

Carson, Clayborne. 1981. *In Struggle: SNCC and the Black Awakening of the 1960s.* Cambridge, MA: Harvard University Press.

Childs, John Brown. 1980. *The Political Black Minister: A Study in Afro-American Politics and Religion.* Boston: G. K. Hall.

_____. 1997. "Transcommunality: A 21st Century Social Compact for Urban Revitalization in the United States." In *Villes et politiques urbaines au Canada et aux États-Unis*, edited by Jean-Michel Lacroix, 181–198. Paris: Presses de la Sorbonne Nouvelle.

_____. 2003a. "Crossroads: Toward a Transcommunal Black History Month in the Multicultural United States of the Twenty-First Century." In "The Writing(s) of African American History," edited by Hélène Le Dantec-Lowry and Arlette Frund, special issue, *Annales du monde anglophone* 18: 49–63.

_____. 2003b. *Transcommunality: From the Politics of Conversion to the Ethics of Respect.* Philadelphia: Temple University Press.

Davis, Angela. 2003. *Are Prisons Obsolete?* New York: Seven Stories.

Ellison, Ralph. 1964. *Shadow and Act.* New York: Random House.

_____. 1986. *Going to the Territory.* New York: Vintage Books/Random House.

Evers, Myrlie, and Manning Marable. 2005. *The Autobiography of Medgar Evers: A Hero's Life and Legacy.* New York: Basic Civitas Books.

Forbes, Jack D. 1993. *Africans and Native Americans: The Language of Race and the Evolution of Red-Black Peoples.* Urbana: University of Illinois.

Frye, Hardy T. 1979. *Black Parties and Political Power: A Case Study.* Boston: Greenwood Press.

Grant, Joanne. 1998. *Ella Baker: Freedom Bound.* New York: John Wiley and Sons.

Grubbs, Donald H. 1971. *Cry from the Cotton: The Southern Tenant Farmers' Union and the New Deal.* Chapel Hill: University of North Carolina Press.

Kahn, Charles H. 1979. *The Art and Thought of Heraclitus.* London: Cambridge University Press.

Payne, Charles M. 1995. *I've Got the Light of Freedom: The Organizing Tradition and the Mississippi Freedom Struggle.* Berkeley: University of California Press.

Port Huron Statement. 1964. Port Huron, Michigan (mimeograph edition, 1963), 33–37.

Sale, Kirkpatrick. 1974. *SDS.* New York: Vintage Books.

Sidney, Wilhelm. 1970. *Who Needs the Negro?* Cambridge, MA: Schenkman.

Standon, Mary. 1998. *From Selma to Sorrow: The Life and Death of Viola Liuzzo.* Athens: University of Georgia Press.

Thoreau, Henry David. [1859] 2000. "A Plea for Captain John Brown." In *Walden and Other Writings*, edited by Brooks Atkinson, 715–744. New York: Modern Library.

Wallace, Paul A. 1986. *The White Roots of Peace*. Santa Fe: Clear Light Publishers.

Williams, Michael Vinson. 2011. *Medgar Evers: Mississippi Martyr*. Fayetteville: University of Arkansas.

NOTES

1 I deeply appreciate the invitation from Hélène Le Dantec-Lowry and Ambre Ivol to participate in this important book project. I thank my wife, Delgra M. Childs, and my collaborator and friend in many ventures, Guillermo Delgado-P., for their thoughtful suggestions. I also thank another friend, Denis Constant-Martin, for his insightful analysis of my concept of "transcommunality" in his *L'identite en jeux: Pouvoirs, identifications, mobilizations* (Paris, Éditions Karthala, 2010). Many years of conversation and shared actions with my friend Hardy Frye, former Deep South Student Nonviolent Coordinating Committee activist and University of California, Berkeley, professor, remain invaluable.

2 This second march, known as "Turn-Around Tuesday," involved a prearrangement by King and the SCLC to do a symbolic partial march to the bridge, then turn around in order to obey a federal court order "restraining" them from crossing the bridge. Most of the participants did not know about that agreement beforehand, and many were dismayed by and critical of it.

3 I am influenced here by the power of Fragment 33 of Heraclitus, which reads, "[The] oracle . . . in Delphi neither declares nor conceals, but gives a sign." See Kahn (1979, 43).

4 Langston Hughes's poem goes in part, "What happens to a dream deferred? Does it dry up like a raisin in the sun or does it explode?"

5 His widow, Myrlie Evers, herself became a well-known activist. She also put together *The Autobiography of Medgar Evers* (2005), with commentary by her and Manning Marable. Also important is Williams (2011). Nina Simone wrote and sang the song "Mississippi Goddamn" (1963) about the assassination. Bob Dylan's song "Only a Pawn in Their Game" (1963) also focuses on the killing of Evers. For a detailed overview analysis of civil rights in Mississippi, see Payne (1995).

6 Today, of course, John Lewis is a highly respected and long-serving Democratic member of the US House of Representatives. At the 2013 fiftieth anniversary of the March on Washington, he was the only main speaker to have actually participated in (and organized) that event.

7 Idela Childs, "The Lincoln Normal School," in *Perry County Heritage*, ed. W. Stuart Harris (Marion, AL: Perry County Historical and Preservation Society, 1991), 29–36. The school is now Alabama State University.

8 For a longer version of these ancestral spirit descriptions, see "Red Clay, Blue Hills" in Childs (2003b).

9 Malcolm X was assassinated on February 21, 1965, just a short while before the major civil rights events in Alabama.

10 Karl Marx and Friedrich Engels found the Great League of Peace of interest through their reading of its description in the work of nineteenth-century anthropologist Lewis Henry Morgan. The Great League also influenced the writers of the US Constitution. Wallace (1986) is a useful introduction to the classic formative period of the Great League. The five original nations in the league, from east to west in what is now New York State, were the Mohawks, Oneidas, Onondagas, Cayugas, and Senecas. The specific founding date of the league is contested.

11 For an important discussion of contemporary issues in part related to the Great League, see Mohawk writer and activist Taiaike Alfred (2005). For those interested in the wider picture of African–Native American connections in the Americas, see Forbes (1993).

12 Initially organized by the New York–based Congress of Racial Equality, the Freedom Riders soon became a broader loose grouping with input from SNCC.

13 The Democratic Party of Kennedy at that time was dominant in the segregationist South, and the Kennedy administration was initially wary of supporting civil rights for fear of losing its white Southern support base. When Lyndon B. Johnson later signed the landmark Voting Rights Act, he remarked accurately that, in so doing, he had lost the South. Soon there was widespread defection of white Southern Democrats ("Dixiecrats") to the Republican Party, in which they and their ideological descendants are now deeply embedded.

14 An important discussion of the Freedom Riders can be found in Arsenault (2006). Ironically, the interstate highway system was initiated by President Dwight D. Eisenhower in the 1950s as a Cold War defense measure to facilitate smooth movement of troops and supplies. He did not envision another kind of troops—those of civil rights activists.

15 For another personal account of this moment in that church, see Sam Carcione's account on the Civil Rights Movement Veterans website: http://www.crmvet.org/vet /vethome.htm. This is a uniquely significant oral history symposium among veterans of the SNCC. See also the important work of Clayborne Carson (1981).

16 The Black Panther Party for Self-Defense would later adopt that symbolism.

17 For reasons still not clear to me, no attack happened, and we departed the building safely hours later.

18 See Standon (1998).

19 For an important analysis of efforts to create an independent black political party in response to conservatism in both the main Democratic and Republican parties, see former SNCC activist Hardy T. Frye (1979).

20 See Sidney Wilhelm's prescient work on the erosion of inner-city economic opportunity and the creation of isolated de facto black "reservations" in his important but neglected book *Who Needs the Negro?*

21 Angela Davis does vital work on the prisons in her *Are Prisons Obsolete?* and in the 1999 "The Prison Industrial Complex" San Francisco, AK Press, audio recording.

22 This speech can be found in Grant (1998). It was given at the Institute of the Black World in Atlanta, Georgia, in 1969.

23 Our slogan, reflecting our basic position, was "Support the Troops, Bring Them Home Now!"

24 From a statement by Marx that he hoped to be an agitating "carbuncle" on the rear end of capitalism.

25 See Childs (1980).

26 Barrios Unidos, now a national organization, was founded in 1977 by its executive director, Daniel Nane Alejandrez, in California.

27 For my analysis of transcommunal cooperation among different communities, see also Childs (1997, 2003a, 2003b).

Intersecting Oppressions: Rethinking Women's Movements in the United States

JULIE AJINKYA

In 2007 Senator Hillary Clinton announced her bid for the U.S. presidency. Amid a generally conservative political climate that claimed the United States had become a "postfeminist" society where the women's movement of the 1960s and 1970s had already won equal opportunity for women, vocal feminists heralded Clinton's candidacy as a desperately needed boost of energy for the ailing women's movement. Women were predicted to unite in a voting bloc that would nominate Clinton as the Democratic Party's presidential nominee in 2008. As the primary race kicked off, however, another viable candidate announced his bid not even a month later—Senator Barack Obama, a young black freshman senator from Chicago. As young women and women of color moved to support Obama in overwhelming percentages, feminist Clinton supporters argued that in abandoning the first viable female candidate for president, they were abandoning feminism itself. There was an immediate spike in the discussion of Second Wave versus Third Wave feminism in newspapers, magazines, and blogs, trying to explain why women were aligning with either candidate. In February 2008 an article entitled "Feminists for Clinton" was posted on the well-followed political blog the Huffington Post, documenting 264 prominent U.S. feminists' support for Clinton's candidacy. The discussion board erupted between Clinton and Obama supporters (Stansell 2008):

UNITED STATES

Human Development Index ranking: .951

Gender-Related Development Index value: .937

Gender Empowerment Measure value: .762

General

Type of government: Federal Republic

Major ethnic groups: White (79.7%); Black (12.9%); Asian (4.4%); American and Alaskan Native (1%)

Languages: English; Spanish

Religions: Protestant (51.3%); Roman Catholic (23.9%); Mormon (1.7%); Jewish (1.7%); other or none (21.4%)

Date of independence: 1776

Former colonial power: Britain

Demographics

Population, total (millions), 2005: 299.8

Annual growth rate (%), 2005–2015: .9

Total fertility (average number of births per woman): 2.0

Contraceptive prevalence (% of married women aged 15–49): 76

Maternal mortality ratio, adjusted (per 100,000 live births), 2000: 11

Women's Status

Date of women's suffrage: 1920

Life expectancy: M 75.2; F 80.4

Combined gross enrollment ratio for primary, secondary, and tertiary education (female %), 2005: 98

Gross primary enrollment ratio: 99

Gross secondary enrollment ratio: 95

Gross tertiary enrollment ratio: 97

Literacy (% age 15 and older): M 99; F 99

Political Representation of Women

Seats in parliament (% held by women): 16.3

Legislators, senior officials, and managers (% female): 42

Professional and technical workers (% female): 56

Women in government at ministerial level (% total): 14.3

Economics

Estimated earned income (PPP US$): M 40,000; F 25,005

Ratio of estimated female to male earned income: .63

Economic activity rate (% female): 59.6

Women in adult labor force (% total): 46 (this figure obtained at the CEDAW Statistical Database)

I support Hillary. The media bias has been [about] Obama the savior and Hillary the bad one. I have never bought into the Obama hype. I supposed that is because I don't live in la la land. I live in reality. I'm not an impressional [sic] youth. I'm a 39 yr old mother who is excited about Hillary being president.—(Clinton supporter)

As a woman of a generation that had to fight hard to make things a bit easier for the current generation, I really fear that our younger women have no idea what is at work here. What we are seeing here is an example of a highly competent woman of substance having to work twice as hard to convince people she is as good as a mediocre man with a golden tongue of vapid chanting hollow messages.—(Clinton supporter)

As a long-time feminist, I will not allow anyone to bully me into supporting someone whom I don't think is the best choice as the Democratic nominee—based solely on her sex. America is at a crossroads—we can have a decent president (Hillary Clinton), a disastrous president (John McCain) or an extraordinary president—Barack Obama, a man with enormous vision, more legislative experience than Hillary Clinton, and most importantly, a modern thinker who understands how to unite us as a nation, as opposed to polarizing us further.—(Obama supporter)

According to you, us women who vote for Obama are sell-outs to the cause of feminism. And that's the biggest lie coming from the Clinton camp. As a woman, I have no qualms about voting for Obama and still feeling like I'm supporting women. People accuse Obama of misogyny, but that couldn't be further from the truth. Obama is a product of all of the women in his life. Raised by a single mother. A father of two daughters. A husband of a strong, working mother in Michelle Obama. He is no stranger to the cause of feminism, and has benefited from it. Stop guilting women into voting for Clinton. This is identity politics at its worst.—(Obama supporter)

Women continued arguments like these for pages upon pages in response to articles posted online about the candidates and feminism. Obama supporters were accused of taking women's struggles in the 1960s and '70s for granted, and Clinton supporters were accused of prioritizing gender above race in identity politics. Attacks across generations often cited references to the *feminist waves*—an approach used in women's studies that describes U.S. feminism as occurring in three sequential periods: the *First Wave* imparts the struggle for suffrage; the *Second Wave* refers to the struggle for social, economic, and political equality; and the *Third Wave* focuses on the intersection of different nongender identities (e.g. race, class, sexuality, and so on) with gender itself (Baumgardner and Richards 2000; Garrison 2000). "Second Wave feminists" assumed that younger feminists voted for Obama because they took their predecessors' struggles during the 1960s–1970s for granted, and "Third Wave feminists" argued that women who supported Clinton over Obama believed in an exclusive version of feminism that only applied to white middle-class straight women.

This chapter takes its cue from the election controversy concerning divisions within U.S. feminism to argue that this "wave approach" obscures important political divisions beyond age and cohort; this approach misleadingly suggests a homogenous group of feminists within each wave, thinking about women's rights in the same way during each given time period, and it misrepresents the extent of diversity within U.S. feminism. If we are truly interested in the development of feminism in the United States we should explore these time periods for similar tensions within themselves that divided feminists and different women's organizations. This chapter makes the argument that one such division that repeatedly appeared in women's activism was the relationship that feminists pursued with the state. While liberal organizations and movements saw the state as an ally and believed in institutional reform, radical organizations believed in finding alternative solutions to the state and pursued community-oriented strategies to fight discrimination. Although this classification continues to describe a major rift in feminist discourse today, women's activism—through issue-based campaigns and organizations—negotiates a more complicated relationship with the state, at times lobbying for institutional or legislative reform, while also protesting the policies that it contests. I will conclude with a discussion of the electoral controversy that began this chapter, in order to demonstrate how this election's attention to *intersectional feminism* might encourage feminists to start bridging their differences.

What is the relationship between feminism and women's movements in the United States? While feminism is a political theory that discursively liberates women from gender-based oppression, women's movements mobilize women behind an action agenda, aimed at procuring some level of tangible change in women's situations. This distinction suggests that feminism does not necessarily lead to the mobilization of women's movements but that women's movements must necessarily incorporate, at a bare minimum, the fundamental feminist conviction that the oppressive circumstances that women face derive from their gender identity, even if it is in combination with other identities. In other words, a welfare rights movement that mobilizes women is considered a women's movement if it acknowledges in its raison d'être that women experience welfare and its reform differently from men; it can, and must, emphasize class-based oppression as well, but its interaction with gender-based oppression must play a definitive role, even if the movement itself does not necessarily designate itself as *feminist*. Likewise, this understanding of women's movements excludes certain women's mobilizations, such as women from the religious Right, if they derive their political beliefs from a larger movement that does not challenge gender inequality. Such women are not feminist, nor do they constitute a women's movement, because they do not struggle against gender-based oppression; they merely form an interest group of the larger political movement (e.g., religious fundamentalism) itself. While the growth of women *in* such movements is an interesting topic that warrants further research in U.S. politics, it is beyond the scope of this chapter.

The group of women who are traditionally referred to as "Third Wave feminists" should more accurately be understood as those feminists who use *intersectionality theory* to a greater extent, as an epistemological tool that connects those women who experience interlocking oppressions at the crossroads of their gender, race, class, citizenship, sexuality, and other identities. Intersectionality theory originated in the scholarship of Kimberle Crenshaw in the late 1980s and was popularized by Patricia Collins's work in the 1990s, but there is evidence of intersectionality in women's activism dating back to abolition in the nineteenth century. Crenshaw introduces the concept of intersectionality to caution against the essentialization of gender as an exclusive category in women's identities; instead, women's multiple identities are posited to intersect and interact, describing women's experiences more thoroughly than attention to any one discrete identity might accomplish (see Crenshaw 1989).[1] She argues that an analysis of discrimination that tries to categorize women's experience along single-axis oppressions loses sight of the multidimensional nature of women's identities: "Consider an analogy to traffic in an intersection, coming and going in all four directions. Discrimination, like traffic through an intersection, may flow in one direction, and it may flow in another. If an accident happens, in an intersection, it can be caused by cars traveling from any number of directions and, sometimes, from all of them. Similarly, if a Black woman is harmed because she is in the intersection, her injury could result from sex discrimination or race discrimination" (1989, 139).

Collins (2000) expands on Crenshaw's understanding of intersectionality by describing how individuals are socially located in the middle of crosscutting systems of oppression and how these systems form mutually constructing features of social organization. While there has been appreciation of women as multidimensional characters throughout American history, an intersectional epistemology failed to substantively develop until the 1980s and has now shifted to a position of prominence in contemporary American feminism.

Looking at intersectionality in this epistemological way, as a *form of knowledge* itself, helps us understand how this concept enables feminism to make sense of women's different locations in society. While intersectionality theory broadly describes oppression coming from multiple directions, its particular application in contemporary feminism takes this analysis one step further and connects those women who belong to groups that have been historically conceptualized as second-class citizens: blacks as slaves, the poor as the voiceless majority, immigrants as foreigners, lesbians as deviants, and so on; these women join together with the understanding that they cannot turn to the state as a solution—as other feminists have in the past—because the state is, for them, a part of the problem.

That said, the extent to which the state is still framed as a potential ally versus an irreconcilable force outlines important divisions within feminist discourse and women's movements in the United States today. These contemporary divisions are reminiscent of divisions within feminist women's movements in the 1960s and '70s that also derived from women activists' different interpretations of the state. Initially, the *liberal* branch of feminism was born out of frustration with sexism in institutional reform and developed as an ideology based on the individualist assumption that women were capable of accomplishing everything men could and that legal reform was the way to remove institutional discrimination that limited their opportunities. Meanwhile, for those feminists who disagreed with institutional reform as the ultimate strategy to win women's rights, the *radical* branch of feminism emerged as an ideology that focused on patriarchy as the systemic oppressive force that violated women's rights and called for a radical realteration of society's order, including gender roles in the public and private spheres (Rosen 2000; Roth 2004).

As Mary Katzenstein (1998) argues in her analysis of feminism in the military and church, the legacy of liberal feminism led to the institutionalization of women's movements that work for reform from *within* the establishment. Liberal feminism's efforts during the 1960s and '70s accomplished a certain degree of legislative and judicial validation for feminism, and many women are now found launching their own egalitarian campaigns for better benefits or against sexual harassment within their own organizations, instead of turning to help from "outsider" women's movements. In this sense, liberal feminism still believes that institutional reform is the answer to gender discrimination, instead of overtly challenging systemic gender relations that curb the percentage of both men in secretarial roles and women in executive positions.

Radical feminism was also reincarnated in the contemporary phase of feminism, but it went through a more fundamental shift in disposition than liberal feminism did. While radical feminism continues to disagree with a state-centric approach, its focus on patriarchy as *the* oppressive force has now shifted to *state systems* perpetuating not only patriarchy but racism, classism, nativism, and heterosexism as well. As will be explained in greater detail below, this critical disagreement in seeing the state as ally or adversary shaped the politics of the 1960s and '70s and has continued to affect the development of feminist consciousness today.

This chapter outlines the development of these divisions within phases of feminism and women's activism, countering the traditional "wave approach" in women's studies, and highlights the strengths and weaknesses of contemporary feminism's intersectional approach. In doing so, I conclude with a set of key questions intersectional feminists might address in order to translate their discursive contributions into an action agenda.

THE EARLY YEARS, 1848–1920

The conflict between gender and race as intersecting oppressions can be traced back to the inception of the women's movement, as suffragist leaders such as Susan B. Anthony and Elizabeth Cady Stanton actually began their activist careers as female abolitionists. Ultimately, however, sexism in the abolitionist movement that refused to consider women's leadership or input drove these women to fight for women's representation and found the suffragist movement. Excluded from both feminist organizations and antislavery organizations that were run by either white women or black men, black women found themselves stranded at the crossroads of their identities and started their own organizations, including the Manhattan Abolition Society and the Colored Female Anti-Slavery Society (see Dicker 2008). Though early women's rights activists at this time used abolitionists' human rights rhetoric on the black male slave and analogously applied it to women, it was most often framed as a question of rights for both white women and black men, with no mention of black women's rights. Black women were instead forced to choose their allegiance to either black rights or women's rights. In fact, though the period is often marked by the leadership of three white abolitionist women, Anthony, Stanton, and Lucy Stone, the hostility directed toward the efforts of the most prominent black women's rights leader, Sojourner Truth, in highlighting the plight of black women slaves, revealed that they expected gender to trump race politics; against this backdrop, women's rights grew to mean white women's rights.

Because of this narrow understanding of feminism as the liberation of *white women*, this phase thwarted the development of intersectional feminist analysis. Certain accomplishments were made along the way to suffrage, such as the Married Women's Property Act of 1860, but the main victory that effectively brought an end to this period of women's activism is the ratification of the Nineteenth Amendment to the Constitution of the United States, granting (white) women the right to vote in 1920. Besides winning this right for white women, the other lasting legacy that this period would leave on women's activism was the marginalization of those women not considered to inhabit the mainstream of America.

THE MIDDLE YEARS, 1960s–1970s

The second period of feminism emerged out of the disillusionment of women activists with both institutional reform in the 1960s and the more radical New Left and civil rights movements. These liberal feminists were looking to build a relationship with the state beyond the voting rights that their predecessors had won in the early 1900s; now they were looking to actually insert women into the state and pursue reform from within. The central liberal-feminist organization, the National Organization for Women (NOW), was founded in 1966 by professional women who sat on state commissions on the status of women, after their proposal for the new Equal Employment Opportunity Commission to take sex discrimination as seriously as racial discrimination was turned down. These women had been activists with political interest groups and unions, among other institutions, prior to the founding of NOW, so they retained their institutionalization and established a branch of feminism that believed women could be equal to men without altering the fundamental structure of society, as long as legal roadblocks (such as employment discrimination) were removed along the way.

Meanwhile, other women who were active in the New Left and civil rights movements were growing frustrated with having their activist potential stymied by their male peers. While these male activists allegedly fought against injustice and discrimination, it became clear to women—who were still expected to take notes and make coffee at movement meetings as secretaries, cook and clean at home while bearing children as wives and mothers, and stay quiet while setting organizational agendas—that it was the forms of injustice and discrimination that *men* experienced on the grounds of race or class but not manifestations that they, as women, endured because of their gender. What progress could women make simply by joining organizations, or working within the state, if women were still relegated to menial tasks once inside?

Women who grew frustrated with both these gender relations in the private and public spheres and the state-centric focus of liberal feminist organizations that fought for institutional reform generated their own version of feminism: *radical* feminism. This branch employed consciousness raising (CR) as its main strategy of empowering women to realize that "the personal is political"—prioritizing an agenda that challenged systemic gender norms in society and women's personal lives, instead of focusing on institutional reform. Women gathered in small groups for these CR sessions and shared life stories, asking deeply personal questions about why things were ordered in their lives the way they were (e.g., why were women sequestered in the kitchen, while men worked outdoors?). The sessions were meant to help women understand that they were not alone in their house arrest under strict gender roles. In Rosen's interviews with participants of such sessions, one woman gives an account of watching another woman in the group "get it": "I'll never forget one night, this marvelous woman. She was very blunt, very outspoken; she was talking about how while she grew up, she wasn't the stereotypical feminine type, and how this caused her a lot of grief. Then she said, 'I realized that it was ok to be a strong woman.' Suddenly there was complete silence, followed by shouts of agreement. It was a very exciting moment. People were getting it, right there, in that meeting" (2000).

These sessions, however, were mainly composed of white middle-class women, which was a reflection of the composition of radical feminism itself. Different groups of women objected to this branch for different reasons. Black women thought that CR sessions that talked about women's dreams to work outside of the home and spend less time with their families were endlessly alienating, because a large majority of black women already worked outside the home to meet expenses and they *wanted* more time at home with their families; they also wanted to discuss the intersecting oppressive forces of race, class, and gender in their experiences. Socialist feminists objected to radical feminists' claims that patriarchy was the fundamental oppressive force with which all women contended, and instead argued that it was capitalism to blame for a class structure that oppressed women. Queer women argued that radical feminists were essentializing the role of gender and that gay women's experiences fell outside of the traditional gender role dynamic.

In essence, because of both feminist branches' failure to consider diversity in women's experiences, marginalized women began forming their own organizations, such as the National Black Feminist Organization in 1973, the National Alliance of Black Feminists in 1976, the Freedom Socialist Party in 1966, and the Radicalesbians in 1970. These groups varied according to the issues and identities they prioritized but retained focus on their own axes of oppression. They experimented with temporary coalitional work from time to time, working on issue-based campaigns such as violence against women, but after these campaigns were over, the groups went back to their original corners and stayed distinct from one another—often addressed as "minority groups" by the dominant white middle-class straight majority, but rarely finding any other similarities in the struggles they faced.

VIOLENCE AGAINST WOMEN

The issue of violence against women is an instructive example of coalition politics during the Second Wave of American feminism. The issue of rape, for example, was a juncture in women's activism that temporarily bridged divisions among feminist liberals and radicals, whites and blacks. It seems logical that radical feminists were among the first paying attention to the issue, using CR techniques to encourage women to speak out about the violence they experienced. In order to make the personal experience of rape a political issue for women to rally behind, "speak-outs" linked episodes of rape (and sexual assault more broadly defined) to systemic problems of male dominance.

Though the strategies of radical and liberal feminists diverged during this period, their political positions merged on the topic of sexual assault. Radical feminists, usually disdainful of electoral and legal reform, put their reservations aside and listened to the concerns of rape victims, who complained of feeling victimized a second time by the criminal justice system after reporting their claims; reforming police behavior required cooperation with the institutionalized strategies of liberal feminism. Liberal feminists took advantage of the CR technique's ability to facilitate massive awareness-raising campaigns. Together, radical and liberal feminists united behind reframing rape as an example of violence—not passion—and efforts to make the postrape experience the least traumatic for the victim possible (Gillmore 2008).

Black feminists, particularly in Washington, D.C., challenged the white leadership of rape crisis centers in black-dominated areas like the nation's capital and insisted that rape was also a consequence of poverty and racism (Bavacqua 2008). In this way, antiviolence campaigns birthed coalitions across class and race, but these coalitions proved difficult to sustain as organizations retreated to their separate spheres after temporary alliances. Breines (2006) describes a notable episode of cooperation between black and white feminists toward the end of the Second Wave. She recounts the murders of twelve black women in predominantly black Boston neighborhoods that encouraged cross-racial cooperation among local feminists in the formation of the Coalition for Women's Safety in 1979. Activist women united behind anger toward the police and media; they criticized these institutions for systemically perpetuating attitudes toward black women that made these crimes possible. They were accused of painting the black victims as prostitutes and using prejudice against such women to excuse their responsibility to solve the crimes. In response to sexism in their racial communities, black women turned to explicitly feminist groups and saw that white women were interested in serving as allies; the coalition proved hard to maintain beyond this single-focus campaign, though, and the alliance eventually dissolved.

The politics of the antirape movement were closely aligned with those of the shelter movement, another widespread women's movement against violence, but one that had a far more entangled relationship with the state. The shelter movement in the United States emerged from a conscious-ness-raising group in Minnesota that started their own crisis telephone hotline to assist women, even taking victims into their own homes until they could find support elsewhere. Eventually, this grassroots network raised enough funds to purchase their own house for battered women, and thus was born the mainstream women's shelter movement in 1974 (Elman 2003). The tangible services that shelters provided drew increased attention from both the state and growing numbers of women in need, until shelters finally turned to the state for funding and increasingly became *institutionalized* with professional staff in an effort to expand their services and *depoliticized* as the state imposed rules and process. Ironically, as funding poured in, services had to download assistance measures onto localities and streamline their provisions to adhere to austerity mea-sures dictated by the government. Shelters lost their grassroots base as staff was forced to worry about grants, efficiency, and "clientele," similar to state social service agencies. These temporary coalitions between liberal and radical feminists failed to translate into more sustainable alliances, because as the state became more involved, radical feminists grew fearful of co-optation.

The divisions within women of color had also become apparent during the rise of the women's shelter movements in the 1970s, when mainstream battered women's shelters were unable to provide services to immigrant women in particular. These shelters failed to provide translation services and could not manage cultural sensitivities regarding violence, divorce, and dietary restrictions. South Asian activists, for example, found women from their own community leaving shelters to return to their abusers instead of remaining in shelters where they felt discrimination from other women. These activists turned around and founded their own organizations and shel-ters, facing the same intersection of discrimination from men in their community who believed they were "corrupted" by American radical feminist ideas and banned them from cultural gath-erings, as well as discrimination from the women in the mainstream shelter movement. Similar to black and Latina feminists who were starting their own organizations during this period, Asians forged their own intersectional alternative as well. Groups such as Manavi and Sakhi were even-tually born in the 1980s, providing counseling, shelter services, and legal support to South Asian victims of domestic violence (Das Dasgupta 2007). Feminists outside of the mainstream were preoccupied with finding spaces for their own distinct intersections, but the political landscape still lacked any serious attempt at articulating the commonality these groups all shared under an intersectional framework.

WOMEN'S ECONOMIC INEQUALITY

Women's activism around economic inequality was divided between two main agendas: inequality between men and women in the workplace and inequality between the growing numbers of women on welfare and society at large. Liberal feminist groups dominated the first front, and successfully won the Equal Pay Act of 1963 and sexual discrimination provisions in the Civil Rights Act of 1964. Their campaigns' focus on institutional reform and the white-collar world, however, effectively alienated working-class women, who were more concerned with the systemic factors of poverty on the second front.

Women in poverty found a home in welfare activist organizations, as opposed to mainstream liberal and radical feminist organizations that still neglected discussions over race and class. Because the majority of welfare recipients were women, welfare rights consequently became framed as "poor women's rights." White and black women on welfare also formed organizations parallel to one another, coming together in city or statewide coalitions, such as the Welfare Rights Coalition in Baltimore and the City-Wide Coordinating Committee of Welfare Rights Groups in New York. One of the most prominent groups of this time, the National Welfare Rights Organization, was founded in 1967 and led by committees made up of welfare recipients who were mostly black women; the NWRO protested cutbacks in federal assistance to poor families and their disproportionate effects on women and children.

The welfare rights movement made several key gains in defending poor people's rights during this time. Chief among them were the campaigns for fair hearings from caseworkers, better recognition for their roles as mothers, and school clothing for their children; these activists' roles as mothers proved to be an important mobilizing tool and common ground for these coalitions with women across race. The issue-based nature of this movement allowed women to organize in greater numbers against the deprivation they all faced, instead of the abstract articulation of gender equality and structural reform that often alienated those dealing with the daily pressures of living in poverty; at the same time, this focus on institutional reform, in terms of benefits and wages, meant that this subset of radical feminists compromised their stance on avoiding state-centric campaigns. Initially, this compromise was understood as a needed trade-off to accomplish policy improvements, but as the state grew more receptive to reform advocacy, the welfare rights movement feared the same co-optation to which the antiviolence movements had fallen prey.

However, the heavy involvement of the state was not to last. In the 1980s an overinflated economy, the oil crisis, the deficit, and the election of a conservative regime under Ronald

Reagan led to a fundamental reconfiguration of state institutions. Katzenstein (2003) argues that this reconfiguration hardly affected the ability of privileged women to hold on to the institution-based associational politics they had developed as insiders, but it severely limited the ability of poor women to organize and defend their own interests. This class bifurcation undid the hard work of the activists in the welfare rights movement; they had come close to establishing welfare as an entitlement and had temporarily won legislative reforms that suggested poor women would be included in the nation's citizenry. Now, increased privatization and delegating federal obligations to the state level pushed poor women back to the margins, while co-opting middle-class liberal feminist efforts.

WOMEN'S POLITICAL REPRESENTATION

As is clear by now, liberal feminism was primarily focused on working through legislative and electoral avenues to accomplish its own understanding of gender equality. A series of legislative reforms were implemented during the 1960s, including President Kennedy's President's Commission on the Status of Women in 1961, the Equal Pay Act of 1963, the 1964 Civil Rights Act and its sexual discrimination protections in Title VII, and President Johnson's Executive Order 11375 in 1967, which imposed affirmative action measures on employment receiving federal funds. By 1971 it was clear that liberal feminists had begun to take political parties seriously with the founding of the National Women's Political Caucus (NWPC). The multipartisan caucus was founded with the primary purpose of promoting women into elected and appointed office at local, state, and national levels of government. They pledged to support female candidates financially, as well as to provide them with strategic assistance and campaign training workshops. Candidates were chosen according to prochoice platforms, which explained why the majority of candidates supported by the caucus hailed from the Democratic Party, in spite of its multipartisan mission.

In spite of the NWPC's efforts at increasing the number of women in public office, the actual levels of representation changed little over the next two decades. Beckwith's analysis (2003) shows that the percentage of women in the House of Representatives in 1974 was 4.4 percent of all House members, while in 1994 it had risen to only 11 percent. Liberal feminists, however, tried to take advantage of the federalist structure of the U.S. government and focused on winning seats for women at the statehouse level, which proved more successful. The same analysis shows an increase from 8.1 percent of total state house legislature women's representation to a more significant 20.6 percent in 1995. The impact of this increase in representation on women's policy concerns is still unclear. For example, this increase at the state level corresponded to the offloading of welfare policy management and shelter services from state responsibility to nonprofit provisions; if the increase in women's representation presumably served the best interests of women, one would think that the shelters' petitions, to both the state and the private sector, for more funding to meet their expanding clientele would have been answered favorably by the state legislature—and it was not.

In the 1980s more organizations emerged to work on promoting women's representation, including liberal women of color organizations such as the National Political Congress of Black Women, founded by the first black woman, Rep. Shirley Chisholm, to be elected to the House of Representatives in 1968. Chisholm had also been a key founder of the NWPC in the early 1970s, but believed that an organization focused on promoting black women in politics was necessary after her experiences with sexism and racism serving in Congress; she founded the NPCBW (which would later become the National Congress of Black Women) after leaving office in 1983. Two years later, in 1985, another group concerned with women's representation was founded called EMILY's List; in response to the realization that democratic women were not receiving the financial support necessary for a viable campaign, female supporters came together to start the organization on the principle that "early money is like yeast" and to fund-raise for prochoice Democratic women to get elected into office. While these organizations prioritized getting more women into public office, radical feminist groups such as the Combahee River Collective of Radical Women still saw a great deal of work to be done on grassroots issues in their communities and felt electing women to office put the cart before the horse. There was no indication that simply electing women to office would necessarily translate into better outcomes for women's interests—especially for women from communities that felt ignored by the liberal feminist agenda.

While radical feminists did not pursue political representation, they did participate in a scheme initiated by liberal feminist congresswomen in 1977: the National Women's Conference, an effort funded and authorized by Congress, to bring feminists from all over the country together in Houston to discuss the status of women and issues of concern to them. Support for the conference was primarily provided by liberal feminist organizations such as the National Women's Political Caucus, Women's Action Alliance, Federally Employed Women, and National Organization for Women.

In spite of these initial indications that the conference might be yet another manifestation of the now well-established division between liberal and radical feminists, as well as further divisions based on race, ethnicity, class, sexuality, and other identities, the conference was a marked success in terms of diverse attendance: not only were a quarter of the attendants women from minority racial communities, but there were also women from numerous ethnicities, all sexualities, variations in socioeconomic status, and even representation from the right-wing opposition (National Commission on the Observance of International Women's Year 1978). At least temporarily, these diverse groups crossed the liberal and radical feminist divide in order to see if the conference could bridge their differences. Five million dollars allocated to the project by Congress enabled women to hold state conferences leading up to the national gathering, in order to elect its 2000 representatives with representative privileges. This funding also included travel support for the delegates to attend the conference in Houston, regardless of socioeconomic standing.

The chief purpose of the conference was to bring these diverse groups of women together to discuss and vote on the twenty-six planks of the National Plan of Action for Women devised by the state conventions. A close reading of the plan's planks, however, demonstrates the continued marginalization of women outside of the mainstream liberal feminism establishment. The practice of only discussing the concerns of nonwhite non-middle-class gay women in auxiliary caucuses such as the "Minority Women Plank" and "Sexual Preference Plank," and not in the large-issue planks such as the "Education Plank" or "Employment Plank," further strengthened the construction of the *default* woman as white, middle class, and straight. In this sense, the diversity of women's identities was treated as an additive concept, instead of an intersectional concept that would also question the intersection of the mainstream woman's gender identity with her white race, middle-class status, or straight sexuality.

For example, the issue of forced sterilization in communities of color was not included in planks concerning violence against women, which was an issue primarily dealt with under the "Battered Women Plank" or the "Rape Plank"—both planks addressed violence only as it pertained to wife battery in the home or sexual assault at the individual level. The "Sexual Preferences Plank" also detailed employment discrimination concerns that were neglected under the "Employment Plank," which discussed discrimination only as it pertained to women as a homogenous group of employees, in terms of equal pay, merit promotion principles, and upward mobility. The majority plank lacked any discussion of the different obstacles faced by lesbian women when even applying for said jobs.

In spite of these discrepancies between minority caucus groups' planks and the mainstream-issue planks, minority communities made two main advances through this conference. First, for the first time, a number of women had the (federally funded) opportunity to come together with the sisters of their respective communities and discuss the problems they were facing in person. Second, from this point onward, instead of expressing minority women's identities as though they were isolated from one another, more women from these communities came together under the umbrella identification of "women of color," which would give rise to more intersectional analysis in the future. The "Minority Caucus" brought women from different racial and ethnic communities together to discuss the commonality of their experiences with what they called "double discrimination." The conference report explained:

> For the first time, minority women—many of whom had been in the leadership of the women's movement precisely because of their greater political understanding of discrimination—were present in such a critical mass that they were able to define their own needs as well as to declare their stake in each women's issue. They were also able to make the media aware of their importance and to forge their own internal networks and coalitions in a way that was far reaching, inclusive, and an historic "first" for their communities, for women and men. (ibid.)

By creating the *permanent category* of "women of color," in which women from different racial and ethnic communities could claim membership, these feminists were, interestingly, addressing the idea of intersectionality without ever explicitly mentioning it. While the discussion of double discrimination was limited to race and ethnicity at this conference, other identities eventually appropriated its analytical traction to forge new coalitions of feminists who felt marginalized—most prominently those who felt marginalized by the liberal feminist agenda of institutional reform, an alliance with the state that had left them behind.

Intersectional analysis was emerging elsewhere around the same time as the conference. Women who had become disillusioned with the liberal feminism of the National Black Feminist Organization, for example, had left in 1974 and founded the Combahee River Collective, a black feminist lesbian organization that was symbolically named after the guerrilla action led by Harriet Tubman in 1863 to free 750 slaves at the site of the Combahee River in South Carolina. Committed to the analysis of interlocking oppressions that shaped the conditions of members' lives, the collective released an important statement in 1977—the same year as the NWC, which they did not attend—that outlined why the concepts of identity politics and intersectionality were vital to understanding the multiple oppressions their members experienced. In their own words, they were "actively committed to struggling against racial, sexual, heterosexual, and class oppression and see as [their] particular task the development of integrated analysis and practice based upon the fact that the major systems of oppression are interlocking." The collective also made clear that the white women's movement had dealt with race, class, and sexuality diversity in only superficial ways; it argued that the main onus was on white women to put more effort into understanding the multiple oppressions that nonwhite women faced: "One issue that is of major concern to us and that we have begun to publicly address is racism in the white women's movement . . . eliminating racism in the white women's movement is by definition work for white women to do, but we will continue to speak to and demand accountability on this issue" (Combahee River Collective 1986). Advocating this position, it would be hard for one to imagine the collective's approval of the NWC's caucus approach to intersecting oppressions—the absence of white women in minority discussions, for example, absolved the former of the accountability that Combahee demanded.

Around this time, the term *women of color* was used more frequently by feminists who started to see commonality in their interlocking oppressions. Frustrated by the same superficial treatment with which their experiences with racism, classism, and, in some cases, homophobia were met by mainstream liberal and radical feminism of the 1960s and '70s, some of the first women to bring attention to these ideas were writers and artists such as Audre Lorde, Cherríe Moraga, bell hooks, Barbara Smith, Beverly Smith, and Merle Woo; among numerous others, they were published in a volume of critical essays, poetry, and fiction entitled *This Bridge Called My Back: Writings by Radical Women of Color*. These women presumably felt liberated from organizational politics and used their personal, expressive art forms to communicate these ideas to the general public.

THE LATER YEARS, 1990–TODAY

In 1991 a young black woman named Anita Hill testified at a Senate confirmation hearing regarding the sexual harassment she received as an employee at the Equal Employment Opportunity Commission. The alleged harasser was Clarence Thomas, a black man who had served as the chair of the EEOC and was under consideration to replace Justice Thurgood Marshall, the first African American to be appointed to the Supreme Court bench. Feminists across the liberal and radical divide became increasingly invested in how the courtroom drama played out, waiting to see how the most senior legal institutions in the country treated sexual harassment.

The liberal branch of feminism from the 1960s and '70s had consolidated in 1983 into the National Council of Women's Organizations (NCWO), a coalition of the predominant liberal national organizations at the time that met in Washington, D.C., to discuss public policy agendas and their persistent commitment to legislative reform. Member groups such as NOW objected to Thomas's nomination even before Hill's allegations were unveiled, in response to his position on abortion rights, but the sexual harassment allegations reinvigorated their stance; they argued that Hill was being treated unfairly by the all-male judiciary committee and that sex discrimination was still rampant in the U.S. workforce. Meanwhile, male leaders in the black community argued that the all *white* male committee was unduly grilling Thomas because of his race. Black women were once again caught between their gender and their race, reminiscent of the intersectional conflicts from the 1960s and '70s.

In 1992 Rebecca Walker, the daughter of renowned black feminist Alice Walker, wrote a groundbreaking essay in *Ms.* magazine entitled "Becoming the Third Wave," in which she out-lined her frustrations over the hearings, bemoaning the fact that young women felt estranged from their mothers' generation and found few other feminist options. She declared that she was not a "post-feminist feminist" as young women had been portrayed by the conservative backlash in the media that claimed feminism was dead; instead, she claimed that she, and others her age, were its "Third Wave."

It was this introduction to "Third Wave" language that misleadingly implied homogeneity in two groups: the young Walker's peers and their "Second Wave" predecessors. In reality, it was older black feminists who felt alienated enough by their mostly white liberal feminist peers and their male black peers to initiate an effort in 1991 called African-American Women in Defense of Ourselves. This group even managed to gather more than 1,600 signatures for a statement against Thomas's confirmation that appeared in the *New York Times* (B. Smith 2000). So while the "Third Wave" traditionally refers to young contemporary feminists, it should instead refer to those women, regardless of age or generation, who address the importance of intersec-tional feminism. Hey-wood and Drake explain the "Third Wave agenda": "A third wave goal that comes directly out of learning from these histories and working among these traditions is the development of modes of thinking that can come to terms with the multiple, constantly shifting bases of oppression in relation to the multiple, interpenetrating axes of identity, and the creation of a coalition politics based on these understandings—understandings that acknowledge the existence of oppression, even though it is not fashionable to say so" (1997, 3).

A number of key feminist anthologies that met these requirements began appearing in the 1990s, such as *Listen Up: Voices from the Next Feminist Generation* and *Colonize This! Young Women of Color on Today's Feminism*, but the young authors credited their feminist consciousness to writers such as Lorde, hooks, Anzaldua, Moraga, and countless other feminists who belonged to the age cohort before them. To call these older women "Third Wave feminists" discredits their important contributions in the 1960s and '70s, and incorrectly assumes that their feminist consciousness sequentially followed the feminism of white middle-class straight feminists from the same time period (Roth 2004).

As feminism experienced these discursive developments, the political climate of the 1980s ushered in important changes in the state. After Ronald Reagan took office in 1981, the new conservative government began to roll back a number of accomplishments that Second Wave feminism had accomplished, including allowing more restrictive conditions on abortions, cutbacks in welfare allowances to single mothers, and less oversight against sexual discrimination in the workplace. Meanwhile, civil society witnessed a growth in conservative women's groups as well; the NWC had not only served as organizing grounds for women of the Left but had also given conservative women the same opportunities to come together and give birth to the New Right. Even the 1990s, under the Clinton administration, failed to usher in any relief for women from communities who were feeling the backlash against affirmative action, welfare policies, and the tightening of immigration control under Democratic and Republican administrations.

For its part, liberal feminism had also gone through a major metamorphosis. While organizations had consolidated into the NWCO, their legislative victories from the 1960s and '70s had successfully multiplied the presence of women in the workplace. As Mary Katzenstein (1998) argues in her analysis of women's activism, feminism became so institutionalized that women argued for their own interests from *within* even the least-likely institutions (such as the military and the church), instead of turning to outside women's organizations for support. At the same time, liberal feminism joined other political causes in a surge toward NGO-ization, as various causes prioritized their professionalization in response to the reconfigured state. Former radical groups, in contrast, retreated from the political scene, abandoning their CR sessions and finding refuge in university collectives. As radical feminists negotiated with campus administrations to change sexist organizational culture, and liberal groups continued to bargain with the state, it became conventional for women's activists to negotiate with authorities to accomplish their feminist goals. In this new era of intersectional women's activism, however, there is less emphasis on the state as a potential partner in negotiations; instead, new women's organizations, such as INCITE, CodePink, and the Third Wave Foundation, place alternatives to state power at the center of their feminist analysis. These alternatives include organizing direct action and protests against state domestic and foreign policy, establishing alternative funding sources for like-minded organizations, training women in self-defense, and holding workshops and political art shows to educate the public and encourage resistance against the state-perpetuated violence against their communities.

VIOLENCE AGAINST WOMEN AND WOMEN'S ECONOMIC INEQUALITY

The capacity of antiviolence organizations that emerged during the 1960s and '70s to serve women from communities outside of that mainstream severely diminished over the next few decades. Not only were shelters poorly equipped to manage women who spoke languages other than English or handle special dietary restrictions, but they also failed to address violence against women of color in all of its forms—not just wife battery or domestic violence but the more systemic forms of violence that women outside the mainstream suffered at the hands of the *state*.

The debate around the Violence Against Women Act, passed in 1994, illustrated these tensions. The act, which had been championed by liberal feminist groups such as NOW, provided $1.6 billion in government funds to strengthen the prosecution of crimes perpetrated against women, increased pretrial detention periods for the accused, and allowed women civil redress for unprosecuted cases. Women of color, however, criticized the act's focus on harsher penalties for perpetrators of violence, which called for thousands more police on *their* streets; women of color saw these measures as only protecting those women whose racial and socio-economic communities were not already targeted by an oppressive criminal justice apparatus. At the same time, the problems of violence that still existed in these communities could not be ignored. In order to address violence against *all* women, they argued, the country needed a more comprehensive plan that focused on community health and safety, without persecuting poor communities of color.

In 2000 women of color from across the country who were frustrated with the efforts of racial justice, social justice, *and* antiviolence organizations' inability to address the overlapping oppressions they faced organized a conference called "The Color of Violence: Violence Against Women of Color" in order to shift the analysis around violence against women to place marginalized women of color at its center (Smith et al. 2006). This conference intended to reclaim the issue of violence and bring women outside the mainstream together in a sustainable coalition with one another for the first time. The conference drew so much attention in its planning stages that the organizers received calls begging for them to choose a larger venue so that more women could attend. In the end more than 2,000 women made it to the conference, while 2,000 others had to be turned away. The energy driving these women to come together in person for the first time and forge new coalitions while drafting an agenda to fight violence against women resembled the spirit behind the National Women's Conference in Houston in 1977, in spite of two major differences.

The first major point of departure from the conference in 1977 was this conference's position toward the state. Angela Davis opened up the conference with a powerful keynote address that outlined the obstacles that women of color, lesbians, and low-income women faced in their struggle against violence and how the state played a particular role in this. She argued, "Given the racist and patriarchal patterns of the state, it is difficult to envision the state as the holder of solutions to the problem of violence against women. However, as the anti-violence movement has been institutionalized and professionalized, the state plays an increasingly dominant role in how we conceptualize and create strategies to minimize violence against women. One of the major tasks of this conference, and of the anti-violence movement as a whole, is to address this contradiction, especially as it presents itself to poor communities of color" (2000, 4).

Women who claimed membership to a group that was treated as second-class citizens by the state, such as blacks, immigrants, the poor, Native Americans, or homosexuals, all had experience with institutional discrimination. Davis argued that it was inconceivable for women from these groups to place their faith in a system that had historically failed them. The perception of the state as an ally in 1977's conference shifted toward seeing the state as a main adversary in the violence this group of women experienced.

The second main point of departure was the shift in strategy away from legislative reform toward grassroots organizing. At the conference in 2000, there was a session called "Depoliticization of the Anti-Violence Movement" where activists came together to criticize the institutionalization and professionalization of the antiviolence movement. During that session speakers recounted stories of the federal government's interference in and co-optation of antiviolence organizations' work, implicitly arguing that liberal feminism had failed to recognize the state's role in violence against women. They also discussed how the depoliticization of the antiviolence movement broke leaders' connections with their communities and even led to the perpetuation of cultural stereotypes and structures that ultimately oppress those same communities—an example was given where leaders of a domestic violence organization were photographed at their annual meeting on Maui wearing plastic skirts, a cultural misappropriation of Hawaiian dress.

Conference organizers decided to found a new organization that would replace institutionalized, apolitical social service models with grassroots organizing against violence in women's communities, called INCITE! Women of Color Against Violence. This organization aimed to change feminist discourse and activism in the United States by communicating that all oppression is connected—for example, by linking the oppression that women of color experience inside the United States with that experienced by "third world women" outside the United States. Radical feminist writers from the 1980s even called themselves "third world women," reappropriating the term to emphasize how they were considered second-class citizens in their own country and deriving lessons from women's movements against violence in developing countries (Lorde 2002).

While scholars rightfully criticize some U.S. women's organizations for not being critical enough of how their country's policies affect women in other parts of the world, arguments that categorically discount all women's organizations' activism inaccurately homogenize feminism in the same manner as the wave approach (for example, see Tripp 2006). Groups like INCITE! and CodePink are consistently critical of U.S. foreign policy's impact on women abroad, particularly its militarization and trade policies that disproportionately harm women. Granted, they are not the predominant women's organizations called to government hearings on women's issues, nor does the media wait with baited anticipation to see which presidential candidate they endorse, but to overlook their activism would be akin to ignoring the Combahee River Collective's contributions in prior decades.

At the INCITE! conference, for example, Anannya Bhattacharjee, a prominent advocate for immigrants and workers' rights, drew connections between immigrant women, women of color, and transnational factors. She described the common vulnerability to the state that women of color share transnationally, as well as how globalization has intensified the push-pull economic factors between countries, making immigrant women particularly vulnerable on either end of that migration: "Immigration laws privilege the entry of highly skilled professionals and their families. A poor immigrant worker faces two options, starve with the children in her home country, or near permanent separation from her children as she migrates to the US to work without legal papers" (2000).

The second INCITE! conference was held in 2002 and built on the first conference's discussion of transnational intersecting oppressions by extending the analysis to themes of global peace and justice, connecting feminist issues with the aftermath of 9/11. Julia Sudbury, an academic activist, claimed her allegiance to communities of color all around the world, arguing that it was important to broaden the concept of violence such that it included not just personal violence such as rape or domestic violence but also state violence such as the "military, border patrols, the police, prisons, the Immigration and Naturalization Service, the bombing of Vieques in naval exercises in Puerto Rico, the bombing of Iraq and Afghanistan, and the violence occurring in Colombia, Chile, and Palestine, all of which are funded by the U.S." (Mantilla 2005). Another activist, Katherine Acey, spoke of her multiple identities as an Arab American socialist working-class lesbian feminist; she cited the example of lesbians and gay groups protesting the fact that a bomb was dropped over Afghanistan after 9/11 with the words "Hijack this, fags" scrawled on its side.

The same year a group of feminists concerned with the U.S. war in Afghanistan and its impending invasion of Iraq founded CodePink, a grassroots organization that fights to stop existing U.S. wars, prevent new wars, and reallocate government spending to health care, education, green jobs, and other "life-affirming activities" (CodePink n.d.). CodePink not only runs campaigns that bring attention to the impact of U.S. policies on women in Iraq, Iran, Pakistan, Sudan, and other countries where conflict disproportionately affects women but also uses a feminist perspective to protest brutality broadly speaking, such as efforts to close down Guantanamo Bay.

Similarly, the third INCITE! conference in 2005 centered on U.S. foreign policy and discursively connected women's experiences in the United States to women in Iraq, Afghanistan, and Palestine. And, for the first time, Arab American women were given notable consideration as belonging to a community of color in the United States. Nevertheless, women activists acknowledged that Arab American women are still grossly misrepresented *within* groups of women of color, citing examples of activists' inclination to "save Arab women" who wear *hijab*. In the same way, campaigns that addressed women's issues abroad were sometimes complicated and controversial. The Feminist Majority Foundation, for example, campaigned since 1996 against the Taliban's treatment of women in Afghanistan, but it fell on deaf ears in the U.S. government. But when the Bush administration needed public support to start its war in 2001, officials courted the FMF, co-opted its language on women's rights in the region, and started selling the war as an effort to fight violence against women abroad (Faludi 2007). INCITE! duly criticized the FMF's uncritical support of this military aggression, arguing that U.S. policies abroad were not a simple solution to the predicament of women under the Taliban. If the state had helped create the problem, in pushing the Taliban to power in Afghanistan, how could it also be seen as the solution?

WOMEN'S POLITICAL REPRESENTATION

Liberal feminists, conversely, still take great interest in the state, particularly through electoral politics. While organizations such as EMILY's List and the National Congress of Black Women continue to promote women's entering public office, nongovernmental organizations also form political action committees (PACs) to endorse political candidates without endangering the parent organization's tax status. Various liberal women's organizations made statements during the primary race mentioned at the beginning of this chapter, releasing documents such as candidate "report cards" on women's rights, or voting records on women's issues. Clinton, an iconic feminist lawyer from the 1970s, wife of former president Bill Clinton, and the current senator from New York, and Obama, a community organizer, lawyer, and freshman senator from Illinois, both competed for women's votes by courting large women's organizations, such as the NCWO and the National Abortion and Reproductive Rights Action League (NARAL).[2] Early predictions in the campaign made infamous claims that white women, as the largest demographic in the Democratic Party at 44 percent, could rally behind Clinton and that she needed only a little additional help from another voting bloc to usher her into the convention as the party's nominee.[3] Instead, the primary season turned into a battleground for divisions within contemporary feminism, with a particular focus on black women's support because they resided at the intersection of Clinton's gender and Obama's race.

Different demographics aligned themselves with one candidate over the other. CIRCLE, a nonpartisan research center that studies youth civic engagement, showed that 60 percent of the youth vote favored Obama, while 38 percent favored Clinton. Age demographics even influenced a population that was otherwise split between the two candidates—white college-educated voters above forty-five years of age preferred Clinton, while those under forty-five chose Obama (Frankovic 2008). Pundit discourse imposed these age discrepancies onto the women's vote, suggesting that the Second and Third Waves of feminism clashed over the two candidates and ignoring that these age divisions were not restricted to women. Some feminists were, indeed, split between the two candidates, but viewing these divisions through the lens of age or cohort obscures the nature of the disagreement between different types of feminists.

These divisions surfaced mainly over the importance of reproductive rights. Liberal feminist Martha Burk authored an online essay entitled "Why Hillary Is the Right Choice for Women" (2008), with the joint support of nine other prominent feminists. She argued that Clinton's leadership in protecting women's reproductive health made her the best candidate for feminists, as though reproductive health was the sole concern for this group. Feminist journalist Laura Flanders (2008) immediately challenged Burk's endorsement and argued that Clinton believed in "different womanhoods." She criticized Clinton's affirmative stance on U.S. policies that harmed women outside of the United States, such as trade policies that created a global sweatshop economy and laws that marginalized certain women within the United States, such as those that banned marriage between lesbian women. While Clinton feminists believed that their candidate's record on reproductive rights made her the best candidate for women, Flanders suggested they were not concerned with their candidate's record on issues that affected *other* women.

In January 2008, after Obama emerged victorious in the first caucus contest held in Iowa and black women started supporting him at an overwhelming 78 percent, prominent liberal feminist Gloria Steinem (2008) wrote an opinion editorial in the *New York Times*, arguing that Obama could not have accomplished what he had if he'd been a woman, because "gender is probably the most restricting force in American life." She went on to argue that race and sex are interdependent and must both be dealt with together, but the position that gender ought to trump racial identification in the minds of voters rang clear in her analysis—for example, she posited a hypothetical where a black woman who has all of Obama's credentials could never be as viable as Obama himself. Not once does she posit the same hypothetical for Clinton, replacing her whiteness with membership in a black racial group.

Kimberle Crenshaw argued against Steinem in the media and highlighted intersectional feminism that considered both race and gender in this election. She argued that the long history of division between feminists—particularly across race, and *not* generation—had resurfaced. Not only were black women voters expected to prioritize their gender identity at the expense of their racial membership, but white female Clinton supporters ignored the intersectional impact that Hillary's race had on her candidacy: "You cannot deny that whiteness is playing a role in this every bit as much as gender is . . . basically the feminists who are making this argument are doing what we've been concerned they've been doing for a long time—they're not acknowledging that race is playing a role in elevating Hillary as much as they claim race has played on the other side . . . we don't have agreement, I don't think, on how difficult the rhetoric [is] making life for those of us who want to organize as women of color and who are feminists" (Crenshaw 2008, n.p.).

A younger black feminist scholar, Melissa Harris-Lacewell, also took issue with Steinem's portrayal of gender in the election. In a news program Harris-Lacewell argued that Steinem's position on gender in the race alienated black women's intersectional experience: "[What Steinem is] trying to do there is [bring] black women into a coalition around questions of gender and asking us to ignore the ways in which race and gender intersect. This is actually a standard problem of second-wave feminism, which, although there have been . . . forty years, actually, of African American women pushing back against this, [they] have really failed to think about the ways in which trying to appropriate black women's lives' experience in that way is really offensive, actually" (*Democracy Now* 2008).

When Steinem tried to clarify that she believed both race and gender were important identities and needed to work in "coalition" with one another, Harris-Lacewell argued that mere coalition work would not be enough: "I do agree . . . that we ought to be in coalition. But I think we've got to be in coalition on fair grounds. Part of what, again, has been sort of an anxiety for African American women feminists like myself is that we're often asked to join up with white women's feminism, but only on their own terms, as long as we sort of remain silent about the ways in which our gender, our class, our sexual identity . . . intersect, as long as we can be quiet about those things and join onto a single agenda" (ibid.).

Harris-Lacewell argued that Steinem's proposed coalition work reminded her of the superficial coalition work from the 1960s and '70s that produced minority caucuses instead of sustainable alliances. This particular election did, however, encourage some feminists to make amends over their interpretation of the state as friend or foe. While radical groups such as INCITE! still refrained from endorsing a candidate, other intersectional feminists, such as Rebecca Walker, spoke out in this election because of its ability to encourage intersectional discourse around race and gender. In essence, the possibility of the country's first female president or its first black president lured women into the electoral arena who would most likely have abstained from another conventional election between two white male candidates.

The candidates themselves essentially refrained from such intersectional discourse, speaking to individual demographics (particularly age, gender, and race) that fell in their respective camps. While individual feminists and pundits continued to argue about the "women's vote," as Hillary won only slightly above a majority of her party's primary turnout, everyone waited to see where women's organizations would fall. Institutional feminist organizations overwhelmingly endorsed Clinton. When a prominent group called the National Abortion and Reproductive Rights Action League Pro-Choice America became the first feminist organization to endorse Obama in May 2007, other liberal feminist groups made their disapproval publicly known.

The founder of EMILY's List, Ellen Malcolm, went on record as finding NARAL's endorsement "tremendously disrespectful of Sen. Clinton" in spite of the fact that Obama had a strong record on choice issues (Goldstein 2008). After Obama won the party nomination, rounds of media speculation suggested that large numbers of Clinton supporters would defect from their party to the Republican candidate, Senator John McCain (Dickerson 2008; Rubin 2008; "Clinton supporters" 2008). Though early polls reported close to 30 percent of Clinton supporters pledging to switch party allegiance on election day, these worries were unsubstantiated as a sweeping majority supported Obama in the end.[4] Ultimately, large numbers of feminist Clinton supporters turned to fund-raising and canvassing for Obama, as his policy positions fell in line with feminist policy positions much more than McCain's did. Liberal feminist groups, such as NOW-PAC, even switched their public endorsement from an earlier Clinton endorsement in March 2007 to Obama in September 2008 (National Organization of Women 2008).

In the end, while disagreement persisted among feminists over the reasons to support either candidate, these divisions challenged traditional assumptions about the roles age, race, and institutionalization played in feminist discourse; the focus on intersectional feminism and common oppressions revealed the complicated, often hidden, history of women's activism and its relationship with the state. The binary of state as friend or foe has lost resonance in the feminist community. Instead, women activists pursue a more constructive, mixed strategy that outlines the state as the actor that has legislative influence over women's conditions; at the same time, some groups rightfully continue to critically analyze the state's role in perpetuating systemic violence against particular communities. Ultimately, the viability of a black male feminist candidate in the 2008 presidential election paradoxically encouraged radical feminists to rethink their position on state-centric approaches, while also digging up historical grievances between the branches of feminism that traditionally dissuaded radical feminists from seeing the state as a solution in the first place. Alice Walker, for example, publicly endorsed Obama in this election: "I feel we desperately need people in leadership who have more of an idea of the real world than any of the people we've had before" ("Writer Alice Walker" 2008).

CONCLUSION

This chapter has attempted to illustrate the historic levels of diversity in U.S. feminism and women's movements that the traditional "wave approach" tends to bury in obscurity. While there have been three established periods of feminism in U.S. history, describing them as waves implies a misleading sense of sequence. In reality, there were parallel associations that worked on similar issue-based campaigns such as violence against women or economic inequality, and there were parallel divisions that highlighted the extent to which women's movements' relationship with the state differed. Ultimately, to tell the story of U.S. feminism properly, we must stop thinking of feminism in age cohorts, and continue to explore how gender intersects with other identities, namely, those of race, class, citizenship, and sexuality.

While the recent presidential election drew the public's attention to multiple identities and overlapping oppressions, future research on intersectional feminism should consider the following set of questions. First, whereas the election encouraged a surge of discourse focused on the intersection between race and gender, it is critical to address the intersection between gender and other identities as well. For example, how do feminists and women's organizations make sense of political candidates' positions on same-sex marriage, U.S. foreign policy, workers' rights, or welfare reform? Intersectional feminist discourse and activism have been especially weak on women in poverty; only connecting race and class introduces poor women of color into the discussion. Though socialist feminists argue that capitalism is at fault for the oppression of women, intersectional feminists largely disapprove of their sole focus on class exploitation and encourage a broader interpretation of oppressive forces. In practice, however, women's movements do not seem to advocate for working-class women who do not come from communities of color, with liberal feminist groups focusing on sexual harassment and equal-pay campaigns for middle-class women in white-collar jobs or groups such as INCITE! organizing mothers of color on welfare.

Second, what does intersectional feminist theory mean for women's movements broadly? While political theorists outline the normative dimensions of overlapping oppressions, movement theorists should consider the ramifications intersectional feminism poses for coalition politics. What are the benefits and drawbacks of organizational coalitions that temporarily align according to common-issue campaigns but then dissolve back to individual corners after victory or defeat? Do intersectional feminists propose forming new permanent organizations that unite groups experiencing overlapping oppressions, *instead* of temporary coalitions and alliances? How would these organizations manage internal hierarchical politics and avoid ranking oppressions during agenda-setting sessions?

Finally, how do intersectional feminists intend to translate their revolutionary discourse into an action agenda? For example, INCITE! calls for an "alternative" to the state, focusing on community-centered solutions, but it is thus far unclear what this alternative model would really look like. Would communities really be able to completely replace state paradigms of policing and corrections, or would communities be expected to advocate for state models that incorporate more communities' input? Could CodePink's example of alliance politics with the peace and justice movement against U.S. wars abroad be held as an exemplar of translating intersectional discourse into action? At present, it seems that direct action against current state policies must be accompanied by constructive alternative suggestions. For example, INCITE! runs community radio shows that educate the public on violence against their communities, as well as self-defense training seminars; advocating for state funding for these programs runs the risk of co-optation, as other women's movements experienced in the past, but also sends the message that the state believes these programs are important in a broader sense—instead of pitting state solutions diametrically opposite to community solutions, a hybrid between the two seems promising. CodePink almost operates as a watchdog group, maintaining a stance critical of U.S. domestic and foreign policy and protesting in public to demand government transparency—another action strategy that tries to transform the state instead of rendering it obsolete or useless.

Despite these questions that remain regarding the future of intersectional feminism, it should at least be clear that feminism is alive and well in the United States. In fact, feminists could use the media's fascination over the recent split in women's votes to inject feminism even deeper into the public's vernacular. A recent radio news program invited Farah Jasmine Griffin (a professor of English and comparative literature and African American studies at Columbia University), Carol Jenkins (a former broadcaster and president of the Women's Media Center in New York City), and Eleanor Smeal (president of the Feminist Majority Foundation) to discuss the lasting legacy of this election on women's rights, feminism, and political participation:

> [This election] inspired people to get involved that haven't been involved. And so women all over this country volunteered hours and hours, they went to states, they did things they never thought they could do. . . . This is the most progressive platform a major party has passed for women's issues and for civil rights issues. But for women, it's in every section of [Obama's] platform.—Eleanor Smeal
>
> What has happened with Hillary's candidacy, and with that sexism in the media, is that the genie is out of the bottle. Women will no longer, ever, go back to that sort of complacent stage where they weren't paying attention and weren't active.—Carol Jenkins
>
> I think the most disturbing trend was our continued use of black and women, as if black women didn't fit into one or the other. . . . One had to be black or one had to be a woman . . . I also think one of the problems faced by black women was the sense that in choosing . . . Obama, that they were voting against their interest as women . . . there's still a great deal of work to do. But I think that all of the women, the women that I know, the women that I worked with over the years, have been committed to coming together, especially at this moment.—Dr. Farah Jasmine Griffin
>
> We have to be—when this is over, we have to be together. And I think we will be, but there were a lot of unkind things said, and a lot of people stopped talking to each other, but I think that increasingly, we're beginning to get beyond that.—Carol Jenkins

These women represent a microcosm of the diversity we find in contemporary U.S. feminism; they vary by race, class, candidate endorsement, and age—to name just a few. While they all acknowledge that wounds must still heal and a great deal of work lies ahead, one thing is clear—U.S. feminism is most certainly not "dead," and the 2008 presidential election made it more of a household concept than ever before.

NOTES

1 In "Mapping the Margins" (1991), Crenshaw explains intersectionality in more detail: "[I] consider intersectionality a provisional concept linking contemporary politics with postmodern theory. In mapping the intersections of race and gender, the concept does engage dominant assumptions that race and gender are essentially separate categories. By tracing the categories to their intersections, I hope to suggest a methodology that will ultimately disrupt the tendencies to see race and gender as exclusive or separable."

2 Author's interview with a senior political strategist who wishes to remain anonymous; this strategist first worked on Clinton's campaign for the presidency and then transitioned to Obama's team (August 1, 2008).

3 See washingtonpost.com online discussion hosted by feminist writer Linda Hirschman, http://www.washingtonpost.com/wp-dyn/content/discussion/2008/02/29/DI2008022902857.html.

4 For poll predictions, see Gallup Polling 2008. Interestingly, the same poll reports that 19 percent of Obama supporters would vote for McCain in a Clinton versus McCain race, which was left out of reports discussing women switching party allegiance.

In the Shadow of the Gun: The Black Panther Party, the Ninth Amendment, and Discourses of Self-Defense

BRIDGETTE BALDWIN

In spite of the British conviction that Americans had no right to establish their own laws to promote the general welfare of the people living here in America, the colonized immigrant felt he had no choice but to raise the gun to defend his welfare. ... Now these same colonized White people, these bondsmen, paupers, and thieves, deny the colonized Black man not only the right to abolish this oppressive system, but to even speak of abolishing it.

—Huey P. Newton, "In Defense of Self-Defense"

I say violence is necessary. It is as American as cherry pie.
—H. Rap Brown, press conference, 27 July 1967

Even in the newly emerging scholarship on the Black Panther Party (BPP) most accounts begin and end with the standard portrait of an organization of angry and violent black revolutionaries. Interspersed between descriptions of their official uniform—"black berets, black leather jackets, black trousers, and shiny black shoes"—and their penchant for back talk in interacting with white authority, looms the most common symbol associated with the Panthers: their supposed fetish for the gun. Even journalist Gene Marine's sympathetic early account, *The Black Panthers*, sensationally advertised the Panthers' supposed agenda as "UNIFORMED, ARMED MEN IN AMERICA! BLACK MEN WHO TALK BACK—AND SHOOT BACK!"[1] However, this one-dimensional portrait tells only half the story of the paradoxically street conscious and yet "book smart" "Bad

Niggas." In their decision to pick up the gun, they simultaneously waged both legal and street battles for the control and self-defense of black communities; battles that extended beyond a simple debate on the right to bear arms guaranteed in the Second Amendment.[2]

Disentangling the Panthers' image from the substantive legal issues raised by their efforts is a troublesome business, precisely because of how deeply that image is imbedded in both public and historical memory. Alongside figures ranging from Stagolee to Muhammad Ali, the pantheon of "Bad Nigga" black heroes includes Huey Newton, who combined both pimp and paramilitary imagery in his infamous photo in a high-back wicker chair, brandishing an African spear in one hand and a rifle in the other—the iconographic metaphor for armed black self-determination in the late 1960s and early 1970s. In particular, this BPP image in the white mind foregrounds memories of that "fateful" day in 1967 when armed male and female Black Panthers ascended the steps of the California state capitol building in Sacramento to protest a bill aimed directly at their constitutional right to bear arms. With the fully repressed reportage of white gun lobbyists who were also there in protest, the mainstream media created a national imagined community of racial fear with headlines like "Blacks with guns invading the legislature."[3] To be sure, the Party's fight for the right to possess firearms was not mere performative protest or political principle alone. Armed confrontations took place throughout the nation, with police but also with Black Nationalists like Maulana Karenga's Us. At the same time, the national spotlight that shone down on those Sacramento steps also created sympathy for, and even allegiance with, the BPP's fight for equal protection under the law, especially among those engaged in parallel struggles for black and working-class self-determination.

From the outset, as well as in retrospect, the Panthers' conscious posture and performance of armed self-defense garnered both positive outcomes (street credibility with urban black youth and, later, Third World revolutionaries) and negative consequences (a distorted image of the BPP as a revolutionary "gang" obsessed with irrational violence).[4] However, historical memory and scholarship are just beginning to open wide enough to locate the Panthers within the more complex social context and theoretical frameworks in which they actually existed and, most important, helped to create.[5] Unbeknownst to many, the BPP's more comprehensive discourse of self-defense, including armed resistance and community "survival programs," were derived from both an international Third World anticolonial context and a national American constitutional one. Although the Panthers did not directly argue their case along such lines, they employed a language as much in line with the Ninth Amendment's preservation of inalienable rights as they did with the more celebrated rhetoric, "By any means necessary." A close analysis of the Panther argument for self-defense reveals one of the clearest articulations in the history of American radicalism of the inalienable "other rights" referred to in that amendment.

THE PANTHERS AND THE U.S. CONSTITUTION: THE LEGAL THEORY

Though BPP members may not have thought about the Ninth Amendment as legal justification for their acts of self-defense, they did read, use, and work within the bounds of the U.S. Constitution as a weapon equal to the gun. They brandished both firearms and copies of the Bill of Rights on police patrol. The Declaration of Independence is liberally quoted in their Ten-Point Platform and Program, "What We Want, What We Believe." And, their People's Constitutional Convention of 1970 was a direct attempt to remake the Constitution itself. In the end, their persistent use of the "mother country-colony" metaphor helped structure their vision of black communities under siege and in need of armed self-defense as one part of their larger program for self-determination. Such an approach aligned them with and drew from Third World revolutionary struggles against white nationalist colonialism, but it also tested the limits of the right of black people to an American legacy of armed resistance against despotism that established socio-legal parameters for the U.S. Constitution.

To be sure, within the Party there was no unified position on the means and meanings of self-defense, as demonstrated by the rift between Huey Newton and Eldridge Cleaver that broke into the open in early 1971. For that rift occurred precisely over self-defense as community protection and development versus self-defense as guerrilla warfare.[6] Still, the Panthers' conscious theorizing and application of self-defense, no matter how sensationally represented or vigorously debated internally, remains an important legacy: a politically radical organization attempted to access constitutionally protected rights to forge community autonomy, seek self-determination, and even bear arms in the face of legally sanctioned injustice. Moreover, the Panthers' deliberate use of the Constitution offers an important starting point for reconsidering the Ninth Amendment as a viable resource for resistance in general terms. It is indeed striking that both the American revolutionaries of the late eighteenth century and the Black Panther revolutionaries of the late twentieth emerged within a context of "colonial" occupation and, from there, devised similar theories of armed self-defense as an expression of self-determination and governance. Through the specific lens of the Ninth Amendment, even the BPP's most controversial acts of armed self-defense were not simply rational or morally justified but constitutionally legal.

In his first of many treatises, Huey Newton's "In Defense of Self-Defense" drew directly from the language and laws of the newly formed United States of America in formulating the program he and Bobby Seale devised almost exactly two hundred years later.[7] The historiography of the American Revolutionary period may be complex and contested, but the Panthers understood it elementally as an era of vigorous struggle between the British mother country and its American colonial outpost. American colonists faced restricted political representation in decision-making about their lives and property and were subjected to legal acts that sanctioned what they perceived as unjust and excessive economic taxation. The founding father John Han-cock summarized such one-sided government when he proclaimed, "They have undertaken to give and grant our money without our consent."[8] The colonists responded with nonviolent protest but also engaged in acts of violent resistance, explicitly understood as self-defense. In the face of colonial occupation, Samuel Adams wrote, "If existence … is at stake, it is lawful to resist the highest authority."[9] His cousin and the future president, John Adams, concluded that "insurrection is always due to despotism from the government" and, further, that it served as legitimate resistance against a colonial regime.[10] In the words of the modern constitutional historian A. J. Langguth, Revolutionary-era boycotts, riots, looting, and other acts of violent self-defense of the era were "legitimate … protest by an oppressed people."[11] The BPP would have agreed, noting in 1967 that "the colonized immigrant felt he had no choice but to raise the gun to defend his welfare. Simultaneously he made certain laws to ensure his protection from external and internal aggressions."[12]

The BPP, then, understood that the revolutionary ideas embodied in the Declaration of Independence and the Constitution emerged out of a larger moment of colonial oppression and resistance. During the writing of the Constitution, the thirteen colonies generally shared the goal of creating a united front. Yet, many were not willing to give over complete control to a new "federal" government. Some argued that if individual rights were not spelled out, they could be subjected to unfettered abuse by that government, while others feared that spelling out specific rights could imply that the states had fewer rights against the federal government than actually had been intended. To resolve the issue the Virginian delegate James Madison, who had initially opposed the addition of the amendments that would be called the Bill of Rights, suggested the addition of a clause dispelling the notion that states had given up any rights other than those specifically delegated to the new federal government. His proposal, later ratified in the form, "The enumeration … of certain rights, shall not be construed to deny … others retained by the people," became the Ninth Amendment.[13]

Indeed, that amendment was a key result of colonial resistance to British occupation. For both the context and language of this part of the Constitution rationalized the resistance of the 1760s and 1770s, and further "legalized" resistance on the very same grounds for any other citizen bound by its constitutionality. And, while legal scholars consider the Ninth Amendment a recent rediscovery, it has been an essential part of the Constitution since the ratification of the Bill of Rights in 1791.[14] Included in the first of those eight amendments were specific rights that the founding fathers believed were fundamental to humanity according to natural law. However, the history and text of the Ninth Amendment suggest that there were more rights reserved to the people than those articulated in Amendments one through eight. The very language used in the document—"certain rights, shall not be construed to deny or disparage others retained by the people"—made clear that the list in the other amendments was not exhaustive.[15] But, the language of the Ninth Amendment serves only as the *source* for these "other rights," leaving no clue as to what these rights might be.[16] Nevertheless, the existence of these "other rights" *preceded* the establishment of the new federal government.[17] Accordingly, many have argued (albeit unsuccessfully), under the Ninth Amendment certain "other rights" exist that not only prevent the federal government from infringing on states' rights, but also all other forms of government from usurping citizens' personal freedoms.[18]

In his essay I take the same theoretical ground in applying the argument to the history—in words and deed—of the Black Panther Party.[19] I do not, however, suggest that the Ninth Amendment "creates" enforceable constitutional rights.[20] Rather, I merely seek to illuminate the existence of these "other rights" deemed fundamental, now protected from state intrusion.[21] While the Bill of Rights originally applied restrictions on the federal government's power, the subsequent enactment of the Reconstruction amendments, particularly the Fourteenth Amendment, also prohibited the states from abridging inherent fundamental personal liberties.[22] To the extent that the Fourteenth Amendment incorporated the Bill of Rights, the "other rights" in the Ninth Amendment are not only applicable to the federal government but also to state police power.[23] Such rights exist within the "customary, traditional, and time-honored rights, amenities, privileges, and immunities … , which come within the meaning of the term 'liberty' as used in the Fourteenth Amendment."[24]

Again, there has been very little discussion about what "other rights" are guaranteed in the Ninth Amendment, and, in fact, the United States Supreme Court has never delivered a majority opinion based exclusively on the text of the Ninth Amendment.[25] Yet in some court cases the amendment has been considered to confirm the existence of rights that are not provided in the first eight amendments. Justice Goldberg, concurring in *Griswold v. Connecticut*, for example, devoted several pages to the Ninth Amendment: "The language and history of the Ninth Amendment reveal that the Framers of the Constitution believed that there are additional fundamental rights, protected from governmental infringement, which exist alongside those fundamental rights specifically mentioned in the first eight constitutional amendments. … The Ninth Amendment shows a belief of the Constitution's authors that fundamental rights exist that are not expressly enumerated in the first eight amendments and an intent that the list of rights included there not be deemed exhaustive."[26] The Ninth Amendment has also emerged as a new textual source for other constitutional rights. By example, it has been used to argue for equal treatment for gays and lesbians,[27] rights to employment,[28] visitation rights for children,[29] and the right to transport "obscene materials" for private use.[30]

Most notably, in *Griswold* Justice Douglas used the Ninth Amendment to grant the right to marital privacy.[31] Douglas opined that "specific guarantees in the Bill of Rights have penumbras, formed by emanations from those guarantees that help give them life and substance."[32] Indeed, he used the Ninth Amendment to advance the idea that fundamental rights are protected by an indefinite source of constitutional provisions, despite the absence of any specific reference to these in the document itself. Still, thus far the Ninth Amendment has never been used to justify what might be considered "acts of violence." However, locating such acts within their social and historical context, as in the case of the BPP and much like the case of the framers of the Constitution, forces a reconsideration of traditional understandings of the Ninth Amendment. It also throws the Panthers and their historical moment into a new light.

Critically, the constitutional protection against the newly established government of the late eighteenth century through "other rights" not found in the first eight amendments is not a gift offered by the Ninth Amendment. Rather, it serves as recognition of the existence of other fundamental and inalienable rights. For this reason, the Ninth Amendment's conception—and its social and legislative context—did become a source of inspiration for later anticolonial struggles. Further, even if it were not referred to directly, the meaning embodied in the amendment offered legal precedent for later acts of self-defense and demands for self-determination. For example, there are striking similarities between the Revolutionary period and what, almost exactly two hundred years later, would be called the Black Power era. Appropriately, in the late 1960s BPP leader Eldridge Cleaver suggested that "there are two things happening in this country. You have a black colony and you have a white mother country and you have two different sets of political dynamics. … What's called for in the mother country is a revolution and there's a black liberation called for in the black colony."[33] When 1960s colonial occupants within the United States interpreted struggles and devised solutions for freedom, they did so at least partly in the language of America's own anticolonial Revolutionary moment.

The BPP emerged during a watershed moment of mass violence—a period of mass violence coming on the heels of centuries of racial violence enacted by state agents and private citizens against communities of color. These acts in turn inspired more-pronounced arguments for black self-determination through armed self-defense. Such arguments not only encompassed but also extended beyond the philosophies generated in late-eighteenth-century colonial America. In the 1960s, black communities across America faced the combined violent forces of lynching, police brutality, unemployment, substandard housing, and inferior social services and educational facilities. Protests for justice and the simple right to life during the southern phase of the freedom struggle met dramatic forms of white retaliation—bombings, arson, beatings, murder. These violent responses were matched in force and effect by countless acts of state-sanctioned violence in the form of police brutality in appropriately described "war zones" during urban riots of the mid-1960s. The BPP's harnessing and reconceptualization of the Constitution, then, was sharpened by insights drawn from social movements that had already made connections between resistance struggles against open racist violence in the United States and colonialism in Africa, Asia, and Latin America. Local demands for an end to police brutality and an increase in social services, for example, were interpreted through Third World philosophies of self-determination in the creation of a more comprehensive project of self-defense against violence and structural abuse.[34]

The 1955 Bandung Conference of nonaligned nations set the stage for an alternative worldview outside a mode of strict Western capitalism or Euro-centric communism, and it would directly influence the BPP's notion of self-defense as explicitly anticolonial. Those in the so-called Third World had begun to make alliances among themselves, creating visions of liberation to combat colonialism and the fight against racism in overdeveloped countries like the United States. Mao Zedong's notion of abolishing the gun by picking it up, the revolutionary violence theories of Che Guevara and Frantz Fanon, and the actual armed revolutions in China, Cuba, and Africa offered activists a solution outside the purview of the emerging nonviolent hegemony taking hold in the United States. However, more popular memories of passive resistance had always existed uneasily alongside the realities of armed groups—including the Deacons for Defense and Justice in the Deep South and the Cambridge movement in the Chesapeake region—which had protected even the most nonviolent of protestors in such a violent world.[35]

At the same time, Robert Williams's organizing of armed self-defense groups in North Carolina against the Ku Klux Klan and the police was immortalized in black radical circles through his essays and his book *Negroes with Guns*. Williams eventually fled to Cuba for political asylum, where he developed an ideology of Black Nationalism and Third World internationalism and was elected provisional president of the Republic of New Africa. Finally, Malcolm X's self-defense ideology, "By any means necessary," his travels throughout the Third World, and his appeals to the United Nations to intervene on behalf of black people in the United States consolidated the American history of black armed resistance and anticolonial self-determination. Malcolm was especially appealing to the BPP because he embraced Fanon's idea of organizing the "lumpen proletariat" into revolutionaries through his more vernacular style of address, which was aimed directly at the so-called street brothers in the community. Moreover, all of these tendencies had made direct links between conditions in the United States and Third World. Foreshadowed by the Revolutionary Action Movement and echoed by the Dodge Revolutionary Union Movement in Detroit, the BPP's comprehensive strategy of self-defense grew out of this larger international revolutionary context. Black struggles for self-determination against racist community control in the United States were thus envisioned as but one plank of the larger platform of "decolonization" taking place throughout the world.[36]

By applying the "mother country/colony" or "internal colony" metaphor to black living conditions in U.S. cities, activists glimpsed the international proletarian likeness between, for example, Saigon and South Central (Los Angeles). For, as Newton acutely observed, "as the aggression of the racist American government escalates in Vietnam, the police agencies of America escalate the repression of Black people throughout the ghettos of America."[37] Urban conditions and race relations had been reimagined within a global context. Kwame Ture (né Stokely Carmichael) and Charles Hamilton's *Black Power* offered a conceptual structure to this more general analysis of U.S. urban "colonial" conditions by asserting that "exorbitant rents," police brutality, "uncollected garbage," and overall neglect in black communities were products of the "white power structure." From these conditions, they concluded, "Black people are legal citizens of the United States with, for the most part, the same *legal* rights as other citizens. Yet they stand as colonial subjects in relation to white society. Thus institutional racism has another name: colonialism."[38] This approach complicated inherent distinctions between the spatially demarcated race relations among "chocolate cities" and "vanilla suburbs" in the

United States and the struggles between Third World colonies of color and European nations, as it sought a wider Third World solidarity. Most important, seeing black urban communities as internal colonies helped to make clear that the only response to systemic and state-sponsored neglect and attack was a comprehensive platform and program of self-determination. This larger anticolonial vision would have a direct impact on the Panthers' interpretation of the U.S. Constitution in the defense of these same black communities.

The revolutionary nationalist "internal colony" vision of the BPP, of course, was also descriptive of contemporary black-white relations in the United States—without, however, the demand for black secession.[39] Whereas the prescriptive approach of early American Revolutionaries and twentieth-century Third World anticolonial activists sought autonomy, the Panthers' internal colony metaphor illuminated actually existing relations in an attempt to gain proportionate representation and equal protection from *within* the nation-state. Thus, even their early armed police patrols were conceived, according to Newton, "within legal bounds."[40] Again, the BPP's application of an anti-colonial critique to black urban conditions specified their larger program of self-determination as protection from governmental infringement as outlined in the Constitution. Specifically, their language and approach to armed self-defense, even if unintentional, was rooted in the language and history of the Ninth Amendment.

To grasp the theory behind the BPP's employment of constitutional rights generally, we must reconsider the meaning of, and guarantees in, the Ninth Amendment in the context of late-sixties America. The right to self-defense/preservation is, of course, an integral part of any notion of freedom in the United States, as outlined in the Declaration of Independence. This right, however, was not included in the language of the first eight amendments, even though it should be a constitutionally protected right.[41] In fact, scholars as early as Locke, Pufendorf, and Hobbes made arguments that self-defense is the "ultimate natural right."[42] Some have even asserted that it is a natural right that "might be used as evidence of" the type of right "originally understood to exist when the Ninth and Tenth Amendments were adopted."[43] Moreover, this argument runs, in order to determine which rights are fundamental, judges must look to the "traditions and conscience of our people" to determine whether a right is "so rooted ... as to be ranked as fundamental."[44] The key issue, from this perspective, is whether a right "is of such a character that it cannot be denied without violating those 'fundamental principles of liberty and justice which lie at the base of all our civil and political institutions.' "[45] A reconsideration of the Ninth Amendment, then, offers constitutional appeal for the self-defense discourse of groups like the Black Panthers precisely because of their particular demand for individual rights and their desire to limit the exercise of abusive government power in the black community.

As noted above, according to the Ninth Amendment no state or federal government can deny constitutionally protected rights, even if these rights are not specifically mentioned in the Constitution. Legal scholars such as Thomas McAfee have argued that the Ninth Amendment was only meant to allow states to trump the federal government's authority and not individuals to trump state power.[46] But the amendment has a more expansive reach. It seems implausible that the founding fathers contemplated the unfettered abuse of citizens' rights by state officials while simultaneously prohibiting governmental infringement by federal officials. Any such interpretation would provide a constricted and limited interpretation of intent, as well as severely circumscribing the Fourteenth Amendment.[47]

While there is, of course, no other constitutional provision allowing individuals to defend against identified enemies, that right, like the right to marital privacy, might be considered fundamental and thus retained by the people under the Ninth Amendment.[48] The Constitution was founded on principles that were dedicated to the basic "rights of men." Clearly, in that document, slaves were not men with those basic rights. And yet it is also clear that "man" is a term that has been reinterpreted under the law over time. The "rights of man" rhetoric of the eighteenth century has been the ground on which many oppressed groups (including groups of women) have fought for inclusion in the American Republic. As such, black people might lay claim to the same rights and privileges in the Constitution as those for whites and not simply wait to see which rights whites were willing to give them.[49] In this same vein, the Ninth Amendment reference to "other rights" might indeed be wide enough to include self-defense. This plausible interpretation would reclassify many acts of self-defense deployed by the BPP as not only necessary but also constitutional. Further, if a reasonable understanding of the Ninth Amendment illustrates that self-defense is constitutionally sound, it might be said that, as the ex-Panther Sundiata Acoli states, "it also makes common sense."[50]

Of course, if we focus solely on Panther acts of armed self-defense, then the argument for a reconsideration of the meaning of the Ninth Amendment will appear displaced or even as a justification for random acts of violence. Yet the Panthers consistently regarded armed resistance as merely one part of their larger discourse of self-defense. When in 1971 Newton offered a critique of what he considered Cleaver's obsession with the gun, he emphatically stated that the BPP understood the need for self-defense in the face of a number of oppressing agents, "from armed police to capitalist exploiters."[51] By examining the relationship between the many components of the BPP's larger revolutionary project of self-defense, we will find them commensurate with the strategies and aims of the Constitution—its rights, justice, liberties, and freedoms.[52] Accordingly, a reconsideration of the meaning and significance of the Ninth Amendment suggests a striking paradox: the militant actions and revolutionary demands of the Black Panther Party were legitimate, reasonable, and within the bounds of the U.S. Constitution.

THE PANTHERS AND THE CONSTITUTION: THE HISTORY

While defenders of capitalism celebrated their system with the symbols of individualism and freedom, the Panthers condemned that system as a mode of production that reinforced what they called "community imperialism." For the economic structure that systematically violated individual rights in ways that specifically oppressed and targeted black communities needed dismantling. In the Panthers' vision, that would happen through a program of revolutionary nationalism in which economic wealth, social services, and political power were deployed in the people's interest. Their socialist political agenda demanded that the government allow black people to control the key institutions both affected by and located within their communities. Thus, the Panthers did not embrace black cultural nationalism because they insisted that integrating black faces or cultural styles into capitalist institutions would not alter the power relations of a socioeconomic system that prized private property and gross accumulation over the well-being of the citizenry.[53] At the same time, the BPP remained both politically idealistic and strategically practical. An often-overlooked aspect of its history is the use of a pragmatic individualist rhetoric that both accessed and critiqued the language of the Constitution. While socialist, the Party program, with its reprinting of the preamble to the Declaration of Independence, represented the group's commitment to the perhaps problematic preservation of individual natural rights in the black community. Moreover, a landmark intervention in political philosophy and policy on the part of oppressed people in the overdeveloped world— even if in style and substance indebted to other black groups—the program set the tone for a comprehensive vision of self-defense that was at its foundation. But, though pulling from Third World anti-colonial struggles, as it was part of a larger appeal to the American state for self-determination from "community imperialism," it was self-consciously constitutionalist and conceived as perfectly legal.[54] Here, then, on the home front of a wider revolution, the Panthers sought the protection of individual natural rights defense from racially unequal surveillance and the suppression of livelihood in black communities.

The BPP addressed the fundamental needs of black people and demanded power to determine their own fate, full and meaningful employment, an end to exploitation, decent housing and education, exemption from military service for all black men, and freedom for all black "political" prisoners.[55] It also demanded an "education [for black people] that exposes the true nature of this decadent American Society. ... [an] education that teaches [black people their] ... true history and role in the present-day society." In addition, the BPP sought basic human resources, making it clear that those resources should be taken from the capitalists and controlled by black people within the black community. Finally, in insisting that oppression end immediately, the platform served as the basis for a course of action. As such, the Panther program embodied revolutionary ideology rooted in black political traditions and committed the Party to establishing fundamental change—within the legacy of the American Revolution.

When Newton and Seale substantiated their anticolonial demands, both legally and historically, by ending their platform with a long excerpt from the opening lines of the Declaration of Independence, they emphasized the words, "whenever any form of government becomes destructive ... it is the right of the people to alter or to abolish it, and to institute a new government." Eighteenth-century colonial rebels and their crafting of a document that spoke of "abuses and usurpations" under "absolute despotism" thus resonated with what these twentieth-century black citizens saw in their urban communities on a daily basis. Importantly, the Declaration's discussion of "inalienable rights" also echoed the Ninth Amendment's language of the unenumerated "other rights" with which American citizens were to maintain individual rights in the face of encroaching governmental power. The American solution to "throw off such government" and "provide new guards for" the people's "security" provided the BPP with a foundation on which to act that was directly relevant to the issue of platform point seven: "An immediate end to POLICE BRUTALITY and MURDER of black people."

The clearest example of colonial-like racial inequality and unequal protection was state-sanctioned racial violence and, particularly in urban locales, police brutality. Thus, in using the internal colony metaphor, the BPP denounced "the racist police who come into our communities from outside and occupy them, patrolling, terrorizing, and brutalizing our people like a foreign army in a conquered land."[56] Accordingly, countless BPP posters and speeches made parallel demands for the United States, typically represented as a pig, to "get out of" Asia, Africa, Latin America, and the ghetto.[57] Thus, point seven was the first issue acted on by the Party. Newton and Seale well understood that police brutality in black communities constituted the clearest example of unequal protection under the law and exposed a fundamental opposition between the needs of the people and the interests of the state.

One of the most astute constitutional critiques of police occupation and practice appeared in the Party organ, the *Black Panther*, in late 1969.[58] Written by an apparent rank-and-file member under the byline "Candy," the essay, titled "Pigs-Panthers," refers directly to the Constitution and excerpts the language of the Declaration to insist that the people possess certain "inalienable rights." The combined use of America's founding documents in fact resonates with the language of the Ninth Amendment and its protection of rights that either preceded or were given in the Constitution. In fact, the only place in the Constitution with phrasing similar to the expression of inalienable rights outlined in the Declaration of Independence is in the Ninth Amendment. Candy notes that if as specified in the Constitution the people direct the actions of the government and "sanction its authority," then the police as the military arm of a governing few "have no right in our community." She charges the police with failing to live up to the Constitution, concluding that the BPP phrase "All Power to the People" was the conceptual basis on which America's founding fathers had built the Constitution.[59] In this way, Panther police patrols were a means of carrying a living Constitution—in defense of the people—out into the streets.

The BPP solution to state violence was the organization of "black self-defense groups"—police patrols—that would survey the (mis)conduct of police officers. The most controversial aspect of these patrols, and what is remembered most about them, is that those on patrol openly carried loaded weapons. While the idea of "niggers with guns" was seen as simply the opportunity to retaliate against unlawful police brutality, again this vision of armed self-defense was not divorced from a larger political philosophy.[60] Newton reasoned that because black people did not own the means of production (land or industrial power), they could not generate what he called a "political consequence" when their desires went unmet. In essence, they had political representatives but no power. The political consequence for an otherwise defenseless people, then, was what Newton called "Self-Defense Power."[61]

This threatening language sounded ominous, retaliatory, even vengeful, but in reality political action committees, like nation-states, can exact consequences. Moreover, the BPP "never used [their] guns to go into the white community to shoot up white people," or "claimed the right to indiscriminate violence."[62] Indeed, the Panthers criticized what they called the "traditional riots and insurrections" of the mid-1960s as antagonistic to the program of organized and systemic self-defense.[63] Picking up the gun was consistently presented as a revolutionary but defensive action in the face of police as an occupying imperial force, who claimed "the right to indiscriminate violence and practice[d] it everyday."[64]

In keeping with their political approach to armed self-defense, the Panthers consistently grounded in the Second Amendment and the California Constitution their critiques of the police and their right to create armed patrols.[65] On patrol, the Panthers carried more than just guns, despite what the media may have reported. They also had law books, cameras, and tape recorders. As important, perhaps, the meaning of the gun for these activists was complex. Drawing on the teachings of Mao, Newton consistently argued that "in order to get rid of the gun, it is necessary to take up the gun."[66] Simply put, black people had to create a *community structure* where "the people" had control of all local institutions, including law enforcement, whereas presently they were victims of all local institutions, most visibly the police.[67] At the same time, as an advertising, recruiting, and teaching tool, as well as an actual weapon, the gun was strategically central to what might be called the BPP's discourse of self-defense.

Even beneath the provocative "kill the pig" rhetoric, Cleaver, for example, maintained the language of the American Revolution in arguing that "black men know that they must pick up the gun, they must arm black people to the teeth, they must organize an army and confront the mother country with a most drastic consequence if she attempts to assert police power over the colony."[68] Standoffs between "a cadre of disciplined and armed Black men" and the police over their conduct endeared the Party to local black communities and attracted the so-called street brothers to a politically engaged vision of revolutionary violence and defiance of authority.[69] However, in advocating the propaganda of the gun, the BPP's primary goal was to teach black people that they had to defend themselves and their legal rights in the face of governmental abuse. Even the term "pig," which was thought to mean the police exclusively, actually referred to, according to Bobby Seale, anyone who "violate[s] people's constitutional rights."[70]

The public display of armed Panther patrols, then, served as a weapon against police violence. Further, the patroller's recitation of the Bill of Rights or the appropriate penal code served as a teaching tool so that community members could learn to defend themselves. The arrests of armed BPP members who acted fully within their constitutional right to bear arms served to "educate the masses," according to David Hilliard, who notes that "Black people did not have their rights guaranteed by the constitution to bear arms in defense of their lives against racist mobs of fascists in and out of uniform."[71] That patrols were required to stay within legal bounds—refrain from cursing, keep guns always visible, and read the law—undermines the image of the Panthers as purveyors of random and irrational violence, Panther scholarship stressing the travails of black underclass culture, or purely psychoanalytic readings of the violent upbringings of individual Panther members. When patrol members read the law out loud to police officers, most pointedly on capitol building steps while obeying the legal right to bear arms, and were then still harassed and arrested, the scene served as important street theater and instruction to black people and white state agents alike about unequal protection under the law. Moreover, if Huey Newton's retrospective account can be believed, the Panthers' patrols helped to decrease acts of police brutality, bringing in more recruits while helping black people perceive the Party as a community not an outside entity.[72]

A point that is frequently missed about the BPP's discourse of self-defense was that for many in the organization, protecting the right to self-defense and to bear arms in particular was as important as the actual use of arms. In Seale's account of one exchange between Newton and a police officer over the right to bear arms, Newton is portrayed as seeing the exchange itself—the spectacle of a black man using the law to his advantage and in defiance against a state agent—as a recruiting tool.[73] At the same time, his declaration to the officer that he not only had the legal right to bear arms but that he would open fire if the police should draw their guns or try to disarm him illegally arguably exceeded the bounds of the Second Amendment. But in the expression of his intentions Newton legitimately exercised his constitutional rights, specifically his right of self-defense. And one could argue that Newton's exchange with that police officer did not exceed the inalienable "other rights" protected by the Ninth Amendment. It is also revealing that the police officer allegedly accused Newton of trying to "turn the Constitution around."[74] Yet such a charge of legal perversion, or anarchy against the law, must be read against the Panther leader's consistent adherence to the law: once the California legislature in mid-1967 passed the bill against carrying loaded firearms within city limits, the BPP put down the gun.

Shortly after this critical moment in its political development, the Panthers underwent an important philosophical shift marked by the change of their name from the Black Panther Party for Self-Defense to simply the Black Panther Party. Some scholars, as well as some of the Panthers' contemporaries, view this name change—followed shortly by an increased focus on survival programs over armed self-defense—as evidence that the BPP was "more reformist than revolutionary."[75] However, when the Panthers changed their name it was not an expression of a weakening of their self-defense vision; rather, it signaled an expanded notion of self-defense based on "a deeper, richer discussion of what the party's vision for the future might entail."[76] In line with the internal colony thesis, the BPP saw that spatially and politically marginalized communities needed a wider array of defense mechanisms and that too many people both inside and outside the Party were focusing on what Panther Captain Crutch called "the purely military viewpoint."[77] Newton tried later to make clear that gun violence was simply the "*coup de grace*" of what black working-class people needed defense against. He added that there were "other kinds of violence poor people suffered—unemployment, poor housing, inferior education, lack of public facilities, the inequity of the draft"—all as "part of the same fabric."[78] Through the survival programs, the BPP's dedication and service to the black community, through a program of defense against these various forms of violence, helped them embark on a new meaning of "inalienable," or, in the words of the Ninth Amendment, unenumerated rights.

The BPP's survival programs in fact enacted a defense system against black hunger, a corrupt legal system, inadequate health care, and extreme unemployment.[79] Under siege by police and internal dissent in 1971, Newton argued that the survival programs were the "only reason that the Party is still in existence," because they served the community and addressed its needs.[80] As part of the "process" of revolution, the first front of attack against a racist, capitalist regime was attacking substandard housing conditions, poor health care facilities, and an indifferent criminal justice system.[81] For example, consider the following excerpt from the diary of a former Panther member: "Poverty and people everywhere. Haven't seen this kind of mistreatment, poor conditions ever before ... Black people need the party to do something ... The pigs came for us again. Trapped us coming from the park on our way back to [the] office. ... Said we had failed to appear for court and had a bench warrant out for us ... They kept us at the ... station until the following day then took us to the ... city jail ... No arraignment or anything just tossed inside and left. No bail on a damn disorderly conduct and failure to appear."[82] In response to such conditions, the BPP established social policy programs to improve black urban life.[83] Under these auspices, its community programs focused on the prolonged and detrimental effects of racism and capitalism in the black community.

These community programs fed thousands of hungry children, established free health care clinics, which included free sickle cell testing, and provided moral support and attorney referrals to black people and their families who were "caught up" in the criminal justice system.[84] Often, however, the history of these community programs lies in the shadow of the notorious gunfights between the BPP and "the pig." Moreover, present-day social welfare programs that stem directly from the Panthers and their era remain under siege, especially those serving oppressed communities; ironically, those attacking such programs construct them as antithetical to the democratic spirit. The Panthers, though, insisted that a fully functional sociopolitical system required at its foundation that citizens be defended from illiteracy, homelessness, disease, and other forms of social inequality. It was in the spirit of this novel political philosophy, as noted earlier, that the BPP joined forces with other radical organizations in late 1970 in the hope of writing such a vision directly into the U.S. Constitution.

The BPP's convening of the Revolutionary People's Constitutional Convention (RPCC) is significant on both symbolic and structural grounds. It was purposefully staged in Philadelphia because, in the words of Panther Chief of Staff David Hilliard, it was "the same place the pigs had theirs."[85] Against the backdrop of local Panther surveillance and bloody police violence, the RPCC brought together approximately six thousand people from a cross-section of progressive organizations representing Third World liberation groups, welfare mothers, high school and college students, gay liberation activists, tenant farmers, and professionals. According to George Katsiaficas, who participated in the convention, instead of meeting the expected police terror, delegates were welcomed into local African American homes and churches. Moreover, once the delegates began to draft reforms, they utilized the model of self-defense made popular by the BPP Ten-Point Program and Platform. One of the major legislative aims of the Convention—in line with the Ninth Amendment—was to limit government intrusion by allocating only 10 percent of the national budget for the military and police, and to "guarantee and deliver to every American citizen the inviolable rights to life, liberty and pursuit of happiness."[86] Though the RPCC project quickly collapsed, it set the tone for later progressive initiatives for equal rights among men and women, bans on the manufacture of genocidal weapons, and the currently powerful prison abolition movement. Most significant, the RPCC put into action the constitutional theory that "the people" possessed "other rights" that could not be trampled upon, and, if those rights were violated, they had the power to create a new government.

The comprehensive discourse of self-defense generated by the BPP, then, revealed the contradictory status of democracy in America in the 1960s and 1970s. Its political philosophy suggested that laws were enforced for the benefit of the powerful. Generally, those in power did not act on behalf of all Americans, most especially the poor and the oppressed. The history of the American Revolution, the establishment of the federal government, and the writing of and subsequent appendage to the Ninth Amendment clearly show that this type of oppressive power was exactly what those who wrote the Constitution sought to prevent. To be sure, there are those who have argued that the framers, including Madison, intended the text of the Ninth Amendment to be merely "a truism"[87] by only stating the already self-evident limited powers granted to the new federal government. Although that may be the case in theory, in reality what the Ninth Amendment leaves open is the relationship between individual rights and government officials. Instead of interpreting the Ninth Amendment as merely a construction of the limiting power of the federal government, it might instead be seen as the source for a range of freedoms for all individuals against state-sponsored benign neglect or direct forms of coercion.

CONCLUSION

The Ninth Amendment stands as a bulwark against implied federal government powers and, most important, the implication that the first eight amendments were the only basic and fundamental rights guaranteed to the people. Although it can be argued that it was the intent of Madison and the other delegates to insert the Ninth Amendment "merely for greater caution," it serves as much more than that. Thomas McAfee summarizes well the magnitude of the amendment's significance, when he states: "What is ultimately at stake is the appropriate foundational account of our constitutional order. Proponents of the more expansive reading of the amendment ultimately ground their reading in the view that, for the founding generation at least, the inalienable rights held an inherent constitutional status because they were rooted in a natural law that was binding over all positive law. The most fundamental rights were withheld from the government, not because the people made that decision, but because God or nature had decreed it, and because such rights were the very basis of the social contract. Because of this, the foundation of American constitutionalism is the very idea of natural rights."[88] The Ninth Amendment represents the recognition of an infinite source of additional "other rights," which are not listed but nonetheless are protected by the Constitution. It was that reservoir of rights that the Black Panther Party tapped in the 1960s and 1970s.

While the knee-jerk response to such an argument might be to associate the revolutionary actions of the BPP with present-day white militia groups, it must be stressed—against the prevailing view—that violence was not the first option advocated by the Party. Instead, the group developed a program of self-defense in response to an oppressive state. Thus, it is important to stress that "self-defense" took on a broad form with violence as only one component in resisting state oppression. This contextual distinction helps to clarify a use of the Ninth Amendment in the cause of progressive change, both historically and in the future. A litmus test for its application would be the conditions of the community from which social movements emerge. In the case of BPP activities, self-defense was not an act of choice to opt out of the nation-state but rather a response to state exclusion from its goods and services. In the case of communities under siege, self-defense was a desire for inclusion and equal protection and an act of supplementary social development.[89]

The communities from which white militia groups and other conservative social movements emerge are not surveyed by the police or denied states' rights simply because of their race; rather, they are targeted because of their disdain for equal protection under the law. Their desire to "take back the country" is predicated on a demand for a racially pure nation-state, while the BPP sought a more equal distribution of wealth and power in a racially mixed, if revolutionary, nation-state. The constitutional idea of equal protection thus runs directly counter to the vision of white militias and hence would not be covered under the Ninth Amendment.

Black communities were truly under siege in the 1960s, and the Panthers sought out community restructuring through police patrols, free health and legal clinics, and breakfast programs for children. If we are ever to understand that combination of activities, there must be an expanded understanding of the historical significance of the Party through more critical analysis of the relationship between constitutional law and such social movements. Such critical analysis will likely lead to the conclusion that, overall, the BPP participated legally within the system, and they should be remembered as an important freedom organization for the black community and for America as a whole. In this light, as a case study, the Black Panther Party offers an example of an attempted reconstruction of jurisprudence that directly reflects the actual needs of the citizenry for whom the law—like the Ninth Amendment to the U.S. Constitution—was written in the first place.

NOTES

I would like to thank Wallace Sherwood, Sean Varano, Soffiyah Elijah, and Jen Balboni for their insightful comments and helpful criticism on early drafts of this essay. I also want to thank Jama Lazerow and Yohuru Williams for their invitation to contribute this essay to the anthology. And, along with them, I greatly appreciate the helpful insights from Rod Bush and the anonymous readers from Duke University Press. Finally a very special thank you to Davarian Baldwin for numerous draft readings and late nights of chai tea.

1 Gene Marine, *The Black Panthers* (New York: Signet Press, 1969), back cover.

2 Eldridge Cleaver, "The Courage to Kill: Meeting the Panthers," in *Post-Prison Writings and Speeches*, edited by Robert Scheer (New York: Random House, 1969), esp. 29.

3 Philip S. Foner, "Introduction," in *The Black Panthers Speak*, edited by Philip S. Foner (New York: Da Capo Press, 1995 [1970]), xxxi.

4 Bobby Seale, *Seize the Time: The Story of the Black Panther Party and Huey P. Newton* (New York: Vintage, 1970), 83.

5 See Kathleen Cleaver and George Katsiaficas, eds., *Liberation, Imagination and the Black Panther Party: A New Look at the Panthers and Their Legacy* (New York: Rout-ledge, 2001); Charles E. Jones, ed., *The Black Panther Party [Reconsidered]* (Baltimore: Black Classic Press, 1998); and, earlier, Kim Kit Holder, "The History of the Black Panther Party, 1966–1972: A Curriculum Tool for Afrikan-American Studies" (Ph.D. diss., University of Massachusetts, 1990).

6 Newton, " 'On the Defection of Eldridge Cleaver from the Black Panther Party and the Defection of the Black Panther Party from the Black Community': 17 April 1971," in *The Huey P. Newton Reader*, edited by David Hilliard and Donald Weise (New York: Seven Stories Press, 2002), 200–8.

7 Newton, "In Defense of Self-Defense: Executive Mandate Number One," *The Black Panther*, 2 June 1967.

8 Quoted from online source at www.historyplace.com/unitedstates/revolution/ causes.htm.

9 Quoted in A. J. Langguth, *Patriots: The Men Who Started the American Revolution* (New York: Touchstone, 1988), 32.

10 Ibid., 159.

11 Ibid., 56.

12 Newton, "In Defense of Self-Defense," in Hilliard and Weise, eds., *The Huey P. Newton Reader*, 134.

13 Alexander Hamilton, James Madison, and John Jay, *The Federalist Papers*, edited by Clinton Rossiter (New York: Mentor, 1999), 478–88. See also Langguth, *Patriots*.

14 Bennett B. Patterson, *The Forgotten Amendment: A Call for Legislative and Judicial Recognition of Rights under Social Conditions of Today* (Indianapolis: Bobbs-Merrill Co., 1955); Calvin R. Massey, *Silent Rights: The Ninth Amendment and the Constitution's Unenumerated Rights* (Philadelphia: Temple University Press, 1995).

15 Patterson, *The Forgotten Amendment*.

16 Charles Black, *Decision According to Law: The 1979 Holmes Lectures* (New York: Norton, 1981), 46; Mark N. Goodman, *The Ninth Amendment: History, Interpretation, and Meaning* (Smithtown, New York: Exposition Press, 1981), 1; *United Public Workers v. Mitchell*, 330 U.S. 75, 94–95 (1947); *Calder v. Bull*, 3 U.S. (3 Dall), 386, 388 (1798); *Loan Ass'n v. Topeka*, 87 U.S. 655, 662–63 (1875); *Ashwander v.* TVA, 297 U.S. 288, 330–31 (1936); *Tennessee Electric Power Co. v.* TVA, 306 U.S. 118, 143–44 (1939).

17 John Choon Yoo, "Our Declaratory Ninth Amendment," *Emory Law Journal* 42 (1993): 967–1043.

18 Some scholars have argued that the Ninth Amendment was not intended to limit state power but to serve only as a rule of construction regarding the extent of the Constitution's enumerated powers. Thomas McAfee, "The Original Meaning of the Ninth Amendment," *Columbia Law Review* 90 (1990): 1215–1305; Massey, *Silent Rights*; Charles J. Cooper, "Limited Government and Individual Liberty: The Ninth Amendment's Forgotten Lessons," in *The Bill of Rights: Original Meaning and Current Understanding*, edited by Eugene J. Hickok (Charlottesville: University Press of Virginia, 1991).

19 The position taken here—that the Ninth Amendment is enforceable against state and federal government officials—can be found in numerous works, including Yoo, "Our Declaratory Ninth Amendment"; Charles Black, *A New Birth of Freedom: Human Rights, Named and Unnamed* (New York: Putnam, 1997); Mark C. Niles, "Ninth Amendment Adjudication: An Alternative to Substantive Due Process Analysis of Person Autonomy Rights," *UCLA Law Review* 48 (2000): 85–157.

20 Laurence H. Tribe and Michael C. Dorf, *On Reading the Constitution* (Cambridge, Mass.: Harvard University Press, 1991), 54.

21 See *Planned Parenthood v. Casey*, 505 U.S. 833, 848 (1992); Yoo, "Our Declaratory Ninth Amendment," 1009.

22 Ibid.

23 Although the current trend is to absorb a few of the Bill of Rights into the Fourteenth Amendment's Due Process Clause, case law has clearly established that the court will look at rights considered "fundamental principles of liberty and justice which lie at the base of all our civil and political institutions" (*Palko v. Connecticut*, 302 U.S. 319, 328 [1937]). As stated in *Planned Parenthood v. Casey*, 505 U.S. 833, 834 (1992): "Neither the Bill of Rights nor the specific practices of States at the time of the adoption of the Fourteenth Amendment marks the *outer limits* of the substantive sphere of liberty which the Fourteenth Amendment protects. See U.S. Const., Amdt 9" (emphasis mine).

24 *Doe v. Bolton*, 410 U.S. 179, 210–11 (1973).

25 Tribe and Dorf, *Reading the Constitution*, 55. Although the courts have had little occasion to interpret the Ninth Amendment, see *Marbury v. Madison*, 5 U.S. 137, 174 (1803): "It cannot be presumed that any clause in the Constitution is intended to be without effect." In interpreting the Constitution, "real effect should be given to all the words [the Constitution] uses" (*Myers v. United States*, 272 U.S. 52, 151 [1926]).

26 381 U.S. 479, 488, 491, 492 (1965).

27 *Bowers v. Hardwick*, 478 U.S. 186 (1986).

28 *Webster v. Doe*, 486 U.S. 592 (1988).

29 *Troxel v. Granville*, 530 U.S. 57 (2000).

30 *United States v. Orito*, 413 U.S. 139 (1972).

31 *Griswold v Connecticut*, 381 U.S. 479 (1965).

32 Ibid., 484.

33 Quoted in Foner, *The Black Panthers Speak*, xxxi. See also Cleaver, "The Land Question and Black Liberation" (April/May 1968), in *Post-Prison Writings and Speeches*, 57–72.

34 The literature on this topic is immense and still growing. For examples from the last decade, see Nikhil Pal Singh, *Black Is a Country: Race and the Unfinished Struggle for Democracy* (Cambridge, Mass.: Harvard University Press, 2004); Barbara Ransby, *Ella Baker and the Black Freedom Movement: A Radical Democratic Vision* (Chapel Hill: University of North Carolina Press, 2003); Martha Biondi, *To Stand and Fight: The Struggle for Civil Rights in Postwar New York City* (Cambridge, Mass.: Harvard University Press, 2003); Gail Williams O'Brien, *The Color of Law: Race, Violence, and Justice in the Post–World War II South* (Chapel Hill: University of North Carolina Press, 1999); Leon Litwack, *Trouble in Mind: Black Southerners in the Age of Jim Crow* (New York: Knopf, 1998); Fitzhugh Brundage, *Under Sentence of Death: Lynching in the South* (Chapel Hill:

University of North Carolina Press, 1997); Joy James, *Resisting State Violence: Radicalism, Gender, and Race in U.S. Culture* (Minneapolis: University of Minnesota Press, 1996); Charles M. Payne, *I've Got the Light of Freedom: The Organizing Tradition and the Mississippi Freedom Struggle* (Berkeley: University of California Press, 1995); Gerald Horne, *The Fire This Time: The Watts Uprising and the 1960s* (Charlottesville: University of Virginia Press, 1995).

35 Singh, "The Black Panthers and the 'Undeveloped Country' of the Left," in Jones, ed., *The Black Panther Party*; Robin D. G. Kelley, "Roaring from the East: Third World Dreaming," in *Freedom Dreams: The Black Radical Imagination* (Boston: Beacon, 2002); Robin D. G. Kelley and Betsy Esch, "Black Like Mao: Red China and Black Liberation," *Souls* I (fall 1999): 6–41; Vijay Prashad, *Everybody Was Kung Fu Fighting* (Boston: Beacon, 2000); Lisa Brock and Digna Castaneda Fuertes, eds., *Between Race and Empire: African-Americans and Cubans before the Cuban Revolution* (Philadelphia: Temple University Press, 1998); Van Gosse, *Where the Boys Are: Cuba, Cold War America, and the Making of a New Left* (London: Verso, 1993); Frantz Fanon, *The Wretched of the Earth* (New York: Grove, 1967); Mao Tse-tung [Zedong], *Quotations from Chairman Mao Tsetung* (Peking [Beijing]: Foreign Languages Press, 1966); Rolland Snellings [Askia Muhammad Toure], "Afro American Youth and the Bandung World," *Liberator* 5 (January 1965).

36 Rod Bush, *We Are Not What We Seem: Black Nationalism and Class Struggle in the American Century* (New York: New York University Press, 1999); Timothy Tyson, *Radio Free Dixie: Robert Williams and the Roots of Black Power* (Chapel Hill: University of North Carolina Press, 1999); Komozi Woodard, *A Nation within a Nation: Amiri Baraka (LeRoi Jones) and Black Power Politics* (Chapel Hill: University of North Carolina Press, 1998); Grace Lee Boggs, *Living for Change* (Minneapolis: University of Minnesota Press, 1998); Williams Sales Jr., *From Civil Rights to Black Liberation: Malcolm X and the Organization of Afro-American Unity* (Boston: South End Press, 1994); Ferruccio Gambino, "The Transgression of a Laborer: Malcolm X in the Wilderness of America," *Radical History Review* (winter 1993): 7–31; William Van Deburg, *A New Day in Babylon: The Black Power Movement and American Culture, 1965–1975* (Chicago: University of Chicago Press, 1992); Joe Wood, ed., *Malcolm X: In Our Own Image* (New York: St. Martin's Press, 1992); James Cone, *Martin or Malcolm and America: A Dream or a Nightmare?* (Maryknoll, N.Y.: Orbis Books, 1991); Maxwell Stanford, "Revolutionary Action Movement: A Case Study of an Urban Revolutionary Movement in Western Capitalist Society" (MA thesis, Atlanta University, 1986); Marcellus Barksdale, "Robert Williams and the Indigenous Civil Rights Movement in Monroe, North Carolina, 1961," *Journal of Negro History* 69 (spring 1984): 73–89; Kalamu ya Salaam, "Robert Williams: Crusader for International Solidarity," *Black Collegian* 8.3 (January/February 1978): 53–60; Malcolm X, with Alex Haley, *The Autobiography of Malcolm X* (New York: Grove Press, 1965); Robert Williams, *Negroes with Guns* (New York: Marzani and Munsell, 1962).

37 Newton, "In Defense of Self-Defense," in Foner, ed., *The Black Panthers Speak*, 40.

38 Kwame Ture and Charles Hamilton, *Black Power: The Politics of Liberation* (New York: Vintage, 1992), 9, 5.

39 At Cleaver's behest, the BPP added a plank to their original platform and program, calling for a United Nations plebiscite allowing black citizens the right to decide on national inclusion or independence. For that amended version, see "What We Want, What We Believe," mislabeled as the "October 1966 Black Panther Party Platform and Program," in Foner, ed., *The Black Panthers Speak*, 2–4. See also Cleaver, "The Land Question."

40 "Patrolling," excerpted from Newton's autobiography, *Revolutionary Suicide*, in Hilliard and Weise, eds., *The Huey P. Newton Reader*, 60.

41 See, for example, *Snyder v. Massachusetts*, 291 U.S. 97, 105 (1934); *Powell v. Alabama*, 287 U.S. 45, 67 (1932) (quoting *Herbert v. Louisiana* 272 U.S. 312, 316 [1926]).

42 See John Locke, *Second Treatise of Government*, edited by C. B. Macpherson (Cambridge, Mass.: Hackett Publishing, 1980 [1690]); Samuel Pufendorf, *De jure naturae et gentium libri octo* [The Law of Nature and Nations], vol. 2., translated by C. H. Oldfather and W. A. Oldfather (Dobbs Ferry, N.Y.: Oceana Publications, 1964 [1688]), 264; Thomas Hobbes, *Leviathan*, edited by Michael Oakeshott (Oxford: Basil Blackwell, 1957 [1651]), 103.

43 J. D. Droddy, "Originalist Justification and Methodology of Unenumerated Rights," *Michigan State University–Detroit College of Law Law Review* 199 (1999): 831.

44 *Snyder v. Massachusetts*, 291 U.S. 97, 105 (1934).

45 *Powell v. Alabama*, 287 U.S. 45, 67 (1932) (quoting *Herbert v. Louisiana*, 272 U.S. 312, 316 [1926]).

46 McAfee, "The Original Meaning of the Ninth Amendment,"

47 Patterson, *The Forgotten Amendment*, 36–43; Black, *A New Birth of Freedom*, 47.

48 Knowlton H. Kelsey, "The Ninth Amendment of the Federal Constitution," in *The Rights Retained by the People*, edited by Randy Barnett (Fairfax, Va.: George Mason Press, 1989), 96–99; see also Patterson, *The Forgotten Amendment*, 107.

49 For example, in the Civil Rights Act of 1964 and the Voting Rights Act of 1965.

50 Sundiata Acoli [né Clark Squire], "A Brief History of the Black Panther Party: Its Place in the Black Liberation Movement," from the Sundiata Acoli Freedom Campaign 1995, Marion Penitentiary, 4/2/85, online at http://www.afrikan.identity.com/sundiata/sun04.html.

51 Newton, "On the Defection of Eldridge Cleaver," in Hilliard and Weise, eds., *The Huey P. Newton Reader*, 201.

52 Hence the BPP-organized Revolutionary People's Constitutional Convention, which proposed a new Constitution with expanded individual rights and limited government intrusion. George Katsiaficas, "Organization and Movement: The Case of the Black Panther Party and the Revolutionary People's

Constitutional Convention of 1970," in Cleaver and Katsiaficas, eds., *Liberation, Imagination, and the Black Panther Party*, 141–55.

53 Newton, "Huey Newton Talks to the Movement about the Black Panther Party, Cultural Nationalism, SNCC, Liberals and White Revolutionaries," in Foner, ed., *The Black Panthers Speak*, 50. Cf. Scot Brown, *Fighting for us: Maulana Karenga, the us Organization, and Black Cultural Nationalism* (New York: New York University Press, 2003), 115–19.

54 Seale, "The Ten-Point Platform," 78, and "Defend the Ghetto," (Brooklyn Panther leaflet), 180, in Foner, ed., *The Black Panthers Speak*.

55 The rationale is offered by Seale, in *Seize the Time*, and by Huey Newton (with the assistance of J. Herman Blake, in *Revolutionary Suicide* (New York: Writers and Readers Publishing, 1995 [1973]), 114–27.

56 Seale, "Defend the Ghetto"; Newton, "Functional Definition of Politics," *The Black Panther*, 17 January 1969, and Hilliard, "If You Want Peace You Got to Fight for It," *The Black Panther*, 19 November 1969, in Foner, ed., *The Black Panthers Speak*, 44– 47, 128–30, respectively.

57 Fliers/posters in Foner, ed., *The Black Panthers Speak*, 53, 180, 221.

58 Candy, "Pigs-Panthers," *The Black Panther*, 22 November 1969, in Foner, ed., *The Black Panthers Speak*, 35–37.

59 The fundamental power of "the people," of course, is embodied in the Tenth Amendment: "The powers not delegated to the United States by the Constitution, nor prohibited by it to the States, are reserved to the States respectively, *Or to the People*" (emphasis mine).

60 Seale, *Seize the Time*, 157.

61 Newton, "A Functional Definition of Politics," *The Black Panther*, 17 January 1969, in Hilliard and Weise, eds., *The Huey P. Newton Reader*, 148.

62 Seale, *Seize the Time*, 71; Newton, "Violence," *The Black Panther*, 23 March 1968, in Foner, ed., *The Black Panthers Speak*, 19.

63 Newton, "Huey Newton Talks to the Movement," in Foner, ed., *The Black Panthers Speak*, 62.

64 Newton, "Violence," in Foner, ed., *The Black Panthers Speak*, 19.

65 The Second Amendment states: "A well regulated Militia, being necessary to the security of a free State, the right of the people to keep and bear Arms, shall not be infringed."

66 Newton, "On the Defection of Eldridge Cleaver," in Hilliard and Weise, eds., *The Huey P. Newton Reader*, 204.

67 Ibid., 207.

68 Cleaver, "The Land Question," in *Post-Prison Writings and Speeches*, 72.

69 Newton, "Patrolling," in Hilliard and Weise, eds., *The Huey P. Newton Reader*, 60.

70 "Bobby Seale Explains Panther Politics: An Interview," *Guardian* (January 1970), in Foner, ed., *The Black Panthers Speak*, 82; further explication of this position can be found on page xxx. For a retrospective explication of how and why the Panthers adopted the term "pig," see Newton, *Revolutionary Suicide*, 165–66.

71 David Hilliard, "The Ideology of the Black Panther Party," *The Black Panther*, 8 November 1969, in Foner, ed., *The Black Panthers Speak*, 122.

72 See Newton, *Revolutionary Suicide*.

73 Seale, *Seize the Time*, 85–99.

74 Quoted in Michael Newton, *Bitter Grain: Huey Newton and the Black Panther Party* (Los Angeles: Holloway House, 1991), 19.

75 Floyd Hayes III and Francis Kiene III, " 'All Power to the People': The Political Thought of Huey P. Newton and the Black Panther Party," in Jones, ed., *The Black Panther Party*, 161; Newton, "On the Defection of Eldridge Cleaver," in Hilliard

76 Kelley, *Freedom Dreams*, 95–96.

77 "Correcting Mistaken Ideas," *The Black Panther*, 26 October 1968, in Foner, ed., *The Black Panthers Speak*, 23.

78 Newton, *Revolutionary Suicide*, 188–89.

79 See Acoli, http://www.afrikan.i-entity.com/sundiata/sun04.html.

80 Newton, "On the Defection of Eldridge Cleaver," in Hilliard and Weise, eds., *The Huey P. Newton Reader*, 201.

81 Ibid, 203; *The Black Panther*, 4 August and 5 October 1969.

82 Steve McCutchen, "Selections from a Panther Diary," in Jones, ed., *The Black Panther Party*, 119, 121.

83 Abron, " 'Serving the People': The Survival Programs of the Black Panther Party," in Jones, ed., *The Black Panther Party*, 177–92.

84 Through the prison bus rides, for example, families could visit family members incarcerated in a far-flung state prison system.

85 "Black Panthers: Panthers Plan New 'Constitution,' " *Facts on File World News Digest*, 15 July 1970, online at http://www.2facts.com.

86 Ibid. See also Katsiaficas, "Organization and Movement."

87 *Griswold v. Connecticut*, 381 U.S. 479, 529 (1965) (Stewart's dissent).

88 Thomas McAfee, "A Critical Guide to the Ninth Amendment," *Temple Law Review* 69 (1996): 91–92.

89 For the contrary view, see John A. Wood, *Panthers and the Militias: Brothers Under the Skin?* (Lanham, Md.: University Press of America, 2002).

SUPPLEMENTARY QUESTIONS FOR ANALYSIS AND LECTURE DISCUSSION

1. Based on the reading, Bold Rule Changes to Break Up Concentrated Wealth, please provide and analyze in detail three ways in which policy changes need to occur in order to break up concentrated wealth in this nation thus reducing economic inequality and class based economic stratification.   Note: Base your answers strictly on the reading.

2. Based on the reading, From North to South in the 1960's, please explain how social protest movements change American Public Policy. How does culture inaugurate and also resist social justice policy implementation? Note: Base your answers strictly on the reading.

3. Based on the reading, Intersecting Oppressions: Rethinking Women's Movements in the United States, explain the concept of Intersectionality and how this impacts women of color in the women's liberation movement. In addition, explain "how individuals are socially located in the middle of crosscutting systems of oppression that form mutually constructing features of social organization." (pg 53) In your analysis explain the three phases of the women's liberation / feminist movement, its current trajectory and impact in today's social justice protest agenda. Note: Base your answers strictly on the reading.

PRE-UNIT REFLECTION QUESTIONS

After each unit, the reader should be able to critically analyze and engage these three core points (Note: Base your answers strictly on the reading and current events related to the readings in the text.):

1. Based on the readings, please provide and analyze in detail three ways in which policy changes need to occur in order to break up concentrated wealth in the United States, thus reducing economic inequality and class based economic stratification.

2. Based on the readings, please explain how social protest movements change American public policy. How does transformation of consciousness initiate social, political, and subsequent economic change. How and why does culture inaugurate and yet resist social justice policy implementation?

3. Explain how the concept of intersectionality is demonstrated in the readings from this section. Think about how this intersectionality impacts women of color, participants in the women's liberation movement, oppressed people, and other marginalized groups who exist at the periphery of society seeking economic, political, and social justice. How do institutions provide the seeds of change and also the tools of systematic oppression? Refer back to the reading "Intersecting Oppressions: Rethinking Women's Movements in the United States," and revisit this quote of "how individuals are socially located in the middle of crosscutting systems of oppression that form mutually constructing features of social organization."

TRANSNATIONAL NARRATIVES: 21ST CENTURY PROTEST AGENDA

Moving from Guilt to Action: Antiracist Organizing and the Concept of "Whiteness" for Activism and the Academy

WILLIAM AAL

As an antiracist organizer and trainer over the last twenty years, I have grasped at any tools that might make my work easier and more effective. Many of us who work at the grassroots level against racism do so because we see it as the fundamental problem underlying and linking other forms of oppression and social injustice in the United States. None of us were born antiracist organizers; we became such as we saw devastating effects that racism has on people of color, on the humanity of white people, and on the moral and spiritual fabric of society. Like others grappling with the pervasive and seemingly intractable problem of racism in this country, I have studied history, Marxism and other forms of political economy, social psychology, sociology—anything that might help one to understand how our society got organized the way it is and what it will take to change it.

I became an "expert" at being racist from having been born and raised "white" in a country that is structured along racist lines. At the same time, because I am a beneficiary of this system, the impact of racism is almost entirely invisible to me. In order to get real insight into the dynamics, it has been necessary for me to read history and analysis by people of color to get the view from "outside." In order to survive each day, whether there is a white person in the room or not, they have to deal with the consequences of a world ordered by white skin privilege. They are the experts on whiteness and its impact on themselves, "white" people, and the United States as a whole.

In the work that I and other trainers and organizers do, it is invaluable to define the concept of white identity as privilege. Many people self-identified as white experience themselves as beyond history and without community. Their culture is one of consumption—of ideas, art, and spirituality, as well as of material objects.

When trying to encourage "white" people to help eliminate racism, it is helpful to encourage them to remember that by fighting racism we act to restore our own humanity and culture as well. We welcome the academic study of whiteness as a way to reclaim history, yet many of us are uneasy with this trend as well. This essay grew out of a concern that "whiteness" as an academic subject of study can easily slip from being the examination of an important social/political category to becoming just another career path. People often start out with a commitment to serve, but the process of professionalization takes them away from the community. This is a pitfall that is systemic to U.S. work culture. I see the same dynamic in the dichotomy between diversity training and anti-oppression organizing. As a "diversity trainer," it is also easy to end up making a career of working in the corporate sector and becoming disassociated from the oppressed communities. In fact, there is a whole generation of people coming through various university programs in multicultural work or "cross-cultural" training or similar fields who are looking for work as trainers or organizers and yet have had very little experience as activists.

I felt very ambivalent about writing for an academic book when first approached. I didn't want my work to become more fodder for the academic paper mill. On other the hand, I have wanted to make a contribution to the antiracist movement in this country by challenging academics to produce materials useful to the struggle for justice and to actively engage—because we could really use a hand!

One lesson I have learned over the years is that in order to eradicate racism activists and organizers need to start working with those who benefit from racist structures and who play the biggest part in maintaining them. So it makes sense for me to use this opportunity to address academics who are overwhelmingly white and are certainly among those who benefit from and maintain the status quo. Therefore, they can play an important part in bringing about change.

There are intellectual projects that could take all of us further. What we need in the movement is a better understanding of how "whiteness" as a set of overlapping identities, structures, and power relations keeps the United States divided along the lines of race, class, and gender. We need to know more about how we got into the predicament in which most of the "white" people in the United States either are unaware of the impacts that their daily lives have on "others," both inside the United States and around the world, or don't care. We need to reclaim our history through an antiracist lens, especially remembering and learning from those of our ancestors who have stood for justice.[1] And we also need to contribute to the process of creating new ways of being together across lines of difference in classrooms, conferences, and the community.

The stories we tell need to be deep, to promote critical thinking, and be both accessible and relevant for people outside the academy. I long for someone to engage with the thinking of Antonio Gramsci, Stuart Hall, bell hooks, Cornel West, Edward Said, Roberto Unger, and others in ways that relate these cultural and intellectual struggles with everyday life. The work of these intellectuals makes an enormous contribution toward revealing the fact that the structures of injustice are not natural phenomena ("the way the world has and will always be") but were created by humans in specific historical contexts and therefore *can be changed*. By helping us understand the formative contexts of daily life and the institutional arrangements that maintain oppression, engaged academics could help foster new ways of thinking about our social/political problems.

STORIES FROM A FEW ANTIRACIST WHITES

To clarify my own thinking, I decided to talk with a few other trainer/ activists around the United States about what the idea of whiteness means to them and what they would want from the study of whiteness. I talked with three people who have been doing antiracist work for many years. Two of them have Ph.D.'s and work in academic settings, though they both have taken decidedly nontraditional paths. Each of us is committed to a form of social justice that includes looking at the intersecting axes of class, gender, and race. We take it as a given that without racial justice, there can be no gender justice and vice versa. At the same time, each of us understands that racism is at the center of much of what it means to be white in America. We understand that our worldview, our sense of what is ours without asking and our knowledge of what we are not supposed to talk about, is structured by our white identities. I asked them three or four questions about their motivations for doing the work, their vision for the future, what they thought about "white studies," and what they would want from such an endeavor. When I mentioned the ambivalence I myself felt about the field, they acknowledged similar feelings. We all have learned a lot from academics and at the same time have been outraged by some of the dynamics described later in this article. These conversations challenge academics to turn some of their own tools of critical analysis on their own work: to examine how they make choices about what to focus on, whose interests the research they are doing serves, and to whom they are accountable.

Mark Scanlon Green is an academic who has also done a lot of antiracist organizing and brings a gender analysis to his thinking about race. His Ph.D. dissertation was on the subject of white males and diversity work. He now works in a private academic setting, working principally with students of color. Mark took up antiracist work, coming out of a complex personal/family history, his identity as a gay man, and a political commitment to change from the age of fourteen. "My choice to focus on white men is personal and political," he says.

> As a white man who has become actively involved in the diversity move-
> ment, I have wondered how it is that I have chosen to challenge the system
> that assigns me higher status and more power than it does to people of
> color and white women. If all the unearned privilege I have is a boon to my

personal and professional development, why would I, or for that matter, any other man in his right mind, choose to work to eliminate its influence? … I have also realized, however, that over the years, many of my political "fellow travelers" were every bit as racist, sexist, and heterosexist as the larger society they claimed they wanted to change. And since racism is at the heart of the American experience, without dealing with it, we can't move forwards with a progressive social agenda. If the Rosetta Stone is found that decodes the process by which some white men, who are at the pinnacle of social status and power, actively engage themselves in changing the system, significant social change becomes possible.

Eventually he ended up feeling attacked from several fronts in the "diversity" arena. He says, "It is much harder for a white man to be out front as a trainer." White people didn't accept his leadership, and people of color didn't trust a white person doing "diversity training." Mark gave up active organizing with white people since he couldn't see social change occurring from doing "diversity work." He doesn't see himself as an activist anymore. He has chosen as his life work to be supportive of people of color getting access to higher education and puts the majority of his academic commitment in that direction, mentoring students from nontraditional backgrounds. He is committed to "academic excellence" not only to help students get access but also to insist that they grab that access, make it theirs in whatever way makes sense to them, and to shine in their competence.

His vision of a world that has dealt with racism is one based on equal access to resources—educational, economic, and political. It has to do with principles of justice as opposed to "equality." He wants academics looking at whiteness to be focused on eliminating the barriers to access within the academy that white people keep putting in front of people of color. The challenge is to make space for people of color on a truly equal footing; liberalism, individualism, and tokenism need to be combated.

Sharon Howell, raised poor, was the first in her family to go to college. She is now an academic as well. A lifelong antiracist, she has been a member and a leader of a non-Marxist revolutionary organization that was dedicated to creating a revolution with people of color in the lead. She works at a large midwestern university and is a leader in her community as an antiracist and antihomophobic organizer. She currently leads the major grassroots effort to rebuild Detroit. Along with Margo Adair, she is a founding member of Tools for Change, a consulting group that conducts workshops around antiracism and economic justice in work settings and for political groups.

Sharon would rather do anything else than have to deal with racism. There are more interesting things to do in the world, she says, like reconstruct Detroit so that it is a city that sustains all its people. But, according to her, racism gets in the way of that project. Detroit was destroyed because of racism. And now the majority of people left in the city are people who can't afford to leave, so—white, black, Arab, Asian, or Latino—they have common ground to stand on. Much of Detroit looks like a war zone. Whole blocks of houses have been bulldozed to the ground because absentee landlords abandoned their properties as economic values went down. There is little blue-collar work left in Detroit proper and its surrounding suburban areas, as the big auto makers have moved toward automation and outsourcing overseas and to other, nonunionized parts of the city. So the racial question has now more clearly than ever become one of class. The folks at the bottom have to deal with each other in order to survive. Yet race still is a "wedge issue" that is used to divide people.

So, for Sharon, it is necessary to deal with racism at all levels, interpersonally, within organizational structures and in "civil" society. Interpersonal racism, the kind that keeps white people and people of color from being able to trust each other because of white people's conscious or unconscious identification with the white power structure, needs to be dealt with to build long-lasting relations of solidarity. A former member of the National Organization for an American Revolution (NOAR), a revolutionary organization dedicated to the revolutionary leadership of African Americans and other people of color, she and her writing partner and political comrade Margo Adair started doing organizational consulting with groups committed to progressive social change in the mid-1980s. They, like Mark, realized that the relationships of oppression that exist in the dominant society are reproduced within those groups. Their analysis of organizational culture as an outgrowth of European American (white) middle-class patriarchal culture led them to look at how patterns of power govern access to resources and structure relations in groups committed to ecological or social justice.

They developed the concept of internalized privilege to help explain why people in positions of power usually don't see how their actions impact others and move through the world with a sense of entitlement. They also put forward the idea of "wonderbreading" which is what assimilation does. In order to make it into the category of "white" and receive its privileges, people were forced to give up their loyalty to their own traditions, language, community, and principles. In this framework, "white" is solely an identity of privilege. Value is no longer placed on community, place, or history but, instead, on access to power and commodities. Business decisions are based on purely economic rationality, without taking into account these other dimensions. Communities are reduced to individuals and families to reproductive units. Culture becomes devoid of richness. Understanding these dynamics reveals what white people have to gain by ridding society of racism. Sharon sees it as important to help people of European descent see how their identification with white privilege keeps them from moving toward racial justice and how their guilt over that compounds the problem even more.

Her vision of a society based on principles of justice has led to work on Detroit Summer, a multigenerational project dedicated to rebuilding the most devastated parts of Detroit. Each summer, youth from Detroit and all around the country work with neighborhood people cleaning up parks, reconstructing homes, and re-creating a vital community. Leadership development and the study of Detroit's history and culture are integral parts of the project. Sharon sees this work as part of her life commitment. Her request to other academics is that they engage in projects of social justice that will inform their writings about social movements and help deepen their commitment to eliminate racism.

Marian Meck Root grew up in "Middle America," in the mainstream Lutheran church. At an early age, she realized the spiritual void left by people's refusal to deal with racism. She is a theologian in a major East Coast city and is part of a feminist theological center that keeps antiracism at the heart of its work.

She and her co-workers are grappling with the spiritual void left by racism, asking the question "How did this happen that we as a (white) people and as individuals are so spiritually afraid and weak?" She believes that when white people begin to address this question, they will begin to unearth some clues about ending racism. It is a project that can't be undertaken individually but, rather, communally. It is one according to her that can't be approached merely from the rational, linear patriarchal side. "It requires going against ... the dominant culture especially of the academy which projects its own fears onto the feminine."

In her exploration of the concept of whiteness she defines white "to mean those of us who have had enough European ancestry to benefit from having white skin and who have been raised to assume that our culture is generic or universal and to act out of a sense of racial and/or cultural superiority even when we deny or cannot see ourselves doing that." She talks about spirituality as in some sense acknowledging mystery and giving up the illusion of control. Pointing out that white folks are very attached to control and domination, she draws the conclusion that we have a hard time with mystery and hence spirituality.

For Marian, Europeans haven't always been this way; it is a historical development of recent vintage. It helps explain our yearnings for spirituality and some of our racist appropriation of other people's spiritual traditions.

While acknowledging the yearning, she notes that spirituality has much to do with ancestors and that white Americans have distanced themselves, literally, from theirs. "We don't know ourselves because we don't know where we come from." Looking back on thousands of years of European history, she sees a progressive disintegration of tribal life, that is, life connected to the land and to ancestors. Without romanticizing tribal existence, she states that there was a felt relationship between the spiritual and the material, between intuition and rational ways of knowing. She calls for a reconnection of mind and body and spirit as well as for a reintegration of our communities. In order carry out this project, we as white people have to forgive our ancestors and ourselves, and we have to hope for forgiveness by people of color without having the right to expect it.

What Marian wants from "whiteness studies" is a critique of Western rational thinking and individualism. This critique would help overcome the dualist splits between mind and body, individual and community, spirit and idea. The critique would embody a way forward to a healing transformation.

As for myself, I am an owner of a small house painting business and work with environmental and economic justice organizations. I am a former member of NOAR, along with Sharon, and am also an associate of Tools for Change. I work on coalition-building with people of color around issues of ecological and economic justice.

I came to an antiracist sensibility when I was ten or eleven. I grew up in a lower-middle-class, single-parent, Jewish family in upstate New York. We lived in a mixed ethnic neighborhood. I saw how much easier our lives were as a "white" family than those of my "black" friends and their families in similar economic circumstances. In the 1950s and early 1960s, we were able to see our cash-poor life as merely a temporary setback on the way to a fully middle-class life. Help from her parents alleviated my mother's temporary unemployment, and she knew that with her college education she would eventually be able to get a better job in the expanding civil service economy. My African American neighbors would have to wait a generation for members of their family to get access to education before being able to obtain that kind of work—and even then economic life would be precarious at best. Experiencing that difference had a profound impact on how I interpreted the success stories that my upper-middle-class Jewish and white Christian friends were given by their families. It made it impossible for me to accept the myths of individual progress or the metaphors of assimilation or the "melting pot" that were the basis of white American cultural hegemony.

As the Vietnam War unfolded, I began to see the links between racism at home and U.S. imperialism around the world. It became clear to me that the reasons racism and its related manifestations of sexism and homophobia were still present in the United States was because "white" people, and "white" men especially, were not willing to give up the position and power that they (we) gained by our white skin privilege. Of course, at the time I didn't have an analysis, only a feeling that something was wrong.

When I first became involved in the movement for racial justice in the 1960s, the social project seemed clear: to eliminate racism as an underlying ordering of public space and to create opportunities for women and men of color to enter into business, academic, and religious spheres on an "equal basis." We started with a basic understanding that racism is rooted in unfounded negative attitudes about people of color (prejudice) tied with the power to oppress them (institutional bias). All that was needed was to "change people's attitudes" and to make sure that policies in educational institutions, restaurants, residences, and banks provided equal access to resources.

In college in the early 1970s, I was exhilarated by the development of the various identity movements, as they allowed people who had been locked out of society to express their humanity to the society at large and begin to claim power for themselves. At the same time, as I watched the tendency of people in those movements to claim their piece of the American pie, I became confused. For me it was the very existence of that pie that required the United States to maintain the race, class, and gender divides, that kept some people rich while the majority remained poor. I also saw something like the pain that "wonderbreading" engendered for my parents' generation affect some African American friends of mine when they started going to college. They lost intimate contact with their childhood friends and sometimes with their families, as they chose to "make it" in academia or the business world. In short, I began to see the limitations of the concept of "equality" since in fact "equality" really meant "play by the rules of the game and don't question the status quo." It didn't allow for the transformation of the social context to include all the experiences and values that are embodied by those who have been locked out. In short, people were being welcomed to join a society whose rules were set by the oppressors.

Since identity politics by itself didn't call for the total transformation of society, only for either a piece of the pie or for carving out autonomous spaces for blacks, Latinos, women, gays, lesbians, or other disadvantaged people, it began to feel in the 1980s that we would have a fractured society that wasn't necessarily a more just one. With my membership in NOAR, I was able to see the power of being in an organization dedicated to the leadership of African American people for the whole country. I was challenged to be a leader in this context and to think collaboratively with people very different from myself. What NOAR was unable to incorporate into its practice was a deep understanding of the subjective side of reality, social power, and cultural differences. Despite our political unity, which included an understanding of racism as the underlying contradiction of the United States, we were still unable to deal with racism and internalized it within our own ranks.

I joined Tools for Change because, as a group, we grapple with these kinds of issues and help organizations deal effectively with them. Central to our work is a focus on the subjective side of politics, which includes the particularities of culture differences, the importance of the sacred, and the dynamics of both formal and informal power. We try to encourage people and organizations to become visionary. Without vision, we find ourselves re-creating the same patterns of life. In this context, I am attempting to develop an organizational development model of "opening the imagination to change," which incorporates vision, addresses issues of power, and encourages critical thinking. In this way I hope to be able to help organizations deal with race and class hierarchies by rethinking their mission and re-visioning the way they do their work. I would like to challenge academics to do the same. It would be an exciting program that turned its critical gaze inward to try to create a real space for people of color.

My own vision for racial justice involves a society that goes beyond celebrating difference, actually embodying cultural differences and gender and gender orientation differences—in short embracing all of its contradictions and highlighting them. People would no longer have to assimilate to make it; equal access would be a given.

WHITENESS AND ACTIVISM

Whiteness as a conceptual framework in a political context first emerged out of a need to confront some of the limitations of antiracist organizing. At the same time, whiteness has been part of the U.S. sensibility since the country's founding. Many groups and strata of "white" people have been conscious of their whiteness and protective of their privileges. The whole process of "assimilation" was one of immigrants coming to the United States and struggling to become "white" in order to access the legitimacy and resources associated with that status. But by the late 1950s white skin privilege was no longer morally unquestioned in public discourse, and by the mid-1960s its legal status was challenged. By the mid-1970s, at least within the movements for social justice, it wasn't supposed to exist. Yet racism has kept its hold on the fabric of our society and in the structures of even those organizations committed to social justice. The rhetoric of antiracism present in these organizations often has actually acted as a buffer against challenges to racism. People have a self-image of being antiracist, yet the middle-class norms that preclude them from admitting mistakes or showing ignorance make it nearly impossible for them to address these issues. When antiracism is addressed, conversations become focused on intentions rather than the impact.

After years of antiracist organizing, we have learned that white people can't ask people of color to do "our" work for us. Many organizers reluctantly came to the conclusion that the issue was white people's inability or lack of will to examine our own privilege. We were reluctant because we didn't want to deal with other white people—we distrusted them, as we distrusted ourselves. Many of us had come to hate our own whiteness as we learned of the legacy of racism. Not trusting other white folks, we felt better being in the company of people of color. We did not want to come to grips with our own history. Some of us felt that we didn't even have a culture. But, in order to eradicate racism, we realized that we had to start working with those who benefit from racist structures and who play the largest part in maintaining them.

Those of us who do antiracist organizing and training have found that white people have developed a lot of avoidance and defense strategies. I see every day how much investment white folks have in holding onto their power. Recently, this was brought home to me again. After a major success in grassroots organizing against the World Trade Organization meeting in late 1999 in Seattle, where a huge coalition of labor, environmental, human rights activists, and community people took to the streets, a lot of money started flowing to continue the organizing. Many of the groups that organized around this event took part in evaluations of the work. Jointly we critiqued our movement around the lack of diversity. Just after the evaluation, one part of the coalition, a mostly white student group was offered money for organizing at the University of Washington campus, which is also mostly white. They never even consulted with a partner youth of color group that had been organizing very effectively on this issue over a longer period. When challenged, the white group said they had never even thought about it. They had merely seen it as an opportunity to do the work. They would have done outreach to youth of color, but they never thought to share resources with or to take leadership from an already existing group. To date, I am not aware of steps taken to approach the youth of color group.

We have seen how white people, especially those who are better educated, are very good at using antiracist language to allow themselves to feel good about themselves without actually having to change. What we have had to develop are some ways to help white people understand what a high price they pay for their privileged position—so that ultimately they can see that the reason to work for justice is also to free themselves.

We have found in our antiracist work that the first hurdle to get around is a paralysis of guilt and defensiveness. Most white people know very well their skin color is tied to social privileges—so they feel guilty and at the same time don't feel personally invested in change. They don't understand very well the historical nature of our racist social structure, and so they find it very hard to imagine real change and what that might look like. Noel Ignatiev's *How the Irish Became White* is an example of academic work that can help "regular white folks" understand whiteness in the context of their own history. It helps them begin to see their own place in all of this. Although it is often very painful, using the concept of whiteness has been helpful in workshops as a tool for breaking through many patterns that hold back white people from organizing together to eliminate racism.

One of the first things I do in antiracist workshops is to ask people about their family backgrounds, to help them get in touch with their own history. From there, we can begin to ask questions like "What strengths do you draw from your family history?" and "What did you and/or your family have to give up to be white?" For people to really become invested in change, they need to get a sense of the violence they do to themselves and others in order to live in this kind of society. They need to get in contact with the grief from which they spend so much time and energy dissociating. When white people understand how much energy they expend to create the kind of amnesia that is a necessary part of whiteness, they can begin to see whiteness as a crippling condition that makes it very hard to imagine what a racially just society could be about. At this point, the transformation for justice is as much for "us" as for some distant and impersonal "them."

At the same time, in order to understand the depth and subtleties of the way racism works in the United States, people need to understand history and be able to make critical analyses of the power dynamics they encounter. By looking at the way that class and race intersect, participants can begin to see the way in which these dynamics hold each other in place. They are introduced to the concepts of position (what social strata you come from), stand (whom you are accountable to), bias (whose interests do your attitudes serve), and impact (who benefits and who loses from your actions). Understanding the difference between impact and intention can help people sort out very thorny situations and can help us move from guilt into action. In these workshops, I appeal to the heart and the imagination and the head. Our own history and our own grief—that is the heart. Understanding the historical nature of whiteness—that is what helps us imagine alternatives. Developing a critical analysis of the power structure and what can be done to change it—that is the head.

WHITE STUDIES IN THE ACADEMY

Many academics have become engaged in the study of whiteness as a part of their political work to fight racism in the academy as well as outside, and they courageously pursue their work in the face of great opposition from more established disciplines. Yet the realities of the academic environment soon become painfully evident. There is little support for new faculty, especially in the social sciences and humanities. There is an attack on Ethnic and Women's Studies and related disciplines, and academic institutions as a whole are less and less open to new types of knowledge.

Marian Root, in her piece "The Heart Cannot Express Its Goodness," invokes James Baldwin's statement that the price of whiteness and membership in the privileged ranks is the loss of community. Both Root and Sharon Howell note that this loss of community forces us to be "self-reliant or perish." Capitalism relies on individualism and competition. The university as a middle-class institution both reinforces and reproduces these values. It is organized by and rewards middle-class values like individualism and competitiveness. Collective work is generally not rewarded or even recognized—yet fighting racism has to be more than anything a collective project. Of course, those who can afford individualism are exactly those who have power. Individualism is taught in most U.S. schools from first grade on; it is embedded in the grading system and entrance requirements for undergraduate and graduate programs. Try to imagine a collective Ph.D.!

I do appreciate that this book is an exception to the rule, due to its having a collective editorial board. And, as I have said before, there are many who enter academia out of a sense of responsibility to communities of color. Unfortunately, there are structural forces at work that make it difficult for such academics to stay connected with those communities.

I have a picture in mind. It is not a photograph of academic reality but, rather, a painting, a view from an outsider's eyes. Academics are forced by the requirements of academic life to search for "new" intellectual terrain to explore and stake out.[2] Identity studies seem to follow a life cycle: as time goes on, important political projects begin to attract people who are looking to find a new niche in which to build their careers. At first, the terrain seems "virginal" and untouched (pick your favorite gender-laden term). So the explorer moves around the new territory, poking into people's history, sociology, psychology, and biology, overturning loose stones and pulling up plants. The explorer seeks to unveil knowledge, and the one who is there first creates a claim on large areas of the terrain. The knowledge belongs to the explorer who "discovers" it. Of course, in culture and social studies, the terrain involves human beings; the "new" knowledge is about their lives, their cultures, and their dreams. The academic in general has no sense of accountability to those who are the "subjects" or "objects" of investigation.

As new investigators arrive, they scour around for new and unusual parts of the territory, perhaps a unique species or perhaps a hidden corner. They compete for control over the territory by writing in a manner that uses the most abstract prose. Papers are written in a language so difficult to access that most of us lose patience. After an appropriate tour de force, perhaps the author gains access to scarce academic resources, a temporary teaching post; perhaps if he or she is lucky, the fabled tenure-track position. The people or group studied has not benefited from any of this process, although later they might get thanked in the credits. Sometimes they find their privacy violated and see sacred aspects of their culture now displayed in books and articles, to be read by anonymous strangers who know little, if anything, about the context in which those mysteries were created. Then there is the worst-case scenario: they find that they no longer have control of an aspect of their lives that previously they had had. Instead, they find an insidious slippage into dependency has been initiated by the whole process. This critique is not new. For example, the field of anthropology has long challenged researchers and applied anthropologists to do relevant and accountable work.[3] Obviously, this particular trajectory has nothing to do with a struggle for social justice or with those of us who try to organize against racism.

Part of the explanation has to do with how academics do their work. The prevailing view of academic work comes from the dominant ideology of empirical science: first discover a phenomenon, then analyze it, and then use it to support your argument (in this case for change). From my experience, this model of advocacy is ineffective either as a way to effect change within organizations or as a way to bring people into movements. No critique by itself has ever sustained transformation over time on either a personal or a group level. Creating a new society requires vision, passion, and commitment. Scholarship that engages reason, the imagination, and the heart and that empowers the community can help that process. Vine Deloria Jr., bell hooks, Stuart Hall, and Howard Zinn are role models for those who wish to follow this path.

Useful scholarship would help us connect ourselves to the historical and social complexes that we refer to when we speak of whiteness. But doing scholarship in the service of antiracism also means that scholars need to pay attention to the language in which they communicate their thoughts and their findings. Unlike academics, antiracist organizers cannot afford to distance themselves from the community, nor can we afford to slip into a language that alienates and excludes. There is no antiracist organizing without connection to the community. So that is one thing academics who are truly interested in whiteness in terms of antiracist work might try to think about: are they writing for tenure committees alone, or are they writing for all of us?

I look forward to an academy that values community, collaboration, and justice as much as rigor, creativity, and novelty. I have been inspired by the words of Roberto Unger in his *Politics:*

> In this work, true satisfaction can be found only in an activity that enables people to fight back, individually or collectively against the established settings of our lives—to resist these settings or even to re-make them. Those who have been converted to this idea of a transformative vocation cannot easily return to the notion of work as an honorable calling within a fixed scheme of social roles and hierarchies, nor can they remain content within a purely instrumental view of labor as a source of material benefits with which to support themselves and their families.[4]

What would a transformative vocation be? What kinds of life and career choices would need to be made? And what kind of institutional structures could we create that would allow activists the time and resources to reflect on their work and academics to engage fully in the practical effort to make society a just and open space? This is a challenge for activists and scholars alike.

NOTES

1 Mab Segrest's *Memoirs of a Race Traitor* (Boston: South End Press, 1994), Lillian Smith's *Killers of the Dream* (New York: Norton, 1978), and Linda Stout's *Bridging the Class Divide and Other Lessons for Grassroots Organizing* (Boston: Beacon, 1996) are all written by southern "white" women committed to racial justice. Each in her own way examines the experience of racism in the South and gauges the effects of racism and sexism on her own life and society. All talk about the possibility and impact of standing in resistance to white supremacy. See also Noel Ignatiev, *How the Irish Became White* (New York: Routledge, 1995), and Howard Zinn, *A People's History of the United States* (New York: Harper and Row, 1980).

2 The Portuguese word *explorador* has two meanings: to explore and to exploit. Sometimes I wonder whether the English word should carry both connotations.

3 See Dell H. Hymes, ed., *Reinventing Anthropology* (Ann Arbor: University of Michigan Press, 1999).

4 Roberto Mangabeira Unger, *Politics, a Work in Constructive Social Theory, Volume 1* (Cambridge: Cambridge University Press, 1987), 13.

The Digital Impact on Social Movements

Digital natives, millennials, Gen Y, Gen 2.0: however you label them, the generation born roughly between 1980 and 2000 has been immersed in revolutionary digital technologies since birth. For those of you who fit into this age cohort, life was experienced very differently in the 1990s, and these techno-logical novelties have had vast repercussions at the individual and societal level. The way people communicate has fundamentally changed with the advent of new information communication technologies (ICTs), from e-mail to Snapchat. Not only can messages, photos, and videos be sent instantly, they have the potential to be spread far and wide through social networks—and the ramifications have been felt in all areas of society.

On a personal level, new technology has resulted in a radical shift in the way individuals view themselves and their social ties. Students of previous generations, for example, interacted in a much more limited though intimate way. Friendships and ways of communicating consisted of conversations in the cafeteria at lunch, bonding through sports or other extracurricular activities, sitting next to someone in class and passing secret notes (on paper!), or having neighborhood playmates. The main vehicle of communication was physically going to friends' houses to see whether they were free to play or using the telephone—the one or two stationary phones inside the house that the whole family shared. In sum, communication was initiated, shared, and sustained among people who knew each other personally, and it took effort on the part of the receiver and sender of information. This has changed in many ways as communication now, for many people, takes place to a great extent through digital venues, especially among youth. For example, in 2009 the average US teenager, on Twitter alone, was receiving or sending more than 3,000 messages a month (Parr 2010). In 2010 researchers at the University of Maryland conducted a study of two hundred students who were asked to abstain from using electronic media for twenty-four hours. Though everything else about their college experience was the same—they were surrounded by other students and their identity was intact—not being connected *virtually* to others horrified the participants. One student stated that he had never felt so "alone and secluded from my life." Another reported, "Although I go to a school with thousands of students, the fact that I was not able to communicate with anyone via technology was almost unbearable" (Ottalini 2010).

Many long-standing, profitable, and dominant businesses are now obsolete as digitized industries have replaced analog ones: Polaroid declared bankruptcy with the introduction of digital cameras in 2001, iTunes replaced Tower Records as the largest music retailer in United States, and the chain bookstore Borders, which at one point had more than one thousand stores throughout the United States, closed after the rise of e-reading technology such as Amazon's Kindle (Kansaku-Sarmiento 2011). These are just three examples, but the business world is littered with cases like these. Can anybody really be surprised that "Cyber Monday," the Monday after Thanksgiving, has overtaken Black Friday as the biggest sales day of the year (Carr 2011)?

Even religion has not escaped the technological revolution: the Catholic Church, one of the institutions that has traditionally been most resistant to change, has finally succumbed to the digital age. The electronic missal enables users to stream Mass online and has made the paper missalette (which contains prayers and Scripture readings) antiquated (Catholic PR Wire 2011). Instead of prayer cards, there is now a touch-screen "Saint a Day." The Vatican Observatory Foundation recently launched the Vatican-approved iPhone app "Daily Sermonettes with Father Mike Manning," and users can pray the rosary in their own "sacred space" through the "Rosary Miracle Prayer" app. Pope Benedict XVI used Twitter for the first time in June of 2011, announcing the start of a news information portal that aggregates information from the Vatican's various print, broadcast, and online media (Donadio 2012). The Vatican also now has a YouTube channel and a Twitter feed (@pontifex) that has nearly 10 million followers in more than six languages. Pope Francis, the current pope, has embraced new media as well. In a papal statement in 2014 he praised the peer-to-peer sharing quality of new ICTs: "A culture of encounter demands that we be ready not only to give, but also to receive. ... The Internet, in particular, offers immense possibilities for encounter and solidarity. ... This is a gift from God" (Fung 2014).

Though the Vatican has not yet released an official response, in September of 2014 Pope Francis engaged with schoolchildren from Detroit via Facebook when they pleaded with him, through a social media campaign, to visit Detroit during his upcoming tour of the United States slated for 2015. They set up a Facebook page called "Let's Bring Pope Francis to Detroit in 2015," which includes personalized letters to the pope and photos of students attending Catholic schools (Montemurri 2014a). At the all-boys Loyola High School (a school that works in the tradition of the Jesuit Order with an emphasis on service), students created a YouTube video asking the pope to visit the area. One student is videotaped making a plea aligned with social justice stating, "You are exactly what we stand for—men for others" (Montemurri 2014b). Though students and the mayor of Detroit (who has vocally supported the students' campaign) are awaiting an official response from the Vatican, the fact that the students assumed using ICTs was the best method to get the pope's attention reveals their awareness that this is one of the key ways the pope connects to and interacts with people.

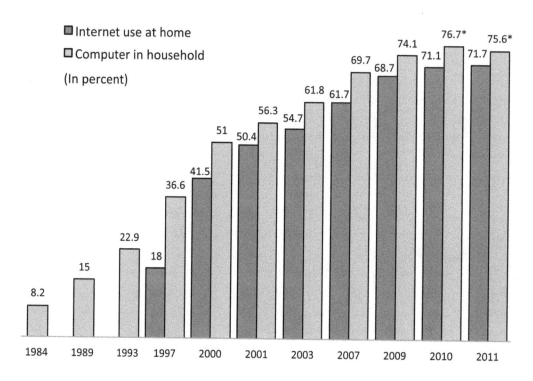

Figure 6.1

US HOUSEHOLD COMPUTER AND INTERNET USE, 1984–2011

*Smaller changes between 2010 and 2011 were due partly to question wording and other instrument changes.

The dramatic and steady increase in computer and internet use over the last three decades has had vast repercussions at the individual and societal level.

Source: US Census Bureau, Current Population Survey, selected years.

NEW INFORMATION COMMUNICATION TECHNOLOGIES AND PROTEST POLITICS

Unsurprisingly, the rise of digital technology and social media also deeply affects contentious politics as well as the organization of and participation in social movements. Over the past several years, there has been an explosion of protest activity among young people around the globe as they embrace a new vision of the future and demand radical changes in the existing economic and political systems. *Time* magazine, in fact, named the protester as its Person of the Year in 2011. We can only speculate as to the reasons for this upsurge in social movement activity, but scholar and cultural critic Henry Giroux emphasizes the influence of the communication field on the political environment:

> Alternative newspapers, progressive media, and a profound sense of the political constitute elements of a vibrant, critical formative culture within a wide range of public spheres that have helped nurture and sustain the possibility to think critically, engage in political dissent, organize collectively, and inhabit public spaces in which alternative and critical theories can be developed." (2012, 39)

In essence, the media ecology can either accelerate—or, conversely, impede—serious political discussion and debate, and ultimately facilitate displays of collective behavior. With new digital technology at their disposal, social movement actors have access to innovative media outlets that help nurture a new political terrain within which they can discuss grievances, disseminate information, and collectively make demands.

There are, of course, many factors to consider when examining recent forms of collective behavior—namely, the austere economic conditions around the globe, political disenfranchisement, and a lack of accountability among political elites. The focus of this book, however, is the use of digital technology in different social movements, communities, and campaigns—from the Indignados in Europe and Mexico, to women seeking social justice, to the Arab Spring in the Middle East and North Africa, to Occupy Wall Street and the DREAMers' quest for immigration reform, to the savvy digital organizing by political groups and communities in the United States. People are challenging political authorities, entrenched dictators, and political and economic systems once taken for granted. On a more micro and individual level, and particularly as it pertains to youth, individuals aided by digital technology are mobilizing to confront skyrocketing debt and current policies regarding immigration through contentious politics.

Indeed, the common thread that runs through all of these case studies in this book is the seminal use of ICTs (this includes the Internet, the World Wide Web, cell phones, texting, Instagram, social media, and social networks) to advance their respective causes. With the recent explosion of e-movements, e-protests, and e-activism, these organizational tools have become an essential component of social movement actors' repertoire. The emergence of social media networking sites is changing the nature of political struggle and social movement activism in the United States and around the world.

This book will explore how new Web 2.0 technologies enable, facilitate, and encourage social movement activity by allowing individual actors to share grievances, accelerate social movement activity, decentralize mobilization efforts, facilitate recruitment efforts through virtual forms of collective identity, and hold authorities accountable for their responses to protest activity with mobile devices.

It is important to remember while reading the case studies in this book that technology is a tool, and therefore it is neutral. It can be used for both progressive and reactionary social movements, and authorities can use ICTs against activists. For example, a government can track Internet use and e-mails and monitor cell phone activity to locate organizers of, and participants in, dissident politics. Corporations can block or limit service, and authorities can discredit protesters by engaging in disinformation or propaganda campaigns, taking advantage of the anonymity that digital media affords. Facebook can be used to build a community around a progressive cause, and it can just as easily be used to bully a classmate. Mobile video recording devices can keep police abuse in check, but they can also be used by terrorist groups to publicize their acts and recruit new members. The most recent example of this is the Islamic State of Iraq and Syria (ISIS), which will be discussed in Chapter 4. This book does not make the claim that digital technologies are all inherently good or progressive nor that they are the only resource to consider when trying to understand social movement activity. But the important role ICTs have played in recent social movement activity is undeniable, and the specific ways their use can translate into motivation, interest, and participation among social movement actors are worth examining.

As we will see throughout the text, social movement theory serves as a toolkit to unpack the conceptual ways in which ICTs influence the political landscape. This book analyzes the many ways that ICTs are changing the structure and tactics of social movements, and the case studies serve as illustrative (rather than conclusive) examples that can assist in updating social movement theories. What we will see is that by applying various theoretical frameworks in a comprehensive and holistic way and by updating them to include theories of new media, we can better make sense of contemporary forms of contentious politics. These are exciting times, both for those fighting for social change and those studying social movements!

WHAT ARE SOCIAL MOVEMENTS?

It is important to take a moment to clarify exactly what social movements are and how they are different from other forms of collective behavior. A social movement is neither a riot nor electoral politics. Rather, it is a sustained collective articulation of resistance to elite opponents by a plurality of actors with a common purpose (Tarrow 1998). According to Charles Tilly (2004), the three main elements of social movements are campaigns (long-term, organized public efforts that make collective claims on target authorities), repertoires (tactics that a group has at its disposal in a certain sociopolitical environment), and **WUNC** (worthiness, unity, numbers, and commitment). WUNC is an intentional effort by participants in a social movement to publicly present themselves and their supporters as worthy of support from other citizens, which Tilly (2004, 23) encapsulates this way: "Social movements' displays of worthiness may include sober demeanor and the presence of clergy and mothers with children; unity is signaled by matching banners, singing and chanting; numbers are broadcast via signatures on petitions and filling streets; and commitment is advertised by braving bad weather, ostentatious sacrifice, and/or visible participation by the old and handicapped. WUNC matters because it conveys crucial political messages to a social movement's targets and the relevant public."

Key to any social movement are mobilizing strategies—"those collective vehicles, informal as well as formal, through which people mobilize and engage in collective action" (McAdam, McCarthy, and Zald 1996, 3). More specifically, Tilly (2006) introduced the concept of a **repertoire of contention,** which refers to the tactical forms from which social movement actors can choose at any given moment. Repertoires vary over time and across cultures, but some of the most widely used have included armed struggle, nonviolent civil disobedience, self-immolation, protests, rallies, demonstrations, teach-ins, global witnessing, and public vigils.

With the advent of the digital revolution, which began in 2004, social movement scholars and organizers have turned their attention to the new range of nuanced tools that activists have in their arsenal. As history reveals, every social movement is in part shaped by the technology available at the time and its influences on the tactics that social movement actors will pursue. Activists have always utilized the latest communication device to recruit, distribute information, and mobilize support, whether it be the pen, printing press, telegraph, radio, television, Internet, or high-speed digital technologies. Manuel Castells (2007, 239) summarizes the critical role of media in protest politics in the following way: "power relations … as well as the processes challenging institutionalized power relations are increasingly shaped and decided in the communication field."

TECHNOLOGY AS A SPARK FOR SOCIAL CHANGE

Technology has always played a critical role in shaping social movement pursuits, as far back as the printing press. In the 1700s, the proliferation of local newspapers, pamphlets, and independent printing presses proved critical to the American Revolution. US revolutionary Thomas Paine kindled the political environment with his widely read pamphlet *Common*

Sense (advocating US independence from Britain). One of the key founding fathers of the United States, John Adams, stated, "Without the pen of the author of *Common Sense*, the sword of Washington would have been raised in vain" (Bernstein and Rice 1987). As Kaye (2011, 229) points out, the nation was founded as a nation by grassroots independent journalists: "Tom Paine was an unemployed or under-employed journalist, who wrote a pamphlet, *Common Sense*, and he said on the back of it, 'I think these are really important ideas but I can't go everywhere in America. If you like this pamphlet, the copyright is off. Copy it, print it up, and give it out to the next person.'" This radical movement toward free sharing of information is very common today with peer-to-peer sharing of digital information (a mechanism that will be discussed and analyzed throughout the ensuing chapters), yet we can see that it began hundreds of years ago via the printing press, the most innovative technology at the time.

More than a century and a half later, moving images became essential to political struggle. In 1930, as a part of his strategy to free India from British rule, Mohandas Gandhi invited reporters and newsreel teams to capture the footage of the 248-mile salt march he organized in 1930. Images of British soldiers beating peaceful marchers with clubs exposed to the world the repression of the Raj (Dalton 2012), swaying public opinion greatly in India's favor, which played a major role in India's independence. During the civil rights movement in the United States led by Reverend Martin Luther King, TV images of police violence, of fire hoses and police dogs set loose on activists engaged in civil disobedience across the South, even targeting children, with the most dramatic episodes occurring in Birmingham, Alabama, also garnered support for the demonstrators and energized the social movement.

Later, US public opinion regarding the Vietnam War changed drastically when footage of the carnage was brought into peoples' living rooms on the evening news, motivating the peace movement (Swerdlow 1992). Similarly, the 1989 images of the peaceful students in Tiananmen Square overrun by tanks as they campaigned for democracy and freedom of speech significantly affected viewers' sentiments toward the Chinese government and military (James 2009).

New media platforms are changing the social movement terrain even more radically than previous technologies. Though communication and information systems have historically been fundamental sources of power and counterpower, and of domination and social change, this effect has been exacerbated by the explosion of digital technologies. As Marshall McLuhan declared decades ago with the introduction of television in the 1960s, "The medium is the message." The form of technology through which information is disseminated and received molds cultures; it introduces a new mind-set that alters the landscape of societies, as well as relationships and forms of interaction among individuals in those societies (McLuhan 1964). What is significant about new social media platforms and social networking sites is that, unlike television, they embody a radically individualistic and freelance format that encourages forms of self-expression.

WE ARE THE MESSAGE CREATORS

New media technologies allow users to become not merely receivers of the message but also the *creators* and *distributors* of messages. Indeed, the latest generation has an unprecedented degree of control over the production, distribution, and consumption of information and therefore over their cultural environment, which also has powerful implications for serious social and political change. The distribution of information is now immediate, worldwide, often free, and in the hands of ordinary citizens. New Internet media platforms and social networking sites, web publishing tools, and the proliferation of new mobile devices—there are currently more cellphones in the United States than there are humans (Kang 2011)—are all altering the political atmosphere.

In this new communication and media setting, almost anyone and anything can be recorded and disseminated without the permission of the elites (be they the professional mainstream press, corporate gatekeepers, the police, the military, or campaign managers). Through an emerging indigenous free press reliant on "**mojos**" (mobile journalists), citizens can broadcast unedited live footage from smart phones, flip cameras, and laptops that have digital audio- and video-recording capabilities. In terms of social movement activity, the ubiquity of camera-ready smart phones allows for authentic transparency, as live-streamers serve as journalist mediators between authorities and protesters. Individuals can also send video shots on mobile phones to international news services, which are then beamed via satellite all over the world, thus connecting mobile amateur journalists to the mainstream press. The images can also obviously be posted onto YouTube, Facebook, and other social networking sites where, if they go viral, can instantaneously capture national attention.

In fact, the very concept of journalism itself is being reconfigured. A perfect example of this happened during the 2011 re-election bid of former senator George Allen (R-VA) against Democratic nominee Jim Webb. As part of its strategy, the Webb campaign had a University of Virginia student follow Allen with a handheld video camera. At one of his rallies Allen introduced the tracker, S. R. Sidarth (who is of Indian American descent) to the crowd as Macaca (considered a racial slur). During the speech Allen interjected, "This fellow over here with the yellow shirt, Macaca, or whatever his name is. He's with my opponent. He's following us around everywhere. … Let's give a welcome to Macaca, here. Welcome to America and the real world of Virginia" (Sidarth is actually a US citizen, born in Virginia). The video of the "Macaca moment" was played more than 400,000 times on YouTube, and bloggers, especially at the *Daily Kos*, amplified the story (Shear 2011). The incident later appeared in an article in the *Washington Post*, illustrating how stories that originate in alternative media often filter into the mainstream media, thereby increasing the visibility and viewership of events. The taping and circulation of this incident helped to foil Senator Allen's re-election bid, with Webb winning by a narrow margin.

Figure 6.2

New media technologies allow users to become not merely receivers of the message but also the creators and distributors of messages.

Mojos, as bearers of breaking news, oftentimes beat the mainstream press to highly relevant stories that can have a political impact. For example, amid the hunt for the mastermind behind the 9/11 attacks in the United States, a Twitter user in Pakistan, @ReallyVirtual, tweeted live as Osama bin Laden was being killed: "helicopter hovering above Abbotta-bad at 1AM (is a rare event)." The news of the assassination circulated on social media immediately and widely. This information was obtainable an hour before President Barack Obama's address from the White House announcing the killing on broadcast television (Patesky 2011). The proliferation of text messages and peer-to-peer sharing of this information via social networks facilitated ad hoc celebratory assemblies at Ground Zero, Times Square, and outside of the White House. This ability for strangers to organize quickly and in real time was facilitated through the several smart phone apps now available.

THE DIGITAL GRASSROOTING OF SOCIAL MOVEMENTS

New technologies are changing more than just the way individuals can share and disseminate information. The actual structure of digitally savvy social movement organizations (**SMOs**) is unique. Traditional movements tended to rely more on a hierarchical model of formal, well-established organizations with charismatic leaders and professional experts, which provided a clear set of grievances and demands as the cornerstone of the collective behavior. More recently, however, collective behavior manifests itself through a more horizontal infrastructure of connectivity. This broadens the public sphere, as citizens can now share grievances and express their opinions through peer-to-peer networks, contributing to the "electronic grassrooting of civil society." Castells (2001) coined this term to describe a new type of "informational politics" in which electronic media become the space of politics by framing processes, messages, and outcomes and results in a new kind of civil society.

These new types of communication flows change the organizational process, as collective behavior is now less dependent on professional leadership and expertise and operates at the grassroots level and in ad hoc settings. Unlike past forms of technology, which relied on the one-to-many flow of information, largely controlled by state or corporate interests (for example, heavy, though not exclusive, reliance on newspaper, television, or radio coverage during the civil rights struggle or the women's suffrage movement), the new media ecosystem is a bottom-up approach to communication. Ordinary citizens, equipped with their tech-savvy sense, now organize and hold politically oriented events to effect social change in both cyberspace and in local communities. Many contemporary social movements have an aversion to naming a specific leader or spokesperson, and some are conscientious about avoiding specific demands. Furthermore, social movement actors are often more flexible than activists who have participated in previous forms of mobilization, in that they demonstrate a proclivity to alter their demands and tactics as protest activities unfold. This approach is made possible by up-to-the-minute information sharing and organizing through new media.

This horizontal structure of social movements, made possible by digital technology, emerged in the early 1990s when the Internet was first utilized for protest activity. For example, the 1994 uprising by the Zapatistas (an indigenous and initially armed group in the southern state of Chiapas) against the Mexican federal government in an effort to protect their indigenous rights and access to land surprised the world, and the only way that the world knew about the revolution was because of the Internet. This new media resource disseminated firsthand accounts of developments in this remote region. The rebellion was not organized over the Internet (as access to computers was clearly lacking in this extremely poor and remote area of Mexico), but commentary, suggestions, debate, and reporting was shared in cyberspace on a peer-to-peer basis, which stirred interest and gained them international support (Cleaver 1998). The Zapatistas handwrote communiqués for distribution to the mass media and gave them to reporters or to friends of reporters, which were then typed or scanned and distributed through the Internet (Arquilla and Ronfeldt 2001).

Another early example is the successful attempt to shut down the World Trade Organization (WTO) ministerial meetings in Seattle in 1999. Despite a lack of face-to-interaction before the major demonstrations, organizations and individuals shared ideas and information as to how to best educate citizens about the WTO and its policies that were deemed harmful to both work-ers and the environment, as well as how to best plan and carry out the rallies. Demonstrators held protests in more than eighty locations in dozens of countries once the information sharing plateaued (Rheingold 2002). They organized these through the website seattle wto.org/N30 (now defunct), which put out action alerts in ten different languages letting those interested know how they could get involved.

GETTING THE MESSAGE OUT

New ICTs have made it easier and faster than ever before for activists to gain support for boycotts, garner signatures in petitions, or simply get the message out to people sympathetic to their cause. Effective online petitions and calls for boycotts abound, and this form of e-ac-tivism is now an integral part of most people's social media activity. There are websites, such as PetitionOnline.com, that host or link online actions as a free service through which visitors can create and maintain online petitions for any cause. Other sites feature action centers that allow citizens to choose from a menu of a variety of actions such as boycotts; online petitions; virtual sit-ins, rallies, and demonstrations; or e-mail or fax correspondence about a particular cause of concern (Earl et al. 2010).

In one particularly effective case, after a fourth-grade class in Brook-line, Massachusetts, read *fie Lorax*, by Dr. Seuss, they discovered on Universal Studio's website that the environmen-tal themes, central to the story, were not going to be addressed in the upcoming film based on the book. The students started a petition on Change.org (host of the world's largest petition platform) demanding the movie company "let the Lorax speak for the trees" (Kristof 2012). The petition went viral and gathered more than 57,000 signatures. The studio, in response to the outcry, updated the movie site with the environmental message (Kristof 2012).

In another example, Molly Katchpole also used Change.org to pursue a cause. She pe-titioned Bank of America on the site to reconsider its plan to add a five-dollar-per-month fee on its customers' debit cards (Dias 2011). The petition drive was successful. Later, she put up another petition against Verizon, which also intended to raise its fees by five dollars a month. This also resulted in a victory when the corporation relented in less than forty-eight hours (Kim 2011). In both cases this online activism saved Americans billions of dollars.

After airline passengers were trapped on the tarmac for eight hours in Austin, Texas, on an American Airlines flight in 2009, one of the disgruntled passengers began an online petition, also using Change.org. The circumstances were horrid, as food and water supplies ran out, toilets overflowed, and patience wore thin. This individual effort snowballed into a national movement for reform across the entire airline industry. Individuals then collectively lobbied Congress to consider the Airline Passenger's Bill of Rights, which it did as the airlines voluntarily accepted the standards proposed by the petition. The bill, passed by the Senate on February 6, was entitled the FAA Reauthorization Bill (Shirky 2008).

A final example of online activism through the use of petitions is a group called Colorlines.com (a think tank that fights for racial justice). The group undertook a three-year campaign to convince mainstream news outlets to stop using the word "illegal" when referring to immigrants living in the United States without the proper documentation, on the basis that the term is racially charged and dehumanizing. They accomplished a major feat when the Associated Press, the largest news gathering organization, agreed to eliminate the use of the "I" word (Rosenfeld 2013). This is of particular significance because the Associated Press feeds hundreds of local television networks and newspapers and serves as a stylebook for all credentialed journalists.

Although large numbers truly make online campaigns effective, get the attention of those being targeted, and often translate into the perceived worthiness of the cause, it is important to keep in mind that these are more "flash campaigns" and not genuine social movements. They are not persistent mobilizations (an essential component for social movements according to Sidney Tarrow), and there is typically no clear sense of collective identity. Nevertheless, they give us insights into the tactics that those seeking social change can utilize, and online mobilization efforts do have the *potential* to transform into social movements. What the above examples also show is that it has never been easier, cheaper, and faster for activists to get their message out, quickly reach a critical mass, and mobilize into a formidable political campaign.

Because of the digital revolution, individuals now have an unparalleled degree of control over the production, dissemination, and consumption of information, which has a significant impact on their efforts to affect social change through displays of collective behavior. Indeed, the emergence of the Internet, social media networking sites, and e-activism are changing the nature of political struggle and social movement activism in the United States and around the world. As the case studies in this book will show, new ICTs are now an essential component of social movement actors' repertoire in their ability to facilitate and speed up the process of organizing, recruiting, sharing information, and galvanizing support among the public.

THE CASE STUDIES

Of course, not all social movements are impacted by ICTs. But the case studies in this book were chosen because of their timely, ongoing nature and because they have received substantial media attention in the mainstream press and on social networking sites. They are of particular interest to students because most are youth based and are related to issues that concern young people—a shaky economy, a dysfunctional political system, and perhaps most importantly skyrocketing student debt. Additionally, the text doesn't discuss only US- or North American-based social movement activity but looks at the global nature of social movements by examining outbreaks of contentious politics in various parts of the world. This provides students with an awareness of how some of the struggles that they may be familiar with in the United States compare and contrast to social movements in other parts of the world.

To understand contemporary displays of collective behavior, this book combines traditional and revised versions of social movement theory and complements them with theories that emphasize the role of digital technology in social movement activity. The case studies inform social movement theory by categorizing and evaluating the influence of new ICTs on the way social movements emerge and succeed, and each chapter outlines which theories are particularly useful given the particular case study.

By looking at the examples and case studies through this lens, we can best analyze and conceptualize the historical, political, and social context within which protest activity occurs, how activists mobilize (what strategies and tactics they employ and why they choose them), how new members are recruited and influenced to participate in often high-risk activities, how groups form alliances and use them to their advantage, the key role that these networks play in the sustenance of contentious politics, and how activists frame issues and use the mainstream and alternative media in addition to social networking sites to help sway public opinion in their favor. In sum, the theoretical frameworks serve as a toolkit that unlocks how a new generation of mobilized citizens is building new collectivities and representing a new type of digitally savvy activism.

STRUCTURE OF THE BOOK

Chapter 1 provides a summary of the history and trajectory of social movement theory as it has been developed and adjusted over the past few decades. It serves as a foundation for the analysis of recent social movements discussed throughout the rest of the book and lays the groundwork for the question, Are these digitally cutting-edge movements and uprisings forcing theorists to re-examine and refocus some of the more conventional explanations of collective behavior?

Chapter 2 explores ICTs as tools for social change outside of formal SMOs. We will see how ordinary citizens, with new powerful digital tools at their disposal, are organizing and mobilizing in ways that are distinct from previous mobilization efforts.

Chapters 3–6 examine specific contemporary social movements to highlight the relevance of new media in contentious politics and to explore how this use of ICTs and new media informs and updates social movement theories. These chapters examine the historical, cultural, social, and political context within which the movements occurred, how activists mobilized (their strategies and tactics), how they recruited and forged alliances with other groups, how they framed their issues and used the mainstream and alternative press to sway public opinion, and the outcomes or consequences of their mobilization efforts. They situate the movements in question within social movement theory and evaluate how well the various theories explain their emergence and evolution. Finally, the chapters will each ask the question, Does this case study give us reason to update or modify traditional social movement theories? At the end of each chapter a "Theory Toolkit" gives the reader a snapshot of the different theories that can be used to analyze the social movement.

DISCUSSION QUESTIONS

1 In what ways are social movements a distinctive form of collective behavior? Can you think of examples not provided in this book that might blur the line between social movements and other repertoires of contention? For example, in some cases, can we perceive armed struggle or war to be a social movement?

2 What does McLuhan mean by "the medium is the message"? How does the digital revolution fit into this schema? How has it played out in a recent social movement that this book does not cover? Are there flaws in his theory?

3 Mojos are important for mobilizing efforts and contentious politics. How can efforts of mojos potentially backfire? Create a scenario where this might be the case.

4 Think of ways in which "flash campaigns" might be considered social movements or turn into a sustainable campaign. Come up with some concrete examples from your own independent research.

The Fragmented Community and Its Transformation

*The **essential challenge** is to transform the isolation and self-interest within our communities into connectedness and caring for the whole. The key is to identify how this transformation occurs. We begin by shifting our attention from the problems of community to the possibility of community. We also need to acknowledge that our wisdom about individual transformation is not enough when it comes to community transformation. So, one purpose here is to bring together our knowledge about the nature of collective transformation. A key insight in this pursuit is to accept the importance of social capital to the life of the community. This begins the effort to create a future distinct from the past.*

• • •

The need to create a structure of belonging grows out of the isolated nature of our lives, our institutions, and our communities. The absence of belonging is so widespread that we might say we are living in an age of isolation, imitating the lament from early in the last century, when life was referred to as the age of anxiety. Ironically, we talk today of how small our world has become, with the shrinking effect of globalization, instant sharing of information, quick technology, workplaces that operate around the globe. Yet these do not necessarily create a sense of belonging. They provide connection, diverse information, an infinite range of opinion. But all this does not create the connection from which we can become grounded and experience the sense of safety that arises from a place where we are emotionally, spiritually, and psychologically a member.

Our isolation occurs because western culture, our individualistic narrative, the inward attention of our institutions and our professions, and the messages from our media all fragment us. We are broken into pieces.

One aspect of our fragmentation is the gaps between sectors of our cities and neighborhoods; businesses, schools, social service organizations, churches, government operate mostly in their own worlds. Each piece is working hard on its own purpose, but parallel effort added together does not make a community. Our communities are separated into silos; they are a collection of institutions and programs operating near one another but not overlapping or touching. This is important to understand because it is this dividedness that makes it so difficult to create a more positive or alternative future—especially in a culture that is much more interested in individuality and independence than in interdependence. The work is to overcome this fragmentation.

To create the sense that we are safe and among friends, especially those we have not yet met, is a particular challenge for our cities and rural towns. The dominant narrative about our cities is that they are unsafe and troubled. Those we label "homeless," or "ex-offenders," or "disabled," or "at risk" are the most visible people who struggle with belonging, but isolation and apartness is also a wider condition of modern life. This is as true in our gated communities and suburbs as in our urban centers.

There is a particular isolation in the spaciousness and comfort of our suburbs. In these neighborhoods we needed to invent the "play date" for our children. Interaction among kids must be scheduled, much like a business meeting. On Tuesday, a mom must call another mom and ask, "Can Alex play with Phil on Thursday, at our house, say about 4? I will call if we are running late. The play date should last until roughly 5:45, to give both children time to freshen up for the family get-together at dinner." A far cry from the day of kids walking home after school and casually seeing who they ran into.

The cost of our detachment and disconnection is not only our isolation, our loneliness, but also the fact that there are too many people in our communities whose gifts remain on the margin. Filling the need for belonging is not just a personal struggle for connection, but also a community problem, which is our primary concern in this book. The effects of the fragmentation of our communities show up in low voter turnout, the struggle to sustain volunteerism, and the large portion of the population who remain disengaged. The struggle is also the reality for the millions of people around the world who are part of today's diaspora—the growing number of displaced people unable to return to their homeland, living and raising their children in a permanent state of transition.

COMMUNITIES THAT WORK FOR ALL

Community offers the promise of belonging and calls for us to acknowledge our interdependence. To belong is to act as an investor, owner, and creator of this place. To be welcome, even if we are strangers. As if we came to the right place and are affirmed for that choice.

To feel a sense of belonging is important because it will lead us from conversations about safety and comfort to other conversations, such as our relatedness and willingness to provide hospitality and generosity. Hospitality is the welcoming of strangers, and generosity is an offer with no expectation of return. These are two elements that we want to nurture as we work to create, strengthen, and restore our communities. This will not occur in a culture dominated by isolation, and its correlate, fear.

• • •

It is not my intent here to journalistically describe what healthy communities look like and where they exist. This is well documented. We have the success stories from Savannah, Boston, Chicago, Portland—all those places where community well-being has been on the rise over time. We have the pockets of authentic community in showcase organizational cultures such as Harley-Davidson and AES.

There is no need for more benchmarking of where the world is working. The reason is partly that we have already heard all the stories, and partly—and more important—that narratives of success give us hope and places to visit, but do not build our community. Social fabric and successful communities elsewhere cannot be imported. What works somewhere else ends up as simply another program here, which might be useful but does not shift the fundamentals that we are after.

What is needed is an exploration of the exact way authentic community occurs. How is it transformed? What fundamental shifts are involved? Too little is understood about the creation and transformation of a collective. I want to explore a way of thinking that creates an opening for authentic communities to exist and details what each of us can do to make that happen. The essence is to take a step forward in our thinking and design about the ways that people in communities come together to produce something new for themselves. By thinking in terms of a structure of belonging, we begin to build the capacity to transform our communities into ones that work for all.

The challenge is to think broadly enough to have a theory and methodology that have the power to make a difference, and yet be simple and clear enough to be accessible to anyone who wants to make that difference. We need ideas from a variety of places and disciplines to deal with the complexity of community. Then, acting as if these ideas are true, we must translate them into embarrassingly simple and concrete acts.

This means a shift in thinking that gives us clues about collective possibility. The shift in thinking is the focus of Chapters 1 through 7. Following that, we come to methodology, which many of you may consider the heart of the book. But without the shift in thinking, methodology becomes technique and practice becomes imitation.

• • •

One key perspective is that to create a more positive and connected future for our communities, we must be willing to trade their problems for their possibilities. This trade is what is necessary to create a future for our cities and neighborhoods, organizations and institutions—a future that is distinct from the past. Which is the point.

To create an alternative future, we need to advance our understanding of the nature of communal or collective transformation. We know a good deal about individual transformation, but our understanding about the transformation of human systems, such as our workplaces, neighborhoods, and towns, is primitive at best, and too often naive in the belief that if enough individuals awaken, and become intentional and compassionate beings, the shift in community will follow.

A FUTURE DISTINCT FROM THE PAST

The core question, then, is this: What is the means through which those of us who care about the whole community can create a future for ourselves that is not just an improvement, but one of a different nature from what we now have?

The kind of future we are primarily interested in is the way in which communities—whether in the workplace or neighborhood, rural town or urban center—create a wider sense of belonging among their citizens.

This is why we are not focused on individual transformation in this book. Individual transformation is the more popular conversation, and the choice not to focus on it is because we have already learned that the transformation of large numbers of individuals does not result in the transformation of communities. If we continue to invest in individuals as the primary target of change, we will spend our primary energy on this and never fully invest in communities. In this way, individual transformation comes at the cost of community.

• • •

The fact that a sense of community has practical importance is probably best established in the work of Robert Putnam in his book *Bowling Alone*. He found that community health, educational achievement, local economic strength, and other measures of community well-being were dependent on the level of *social capital* that exists in a community.

Geography, history, great leadership, fine programs, economic advantage, or any other factors that we traditionally use to explain success made a marginal difference in the health of a community. A community's well-being simply had to do with the quality of the relationships, the cohesion that exists among its citizens. He calls this *social capital*.

Social capital is about acting on and valuing our interdependence and sense of belonging. It is the extent to which we extend hospitality and affection to one another. If Putnam is right, to improve the common measures of community health—economy, education, health, safety, the environment—we need to create a community where each citizen has the experience of being connected to those around them and knows that their safety and success are dependent on the success of all others.

This is an important insight for our cities. If you look beneath the surface of even our finest cities and neighborhoods, there is too much suffering. It took the broken levees of Hurricane Katrina to expose to the world the poverty and fragile lives in New Orleans.

A BRIEF STATEMENT OF THE NEED

I live in Cincinnati, Ohio, which like most of our urban centers can be seen as New Orleans without the flood. While it has abundant assets and irreplaceable qualities, it also has challenges that are impossible to ignore, try as we might. Wherever we live, we are never more than a short ride from neighborhoods that are wounded with disinvested buildings and populated by those who live on the margin. To not see the struggle of those on the margin, to think this is the best of all possible worlds or that we are doing fine, especially if our particular street or neighborhood is safe and prosperous, is to live with blinders on.

We choose to live with blinders for good reason. There is great attraction to the suburban, upscale rural life or to residing in "hot" places. We are constantly reminded of the allure of gated communities, quaint and prosperous small towns, nationally acclaimed golden cities. The streets we most frequently hear about in these areas are clean and busy with pedestrians, their housing a string of jewels, center city vital and alive, and neighborhoods the source of great pride.

These prosperous places, though, are only the partial story. Take it from Jim Keene, a very wise and successful public servant. He has brought his humanity and vision into the cauldron of building community as city manager for Berkeley and Tucson, and now works for an association to build the capacity of other city managers. Jim once said that for every city that prospers, there is another city nearby that is paying the price for that prosperity.

We know we have a shrinking middle class, a growing separation between the well off and the underclass. You cannot look closely at even the great cities in the world without seeing serious underemployment, poverty, homelessness, neighborhoods with empty buildings, deteriorating environment, youth hanging out on street corners day and night, and concerns about public safety.

We know about the dropout rates and deplorable conditions of our urban schools and the difficulty of achieving affordable health care for all. The list goes on. But this is not the point. The question here is not about the nature of the struggles; it is about the nature of the cure.

So the focus in this book is about community transformation; it is about both those communities and places that are paying the price *and* their more prosperous neighbors. For even in prosperous places, the idea and experience of community are elusive. If you look closely, you realize that the social fabric of our culture is more fragile than we imagine.

PART ONE

THE FABRIC OF COMMUNITY

The social fabric of community is formed from an expanding shared sense of belonging. It is shaped by the idea that only when we are connected and care for the well-being of the whole that a civil and democratic society is created. It is like the Bodhisattva belief that not one of us can enter Nirvana until all others have gone before us.

What makes community building so complex is that it occurs in an infinite number of small steps, sometimes in quiet moments that we notice out of the corner of our eye. It calls for us to treat as important many things that we thought were incidental. An afterthought becomes the point; a comment made in passing defines who we are more than all that came before. If the artist is one who captures the nuance of experience, then this is whom each of us must become. The need to see through the eyes of the artist reflects the intimate nature of community, even if it is occurring among large groups of people.

What is extraordinary appears to us as a habit, the dawn a daily routine of nature.

Abraham Joshua Heschel

The key to creating or transforming community, then, is to see the power in the small but important elements of being with others. The shift we seek needs to be embodied in each invitation we make, each relationship we encounter, and each meeting we attend. For at the most operational and practical level, after all the thinking about policy, strategy, mission, and milestones, it gets down to this: How are we going to be when we gather together?

What this means is that theory devolves down to these everyday questions out of which community is actually lived: Whom do I choose to invite into the room? What is the conversation that I both become and engage in with those people? And when there are more than two of us together at the same time, how do we create a communal structure that moves the action forward?

It is in these kinds of questions that accountability is chosen and care for the well-being of the whole is embodied. Individual transformation is not the point; weaving and strengthening the fabric of community is a collective effort and starts from a shift in our mindset about our connectedness.

MoveOn.org and the Tea Party

This chapter examines two SMOs, or, as we will see, what can more accurately be described as **social movement communities** (a term that Wollenberg et al. 2006 use). They are on opposite ends of the political spectrum: MoveOn.org, which is a left-wing organization that advocates for progressive causes, and the Tea Party, which is a conservative entity that is more reactionary in its agenda.

In a snapshot, MoveOn.org is known as one of the original and most successful digital public policy advocacy groups. It has been hailed for its pioneering tactics in support of progressive issues, and it raises large amounts of money to support Democratic candidates. MoveOn.org is made up of MoveOn.org Civic Action, which is a 501(c)(4) nonprofit corporation, and MoveOn Civic Action, which focuses on education and advocacy as they pertain to national issues. It also has a federal political action committee that contributes to the campaigns of many candidates across the country.

The Tea Party arrived later on the scene and in some ways, like MoveOn.org, resembles a social movement community more than a formal social movement in the typical sense, though its structure is more disparate and harder to classify. In essence, the Tea Party is an umbrella organization, an amalgam of somewhat loosely connected groups that consist mainly of libertarians, religious conservatives, independents, and some citizens new to politics who are frustrated with the contemporary political landscape. What unites the various groups is a shared, yet loosely held, set of beliefs. They are sometimes linked to national organizations such as the Tea Party Express and the Tea Party Nation, though they mostly operate independently (Williamson, Skocpol, and Coggin 2011). Other associated groups operate exclusively online, such as the National Tea Party Federation, whose goal is to enhance and facilitate communication among the various groups affiliated with the Tea Party.

These two very different organizations give us some important insights into contemporary forms of social movement organizing in the United States that cut across both contentious and institutional politics. Both groups rely on some traditional methods that have been used in previous social movements, while concomitantly adopting other more innovative tactics. They demonstrate that what is often perceived as a zero-sum game between new and old activism is a false dichotomy: online and offline activism often reinforce each other. There are strong similarities between the organizational structure of MoveOn and the Tea Party as well as the combination of online and offline strategies they employ—they are both hybrids of sorts when it comes to promoting social change. This chapter invites us to think theoretically and conceptually about what constitutes a social movement in the digital age, which subsequently raises questions as to how to best theorize the tactics and strategies of nuanced groups such as these.

Furthermore, a central concern of this chapter is how online sharing of information and e-activism lead to mobilization on the ground, or the spillover effect. We consider whether virtual activism replaces, complements, or has no effect on concrete forms of participation for social and political change.

Figure 8.1

MoveOn's model for electronic recruitment shows how "weak" virtual ties can lead to activism in the streets.

A comparison of the two groups also raises the question of how to de-fine grassroots organizations and their relationship to the public sphere, or communicative action, as posed by Habermas (1993, 1989). Chapter 1 noted his concerns about the shrinking role of the public sphere with the onset of television and the encroachment of professional experts (elites in the media and other major corporations) and contended that they have come to dominate public dialogue and debate, and civil society in general. However, the arrival of the Internet and digital technology prompts us to update his theory as the old top-down and hierarchal structures and modes of communication are being challenged, in some ways, by grassroots entities. MoveOn and some of the Tea Party groups are examples of Castells's (2001) informational politics that result in the electronic grass-rooting of democracy.

MOVEON.ORG

MoveOn emerged in the late 1990s in cyberspace via an online petition. In 1998, during the height of the Monica Lewinsky scandal, Silicon Valley computer entrepreneurs Wes Boyd and Joan Blades created an online petition that called on Congress to censure but not impeach President Clinton. Boyd e-mailed it to thirty friends, and within two weeks more than half a million people had signed the petition (Bennet and Fielding 1999). A few years later he heard from Eli Pariser, who had created an online petition urging moderation and restraint in responding to the September 11 terrorist acts. This petition also exploded in popularity, and at Boyd's suggestion the two merged their websites, and MoveOn.org was born (Markels 2003). The organization currently has more than 5 million members, and its running slogan is "Democracy in Action."

MoveOn's main strategy is to activate people on a few different issues at a time, often for short durations as legislative battles change, and this model allows it to play an important role as a campaign aggregator—inviting people in on a particular issue and then introducing them to additional issues (Markels 2003). According to Boyd, what unites MoveOn activists is support for progressive issues and a different type of politics, and the Internet is an essential tool for staying politically connected.

The organizational features of MoveOn are representative of contemporary social movements as theorized by new social movement theorists such as Melucci (1996): they are constituted by loosely articulated networks that permit multiple memberships and part-time participation, and there is little if any distinction between leaders and rank-and-file members, members and nonmembers, and private and public roles. MoveOn is often members' first step into political action, and what brings them to take that step is typically an e-mail message sent from one of the organizers or forwarded from a family member, friend, or colleague. This resonates with Castells's (2001) concept of informational politics and Giugni's (1998) research on the importance of electronic forms of communication among trusted sources that would-be participants in a social or political cause may not receive otherwise. For many members contributing money to a candidate or a political ad in response to an e-mail is the first time they participate in politics outside of voting (Boyd 2003).

MoveOn's success also highlights the importance of flexible and contingent forms of (wired) collective identity that developing theories of new media address, in particular Giugni's work noted above. Pariser explains:

> Every member comes to us with the personal endorsement of someone they trust. It is word-of-mouth organizing in electronic form. It has made mixing the personal and political more socially acceptable. Casually passing on a high-content message to a social acquaintance feels completely natural in a way handing someone a leaflet at a cocktail party never would. The "tell-a-friend" phenomenon is key to how organizing happens on the Net. A small gesture to a friend can contribute to a massive multiplier effect. It is a grassroots answer to the corporate consolidation of the media. (Boyd 2003)

As the statement shows, the way information is sent, received, and accessed represents a more pluralistic, fluid, and issue-oriented group politics among many contemporary activists that theories of new media, as well as theories of new social movements, recognize. Members and organizers of contemporary forms of collective behavior increasingly operate outside of state-regulated and corporate-dominated media and rely on innovative actions mainly mediated across electronic networks. These in turn enable new forms communicative action that assist in recruitment efforts and can result in concrete forms of mobilization. This exemplifies the grassrooting of civil society that Castells (2001) describes, and it is also illustrative of H. Jenkins's (2006) conceptualization of the importance of civic media in participatory democracy and the spillover effect. These new outlets for organizing can help update resource mobilization theory and illustrate how collective identity is established in new ways, thus calling for a modification of cultural theories to account for weak ties that lend to activism in the streets.

NEW TECHNOLOGY CAMPAIGNS

In terms of campaigns, from its inception, MoveOn's website has distributed e-mail action alerts that inform its members of important current events and has provided petitions and contact information of members' elected officials so that members can respond to those events. Its first campaign supported candidates running against impeachment backers. In 1999, in less than twelve weeks, it signed up over 500,000 supporters and received pledges of $13 million (Burress 2003). As a great example of e-activism, in June of that same year it set records for online fundraising by collecting more than $250,000 in five days, mostly in individual donations under $50 (Potter 2003).

Once the Clinton impeachment trial ended, MoveOn centered much of its energy on the peace movement in the wake of the 9–11 attacks. It hosted the online headquarters for the Virtual March on Washington—an act of online civil disobedience to protest the imminent invasion of Iraq. It was sponsored by the WinWithoutWar Coalition, which serves as an online umbrella organization for the peace movement. Using e-mail connections to coordinate and organize a protestor base, on February 26, 2003, more than 200,000 individuals signed up and made more than 400,000 phone calls and sent 100,000 faxes to every senate office in the United States with the message DON'T ATTACK IRAQ! (MoveOn 2004). Every member of the US Senate also received a stream of e-mails, clogging virtual mailboxes in Washington, DC.

Another tactic MoveOn has used repeatedly as part of its repertoire is candlelight vigils, organized completely online. The March 16 vigils against the pending invasion of Iraq involved more than one million people in more than 6,000 gatherings in 130 countries and were organized in six days by MoveOn over the Internet (Stewart 2003). The online resource Meetup made the event possible, speeding the flow of politics, what Bimber (2003) refers to as accelerated politics. MoveOn's fundraising ability also contributed to the antiwar effort. In less than one week, members raised $37,000 over the Internet to run an advertisement in the *New York Times* on December 11, 2002, thus using alternative media to infiltrate mainstream media in an effort to influence public opinion. In February 2003 MoveOn solicited donations to raise $75,000 in just two hours to place an antiwar advertisement on billboards in four major American cities with a similar message (Stewart 2003).

Although resource mobilization theory has always directed attention to the need for financial backing for political mobilizing efforts, typically the assumption was that most of this would consist of large sums of money from organizations or wealthy individuals. With new technology, however, organizers of a political campaign can instead, as this example shows, raise large sums of money through relatively small donations, and quickly, through word-of-mouth sharing of information online. This beckons us to modify resource mobilization theory to account for these new digital tactics for garnering resources.

After the invasion of Iraq began, MoveOn members petitioned their congressional representatives to continue the inspections for weapons of mass destruction. More than one million signatures were collected in less than five days and were delivered to the UN Security Council. Signatory names and comments were also sent to the petitioners' respective congressional representatives. Additionally, on a single day 200,000 people called their representatives, and, in the run-up to the Senate vote on the Iraq resolution in October of 2003, MoveOn volunteers met face to face with every US senator with "Let the Inspections Work" petitions (Utne 2003). The organization also started to more aggressively engage in political campaigns, urging its supporters to donate money to Democratic House and Senate members who had opposed the Iraq resolution.

In sum, during the above campaigns MoveOn excelled at garnering available resources, people, and computer skills to increase sociopolitical awareness, influence public opinion, mobilize citizens and network with other SMOs, and help elect progressive candidates. It did so by using new technology to tap into submerged networks that could participate in Internet-mediated forms of civic engagement. Therefore, theories of new media best explain the success of MoveOn. Resource mobilization theory also informs our understanding of new groups such as MoveOn.org with its attention to traditional resources that activists have at their disposal such as labor power, financial backing, and support of allies and influential elites.

CULTURAL AND SYMBOLIC TACTICS: COMBINING NEW AND TRADITIONAL MEDIA

Cultural and symbolic forms of political expression, as advocated by cultural theorists of social movements and certain strands of the new social movement school of thought, are viewed as key variables to a social movement's success. These tactics played another central role in MoveOn's repertoire of contention.

For example, the group used celebrities for political purposes. One of the group's first interactions with Hollywood came when filmmaker and cofounder of Artists United to Win Without War Robert Greenwald organized celebrities to join the Virtual March on Washington (Brownstein 2004).

Over one hundred celebrities joined as members of this group, including Matt Damon, Martin Sheen, and Mike Farrell. One of the most direct and visible forms of protest occurred when filmmaker Michael Moore spoke out against the war at his acceptance speech at the 2003 Oscars only a few days after the invasion: "We live in a time where we have a man sending us to war for fictitious reasons. Whether it's the fictitious duct tape or the fictitious orange alerts, we are against this war. Mr. Bush. Shame on you. Mr. Bush, shame on you" (Zakarin 2013). That same night at the Oscars ceremony, Susan Sarandon and Tim Robbins flashed peace signs to photographers. Actor Sean Penn went even further in resisting the war by traveling to Iraq in 2002. On his return he commented, "I cannot conceive of any reason why the American people and the world would not have shared with the Iraqis the evidence of the claim to have weapons of mass destruction. I think that the more information we push for, the more information we are given, the better off we are all going to be, and the right thing will happen" (Zakarin 2013).

Other celebrities who traveled internationally also spoke out against the impending invasion. For example, actor Dustin Hoffman publicized his displeasure during an awards ceremony in London, claiming, "This war is about what most wars are about: hegemony, money, power and oil." In Berlin actor Richard Gere spoke out as well, saying, "We have to say 'stop,' there's no reason for a war. At the moment, Hussein is not threatening anybody" (Zakarin 2013). Perhaps the most radical departure from the US government's agenda was the country music trio the Dixie Chicks at a concert in London. Lead singer Natalie Maines opined that she was "ashamed" that President Bush was also from Texas, where she was born and raised. Upon return to the United States, several country stations refused to play the Dixie Chicks' music in retaliation for her remarks.

MoveOn also has given substantial financial support to a number of Greenwald's films and documentaries to promote more independent and critical voices outside of mainstream and corporate-dominated media. Its website offered his *Uncovered: The Next War on Iraq* DVD as a premium to members who pledged thirty dollars or more, and approximately 8,000 individuals made pledges within the first three hours. More than 2,600 members hosted screenings in their homes and at community venues, and the movie was ultimately distributed in theaters across the country (Deans 2004).

House parties are another innovative tactic MoveOn uses to broaden the public sphere and the realm of civil society by combining the private and public spheres. It also adds to the explanatory power of theories that focus on the importance of collective identity (for example Snow et al. 1986; Benford 1993) and of morally and ethically based reasons for participation in collective behavior that some of the new social movement theories recognize (Giddens 1991; Tomlinson 1999; Johnston 1994). A few years later MoveOn provided free copies of Greenwald's

Figure 8.2

House parties are an innovative tactic MoveOn uses that broadens the public sphere and the realm of civil society by combining the private and public spheres.

Iraq for Sale and *The Ground Truth* documentaries for members to show at house parties. After viewing the films attendees made phone calls and wrote letters to voters. MoveOn also helped Greenwald finance *Outfoxed: Rupert Murdoch's War on Journalism.* Taking advantage of the mainstream media, it also took out a full-page ad in the *New York Times* declaring, "The Communists had *Pravda.* Republicans have Fox" (Deans 2004).

In other cases various directors and film producers helped MoveOn construct homemade advertisements once sufficient funds were raised by its members. The "Real People" ads, for instance, were created by documentary filmmaker Errol Morris and featured ordinary members of the Republican Party explaining why they were crossing party lines to vote for Democratic nominee John Kerry (Deans 2004). This was the first time both the content and the funding for an ad campaign came from the grassroots membership of an organization, typical of social movement communities operating without an established vanguard (Wollenberg et al. 2006). The "Bush in 30 Seconds" ads challenging administration policies were shown during his State of the Union address. Grammy- nominated musician Moby helped to design them, held a competition for members to submit ads, and recruited a panel of celebrity judges that culminated in an awards show in New York City to raise funds for other anti-Bush television ads (Stevenson 2004).

This example shows us that the roles of leaders, spokespersons, formal SMOs, and elite allies—all of which played a prominent role in the development of the resource mobilization framework—are less relevant for many contemporary mobilizations. Theories of new media and some components of the new social movement school of thought are more useful because they highlight the decentralized and more egalitarian structure of today's contentious politics (Melucci 1996 most directly brings this to our attention). Also helpful is Mann's (2000) conception of the interstitial location, where activists promote their agendas outside the formal political system and traditional institutions.

The organization and its supporters also combatted infringement of corporate and elite domination of the cultural sphere in the fight against censorship when theaters across the United States were being pressured by right-wing groups to bar *Fahrenheit 9/11*, Michael Moore's controversial film. It asked members to pledge to see the film on opening night with other members to send a message to theater owners that the public supports Moore's message of peace (Moveon.org, e-mail to all members). Bridging the offline and online worlds and combining entertainment with serious political discussion, more than 4,600 parties were thrown across the United States, and at each Moore spoke to members over the Internet about his movie and his hope they would each bring at least five nonvoters to the polls for the upcoming November 2004 election (Brownstein 2004). This novelty bridges entertainment, activism, and institutional politics.

During the ten-week Don't Get Mad, Get Even! events preceding the 2004 election, MoveOn and America Coming Together held rallies and rock concerts that incorporated celebrity appearances by artists, authors, and actors. As part of the Rock the Vote tour, they jointly held a concert in New York City right before the Republican National Convention that featured rock stars such as Bruce Springsteen, the Dave Mathews Band, Pearl Jam, REM, the Dixie Chicks, Jackson Browne, and John Mellencamp. Some MoveOn members threw house parties to watch the concert, at which members wrote letters to swing-state voters. Additionally, relying on mainstream media platforms, "Don't Get Mad, Get Even!" television advertisements featured celebrity activists such as Matt Damon, Rob Reiner, Woody Harrelson, and Al Franken (Carty 2010).

Thus, MoveOn combines conventional forms of organizing with more nuanced tactics. Rock concerts that support their cause, pledging to view Michael Moore's film, and throwing house parties each serve to open up the public sphere more broadly to ordinary citizens (which Habermas feared we are losing to corporate and elite control) and are also displays of symbolic forms of protest. With this in mind, we can modify some of Habermas's theory to account for new tactics, many of them aided by new technology (for example, the organization of house parties through web-based tools). Parts of new social movement theories help in our assessment of how MoveOn operates as these kinds of activities also serve to politicize new areas of social life.

BRIDGING ONLINE AND OFFLINE ACTIVISM

MoveOn continued its grassroots mobilization during the 2006 midterm election. Recognizing the essential role of on-the-ground (public) efforts to complement e-activism, it trained and supported volunteers on the ground to organize rapid responses to events and to hold news conferences, editorial board meetings, and rallies to target vulnerable Republican incumbents. As both political-process and political-mediation scholars would suggest (for instance Meyer 2005; Tarrow 2001; Soule and King 2006), politicians are vulnerable during election years and swaying public opinion is key, and these two theories assist us in clarifying MoveOn's strategizing. According to a Yale University study, the emphasis on face-to-face voter mobilization through social networks increased turnout by seven percentage points (Middleton and Green 2007). Prior to the election MoveOn members held more than 6,000 actions in these districts and organized 7,500 house parties (MoveOn 2007 annual report).

Members also donated enough money to establish the Call for Change program that used web-based tools and a call-reporting system to reach voters. Once again circumventing professional pollsters (and once again Mann's [2000] interstitial locations is fitting here), the web-based "liquid phone bank" allowed MoveOn members to call from wherever they lived into wherever they were needed within a day or two. Middleton and Green (2007) found that the phone bank was the most effective volunteer calling program ever studied and that it increased voter turnout by almost 4 percent.

Also during the 2006 election, a successful framing approach allowed MoveOn to combine parody and serious political discourse. Cultural as well as new social movement theories (Gamson

1992) that evaluate the effectiveness of social movement activity by their framing of issues are applicable here. For example, activists deployed the metaphor of being caught red-handed by displaying giant foam red hands and signs as they followed their representatives to town hall meetings, appearances, and fundraisers, questioning their allegiance to special interests. In Virginia Beach, members attended every Coffee with Thelma event that Representative Thelma Drake held and asked questions about her allegiance to special interests. In Louisville, Kentucky, members rallied at a gas station to tell voters about Representative Ann Northup's ties to big oil with flyers describing war profiteering. Members in Fayetteville, North Carolina, attended a defense contractor tradeshow that Representative Robin Hayes sponsored. During this campaign alone local media wrote more than 2,000 stories about MoveOn's actions (MoveOn.org 2008 annual report), and, of the nine long-shot races members targeted, five won. As an overall tally, in 2006 Democrats supported by MoveOn lost four and won eighteen races, which helped build a Democratic majority in the Senate (Center for Responsive Politics 2006).

The red-handed campaign represents what MoveOn does best—framing issues in a way that resonates with voters and taps into their frustration, using humorous and innovative techniques by employing diagnostic and prognostic framing (Snow et al. 1986). Its success at harnessing popular entertainment to broadcast alternative voices, whether in the form of rock concerts, fundraisers, Bush-bashing ads, publicity stunts, or supporting alternative forms of media, and doing this jointly with representatives of the artistic community, is something MoveOn has excelled at.

THE IMPORTANCE OF SOCIAL MEDIA

As MoveOn evolves and relies on new resources and tactics, new media are becoming increasingly important to understanding how it now operates. The group still uses e-mail extensively but now also relies heavily on other forms of social media. In response to the negative ads against President Obama by Republican Super PACs that played out on television during the 2012 elections, for example, MoveOn stated in a March 1 e-mail,

> Over the last year we've been quietly developing a groundbreaking plan to counter these lies through social media sites like Facebook and Twitter—where millions of people now get their news, bypassing the corporate media. The results so far have been amazing. There have been 65 million views in the last year. We increased our web traffic tenfold. And we tripled our audience of Facebook fans who can spread the word. But to counter Fox's lies this election we need to raise $200,000 to pay for the researchers, editors and developers necessary to ramp up.

A link was included at the end of the e-mail asking members to chip in fifteen dollars to help fund the efforts.

MoveOn's recent strategizing has some theoretical implications for our understanding of contentious politics. It illustrates that people are now receiving news through sources outside of corporate-dominated media, and the news that they are receiving through digital outlets such as Facebook and Twitter is being shared in a horizontal fashion, through peer-to-peer networks. Therefore, SMOs' direction of social movement activity and dispersion of information is being complemented by these informal and decentralized hubs of activity, informing us how we can update resource mobilization theory put forth by Tilly (1978) and McCarthy and Zald (1973). We can complement this work with recent analyses that incorporate theories that focus on new media. Most prominently, Castells's (2001) notion of an explosive informational politics and grass-rooting of democracy, McAdam and Paulsen's (1993) recognition of the importance of weak social ties forged in the virtual sphere that spread information about mobilization efforts in support of a cause, Bimber's (2003) reference to accelerated pluralism, and Kahn and Kellner's (2003) emphasis on the importance of virtual public spheres in initiating and sustaining momentum for social movement activity all come into play.

Another e-mail read, "This is the strategy. Every day, a team of 50 of MoveOn volunteer editors will collect the most timely and persuasive progressive news and opinion from around the web. Graphics debunking Republican lies about the economy. Live video coverage of the Occupy movement.... Then we'll push the most timely and persuasive stuff out to hundreds of thousands of people, who share it with millions more. We believe that people-powered media, funded by people like us, can be a secret weapon against the conservative noise machine" (March 9, 2012). This statement further indicates how reliant social movement actors are on web-based tools to share information, create a critical mass of support through peer-to-peer sharing, and create new sources of collective identity and community, thus broadening the public sphere on which much of Habermas's (1989, 1993) theorizing is based. It also supports Bennett and Iyengar's (2008) claims that new forms of grassroots civic engagement though online forms of communication can be resistant to state and corporate regulation.

MoveOn continued its distribution videos that spoof serious political challenges during the 2012 presidential election. It launched a video, "Mitt's Office," in which actor Justin Long played Mitt Romney—depicting him as caring only about the 1 percent. The e-mail that disseminated it asked members to share the video with friends and family on Facebook or via e-mail (December 26, 2012). That same month it asked members to protest laws that would restrict voter registration drives and early voting and require voters to present photo IDs at the polls, and it urged them to donate money to try to prevent the laws from passing (January 13, 2013). Supporters protested outside of federal courthouses to contest the ruling on *Citizens United* (which allowed corporations, as well as unions, to donate undisclosed and unlimited amounts of money to candidates running for office), and MoveOn sent a petition to call on President Obama to sign an executive order that would require corporations that do business with the government to disclose their political spending and declare support for a constitutional amendment to get big money out of politics permanently.

After President Obama announced a federal investigation into Wall Street in his January State of the Union address, an e-mail from MoveOn stated, "This is truly a huge victory for the 99% movement. Hundreds of thousands of us signed petitions, made calls, and held signs outside in the cold to make this issue something that President Obama couldn't ignore. Here's some of what MoveOn members and our allies did to bring about this victory" (January 26, 2012). It went on to note that members engaged in Facebook and Twitter activity, and it included a link where readers could post a message of thanks on the White House Facebook wall. It then stated, "And, we need to keep pushing for more wins for the 99%, including our campaigns to get big money out of politics and tax the rich fairly.... MoveOn doesn't get big checks from ban CEOs! So please click here to donate to keep the momentum going" (January 24, 2012).

MoveOn is not as grassroots as it may appear, however. For instance, it works in collaboration with powerful progressive groups such as the American Civil Liberties Union, America United for Change, and United for Peace and Change. Though it does not receive any funding from corporate donors, it has received substantial financial support from international financier George Soros, who spent millions of dollars opposing President George Bush's re-election in 2004 (Drehle 2008). One difference from those funding Tea Party organizations, as we shall see later in the chapter, is that his motivation, as a peace activist, is to support a cause rather than to influence a political party.

In conclusion, MoveOn perhaps can best be conceptualized as a hybrid in terms of its status (part insider/part outsider) and a chameleon in terms of tactics (disruptive yet also engaged in the institutionalized side of the continuum of contentious/institutional politics). Though the social movement organization, or community, emerged as a dissident organization, it eventually evolved into more of a political advocacy group that supports pinpointed candidates for office and operates in an ad hoc fashion without a traditional organizational structure. The case of MoveOn also illustrates that nuanced ICTs have not replaced traditional models of organizing nor replaced activism in the material world. Rather, they have altered the contours of mobilizing strategies and participatory democracy in important ways that vary along the spectrum of contentious and electoral politics. What makes this entity additionally intriguing is the way its online operations allow it to not only straddle the virtual and material spheres in terms of collective identity, organization, and mobilization, but to also engage in both protest and institutional politics.

The case of MoveOn.org leads to the logical question of whether this new type of SMO is an anomaly or can we expect other SMOs to adopt similar ways of organizing and mobilizing. To address this query the next section provides an analysis of the Tea Party, which many view as the conservative counterpart to MoveOn (though it has a more institutionalized structure and forms of financial and strategic backing). An examination of this group allows us to draw some comparisons to, and differences from, MoveOn in terms of agenda and organizational style, and it poses similar theoretical questions that can aid our understanding of contemporary forms of collective behavior.

Figure 8.3

The multiple groups that constitute the Tea Party have been able to take advantage of current political trends, in part by forming networks with other constituencies.

THE TEA PARTY

The Tea Party has been compared to MoveOn.org in terms of its organizational structure and the tactics it employs (though as we will see some of these comparisons are not accurate). In fact, FreedomWorks and other groups behind the Tea Party have long declared their intention to create the equivalent to MoveOn. Broadly, TEA (taxed enough already) Partiers hope to spearhead a movement that aims to reduce government spending and taxes, through an umbrella organization made up of various politically conservative groups and factions. It is this ideological connection that fosters a sense of collective identity among the disparate groups and individuals.

The Tea Party is also flexible and at face value, at least, leaderless, as it is composed of unconnected collections of local chapters with varying agendas. This organizational structure clearly resembles that of a new social movement: an assembly of roughly affiliated groups consisting of supporters rather than members in the traditional sense. Wollenberg et al. (2006) refer to these types of organizational structures as "social movement communities" rather than SMOs, and these are also at the forefront of Khan and Kellner's (2003) research on virtual public spheres as well as Bimber's (2003) work on the accelerated pluralism that new ICTs allow for. Therefore, as with MoveOn, we are encouraged to revise and update resource mobilization theory in some ways to account for these new types of horizontal structures, and we should also update cultural theories to understand what constitutes collective identity and how it is created.

In addition to the Tea Party Nation and Tea Party Express affiliations mentioned earlier in this chapter, there are other core groups that represent the interests of Tea Partiers. For example, Tea Party Patriots is a for-profit organization that organizes national conferences. It was born out of resistance to the Wall Street bailouts and what members view as runaway government spending. At the center of its agenda is an endeavor to restore the founding policy of the constitution, limited government control, and a free market economy (Kroll 2012).

Tea Party Express is a political action committee that actively campaigns in support of specific candidates. It is extraordinarily successful in this capacity. According to the Federal Election Committee, it raised $6.6 million during the 2010 midterm elections, making it the single biggest independent supporter of Tea Party candidates (Williamson, Skocpol, and Coggin 2011). Similar to MoveOn's success in the 2006 and 2008 elections, the Tea Party's influence was undeniably decisive in the 2010 elections, as supporters propelled Republicans to huge gains in the House, helped secure Senate victories for some barely known candidates such as Rand Paul, and captured seven hundred seats in state legislatures (Tanenhaus 2012).

THE TEA PARTY'S IMPACT ON ELECTORAL POLITICS

Political process theory (Tarrow 1996; McAdam 1982; C. Jenkins and Per-row 1977) argues that social movement agents have an advantage when the existing political system appears to be vulnerable to challenges, and this is especially true during times of electoral instability. This advantage is further enhanced when opponents can manipulate competition between key figures in the polity. The multiple groups that constitute the Tea Party have been able to take advantage of current political trends, in part by forming networks with other constituencies, and therefore resource mobilization theory is particularly relevant to grasping and assessing the success of the Tea Party.

For example, joining forces with the Campaign to Defeat Barack Obama (a Tea Party–linked political action committee), the Tea Party entered Governor Scott Walker of Wisconsin's recall fight in the wake of his attempt to curtail collective bargaining rights for public workers. Copying MoveOn's example, Tea Party groups used both digital and mainstream media to pursue the cause. Through e-activism it blasted several e-mails to supporters and launched a $100,000 money bomb fundraiser to help defend Walker, and it ran television ads defending his policies (Kroll 2012). In the summer of 2011 Tea Party Nation, together with Tea Party Express, launched a four-day bus tour across Wisconsin defending six Republicans facing recall elections for their roles in the collective bargaining battle (the Walker recall election will be discussed in more detail in a later chapter). Just like MoveOn, the Tea Party groups' use of new information and media technologies is often complemented by contentious politics in the material world.

One of the Tea Party's first successes was when barely known Republican Scott Brown ran a grassroots campaign in the Massachusetts special election to win the seat vacated by Ted Kennedy, which had been held by Democrats since 1978. Resource mobilization theory contributes to our understanding of this victory given the financial backing provided by wealthy Tea Party advocates who used digital means to fundraise. They emulated some of MoveOn's tactics by organizing an online money bomb (raising more than $1 million online in twenty-four hours) and orchestrated an "on the ground" get-out-the-vote campaign (Stauber 2010). This again combined online and offline activism, and it forged institutional and extrainstitutional political activity. In another simulation of MoveOn's approach, through its Take America Back website it offered a web-based call center through which members could talk to voters from anywhere.

ALLIES AS A KEY RESOURCE

One of the distinctions between the Tea Party and MoveOn is the Tea Party's reliance on powerful allies (as already noted, the Campaign to Defeat Barack Obama was key to the struggle in saving Walker's job)—though this is not to deny that MoveOn also has some wealthy financial backers. One of the major groups funding and organizing the Tea Party is FreedomWorks (formerly chaired by Dick Armey, former Republican Speaker of the House). This SMO provides abundant resources in terms of money, advice, knowledge, and personnel to invigorate and sustain the movement. It helped to organize the first Tea Party March on Washing-ton on September 12, 2009, in conjunction with Glenn Beck's 912 projects and the Tax Day Tea Party campaign (such as Fox News) for the event (Bai 2012). It also utilized main-stream media to try to influence public opinion and promote civic engagement. On May 13 Beck launched this project on his Fox News program. He also mobilized it through a social networking site built by his production company, Mercury Entertainment Group (Rose 2010). The 912 demonstrations were planned over the Internet, with local chapters coordinating activities through digital tools such as Meetup.com and Ning.com. The occasion was de-signed to build national unity around his stated nine principles and twelve values rooted in commitment to the United States and good morals and ethics (labeled the "Take America Back" convention).

Americans for Prosperity, another core group behind the Tea Party, together with FreedomWorks provided funding for the ensuing eight hundred Tea Party protests held across the United States during the Tea Party Express bus tour (Bai 2012). Fox News gave extended coverage of the cross-country caravans that appealed to the media through the use of historical costumes, props, and catchy slogans (Rose 2010). The unpredictable protests, accompanied by

Figure 8.4

Protesters rally against government taxation and spending policies at the US Capitol on September 12, 2009.

symbolic displays of rebellion and disruptions of town hall meetings, as part of the Tea Partiers' repertoire, were also media friendly in their spontaneity and entertainment value. These symbolic forms of political protest parallel some of the tactics that MoveOn uses, and new social movement theories and constructionist theories can help us make sense of them. The use of symbolic displays of grievances and demands, and framing issues in a clear way that resonates with disgruntled citizens is something that both groups have mastered. They also open up the public sphere for more discussion and innovative forms of communicative action (using Habermas's 1993 terms).

The events that the Tea Party hosted and the rhetoric they engaged in are good examples of both frame alignment and frame amplification as promoted by social movement theories that focus on cultural aspects of social movements at the micro level (Snow et al. 1986 in particular). This is a tactic that activists can use to tap into deeply held morals, values, and beliefs that are congruent with other SMOs and that are embedded in the general population. Participants also used frame bridging to resonate with other organizations calling for resistance to the federal government. They also situated diagnostic framing in a way that promoted a critique of what they perceived to be the radical socialist agenda of the Obama administration. Other prognostic and motivational frames were embedded in a call to arms, with slogans such as "take your country back" and "what we need is revival and revolt!" (Rose 2010).

HOW TO DEFINE THE TEA PARTY: ASTROTURF OR GRASSROOTS?

Some of the organizations that are affiliated with and support the Tea Party are corporate, while others are more grassroots in nature, and this led to some criticism of the Tea Party. Critics argue that its attempts to frame itself as a grassroots and ad hoc popular uprising are contrary to the reality of how the Tea party is structured and funded. For example, the supposed spontaneous interruptions and heckling of both Democrats and moderate Republicans during the 2009 town hall meetings were not entirely unrehearsed. Much of this was orchestrated and funded by well-established insider groups such as FreedomWorks and Americans for Prosperity. It is the Koch brothers (David and Charles) who provide most of the funding for both of these groups. They own 84 percent of Koch Industries, which is the second-largest privately held US company, and they financially back a number of libertarian and conservative organizations and think tanks, such as the Cato Institute, as well Tea Party candidates, through their political action committee (Fisher 2012).

The Tea Party groups that participated in the caravans also received advice and encouragement from Beck's (no longer available) national website (912project.com), and other conservative leaning websites such as ResistNet.com (also no longer in service) provided talking points. FreedomWorks suggested particular questions Tea Party representatives should ask at the town halls and maintained a link detailing how members could infiltrate the meetings, spread inaccurate information, and harass members of Congress, and thus the strategy was actually very top down. Although most supporters consider the movement to be populist, FreedomWorks, as mentioned earlier, is a well-funded, well-connected, DC-based think tank. The organization spent more than $10 million on the 2010 elections on campaign materials alone and set up a Super PAC through which it donates hundreds of thousands of dollars to politicians (Coffey 2012).

Despite these top-down tactics, Tea Party participants assert that the movement is a mainstream resurgence among powerless, ordinary citizens. Detractors, however, view their primary agenda as one attempting to preserve their collective privileges, as most activists are middle-aged, middle class, and white. They contend that the Tea Party engages in reactive rather than progressive politics, responding to threats to their sense of entitlement and sometimes engaging in racist or xenophobic rhetoric. An example of this is displayed in an e-mail sent out in August 2010 by Tea Party Nation to its 35,000 members, asking them to post their "horror stories" about undocumented immigrants on its (now taken down) website (Young 2010).

Thus, although Tea Partiers brand the movement as a grassroots uprising, others view it as a tool of the Republican Party that has been used and co-opted by powerful political actors connected with the political establishment in the Beltway (Pilkington 2011). MSNBC talk show host Rachel Maddow describes the movement in the following way: "They're called Fox News Channel tax day Tea Parties because all the big Fox News Channel personalities appeared at

_____ THEORY TOOLKIT _____

MOVEON AND THE TEA PARTY

We can apply a few of the theories discussed in Chapter 1 to the emergence and evolution of MoveOn.org and the Tea Party:

- **New social movement school of thought, cultural theories, resource mobilization theory, and political process theory.** These theories are all very useful in aiding our understanding of these new hybrid types of organizations. Each in some way informs us about how these two groups operate in both the realm of institutional politics (challenging vulnerable candidates for office; i.e. political process theory) and extrainstitutional politics (rallies, marches, the use of celebrities, house parties, etc.; strands of new social movement theories). Most important and applicable to these two cases are cultural theories that address the critical role of collective identity and framing.

- **Theories of new media.** As used in a complementary fashion to resource mobilization, these theories demonstrate (1) the importance of the peer-to-peer sharing of information within these two groups and across broader spectrums of society without heavy reliance on the mainstream media, (2) ways in which recruitment may be easier for contemporary social movement actors, (3) how weak ties forged in cyberspace can develop into strong ties with on-the-ground mobilization efforts and protest activity, and (4) nuanced forms of organizational flexibility that allow for more grassroots forms of participation and a broader spectrum for conversation and discussion.

tax day Tea Party events. They were Fox News endorsed and promoted and, in some cases, hosted events. They didn't just cover the Tea Party protests. They ran ads for them. They used Fox News Channel staff production time and ad time on the air to promote the events. They ran tea party promotions" (MSNBC 2006). This free access to traditional media helped catapult the movement into national consciousness and related it to public sentiment of frustration with the government. MoveOn had done this earlier; however, it relied more on the Internet and digital media as a resource, as it does not have the connections to, or much support from, corporate-owned media.

HYBRID SMO

Regardless of these differences and criticisms, each organization extensively employs both e-activism and contentious street protests as a part of its repertoire, and both straddle electoral and contentious politics by taking advantage of the shifting political context to influence public opinion, which political mediation theory highlights the relevance of (Soule and King 2006). In sum, although the 2012 election did not bode well for Tea Party candidates and it appears that the organization may have lost its momentum, it is important to acknowledge that social movements ebb and flow, and the Tea Party might very well bounce back in the next election. Regardless of what the future brings, through their framing devices Tea Partiers have been able to persuade many citizens that the issues they raise are urgent, that alternatives are possible, that they have the moral high ground, and that citizens can be invested with agency. This has served well as a recruitment mechanism. Their injustice frames explicitly appeal to moral principles for organizational outreach by resonating with deeply held values and beliefs among the general population and linking them to movement's causes. Framing their grievances as a threat to the very existence of "everyday Americans" helps to create a sense of collective identity among Tea Partiers and their supporters who see changes in the economic, political, cultural, and social spheres—and specifically the changing demographics—as a threat to their entitlements. Although different groups work on different issues, there is a very strong emotional thread that holds them together, which indicates that a vehement sense of solidarity cuts across the various segments of participants. This is typical of Mann's (2000) conceptualization of contemporary social movements within the rubric of the new social movement theories that focus on forms of collective behavior that bring diverse groups together to support emotionally charged issues and promote new sets of values in a collaborative way.

The Internet and digital technology were essential resources for the emergence and outburst of Tea Party activism because it was in the virtual world that ordinary citizens first began to spread their message. By establishing weak ties in cyberspace, like-minded people were able to communicate with one another and show support for the causes that the Tea Party supports. This shows how the public sphere and sources of connectivity are changing because of the digital revolution, which allows for information to be created, disseminated, commented on, and circulated through diffuse networks. It also demonstrates how these in turn lead to on-the-ground local forms of participation in political and social issues. Therefore, theories of new media are important supplements to resource mobilization and cultural theories, in particular, their attention to what H. Jenkins (2006) calls the spillover effect.

CONCLUSION

Although different in their ideologies, tactics, and funding, what MoveOn and the Tea Party have in common is that they both take advantage of new ways of organizing and mobilizing their devotees through digital means. They both also rely heavily on different types of media in the hopes of influencing public opinion. Each has raised abundant amounts of money for advertisements and political campaigns. To impact the realm of institutional politics, MoveOn and the Tea Party have also pressured officeholders through e-mail and face-to-face lobbying efforts, and they have taken advantage of the vulnerability of politicians during election years.

And, finally, both entities successfully used framing to pitch their concerns in a way that reso-nated with frustration among voters and citizens on both sides of the political spectrum.

MoveOn's and the Tea Party's mobilization endeavors therefore represent the growing symbiotic relationship between e-activism and local organizing, as they both work in the blogosphere as well as in real communities to impact institutional and extrainstitutional politics. Their strategies underscore the need to expand conceptualizations of Habermas's conception of the "public sphere" and participatory democracy.

DISCUSSION QUESTIONS

1   In what ways are MoveOn and the Tea Party hybrids when it comes to social change? Analyze another group that you consider to be a hybrid, and discuss how its tactics, strategies, and goals compare and contrast to those of MoveOn and the Tea Party.

2   How do the two entities resemble new social movements in some ways, but are actually top-down in other ways? Is either group really an outsider? Are there other advocacy groups you can locate that may be subject to similar criticisms?

3   Examine a social movement that utilizes cultural and symbolic tactics similar to those of MoveOn and the Tea Party. In your opinion, are these effective (especially groups that use somewhat "radical" tactics meant to shock or disturb). Do they do a better job of pulling people into the movement, or do they drive people away?

4   What other causes or social movements rely on celebrities to promote a cause? What are the pros and cons of using celebrities for political issues? How might this backfire? Give specific examples.

SUPPLEMENTARY QUESTIONS FOR ANALYSIS AND LECTURE DISCUSSION

1. Based on the assigned reading: Moving from Guilt to Action: Antiracist Organizing and the Concept of "Whiteness" for Activism and the Academy what are the consequences of "white privilege" on an institutional and social / cultural level? What can one do with this privilege to eradicate systemic inequality and serve as a vehicle for change based on the assigned reading and the film shown in class by Tim Wise -The Pathology of White Privilege, please analyze.

2. Based on the assigned reading: The Digital Impact on Social Movements, please explain the impact or lack thereof of on line political engagement. (Please provide examples from the reading assigned and those in recent historical context from the past decade.) Is this merely a form of "slacktivism" - on line political protest / engagement or is it promoting long term political transformation via internet engagement and contestation of the public sphere. Based on the readings what argument do you feel has more substance.

3. Based on the assigned reading: The Fragmented Community and its Transformation, the problems of community and possibility of community rest with our ability to move away from social isolation and create social capital and subsequent community transformation. Please explain what this means according to the analysis from the assigned reading. How do we create a sense of belonging in our communities in an era that is increasingly fragmented and disengaged. This fragmentation has created within us, "broken pieces" which has produced communities separated into "silos". What does this mean and what is the impact of this assertion explored in this assigned reading. What is the solution? According to the analysis provided in the reading, how do we create communities that work for all? (Based on the reading and film shown in class by Peter Block)

4. Based on the assigned reading: MoveOn.org and the Tea Party, what is the systemic impact of the Tea Party Movement in American Politics and subsequent Public Policy transformation? What have been the long term cultural shifts and ideological belief system changes that have transformed public consciousness, as a result of, Tea Party Activists? Can you compare and contrast another social justice movement to the Tea Party Movement and explain the difference or similarities of the two contrasting movements.

PRE-UNIT REFLECTION QUESTIONS

After each unit, the reader should be able to critically analyze and engage these three core points (Note: Base your answers strictly on the reading and current events related to the readings in the text.):

1. Based on the readings, please provide and analyze in detail three ways in which policy changes need to occur in order to break up concentrated wealth in the United States, thus reducing economic inequality and class based economic stratification.

2. Based on the readings, please explain how social protest movements change American public policy. How does transformation of consciousness initiate social, political, and subsequent economic change. How and why does culture inaugurate and yet resist social justice policy implementation?

3. Explain how the concept of intersectionality is demonstrated in the readings from this section. Think about how this intersectionality impacts women of color, participants in the women's liberation movement, oppressed people, and other marginalized groups who exist at the periphery of society seeking economic, political, and social justice. How do institutions provide the seeds of change and also the tools of systematic oppression? Refer back to the reading "Intersecting Oppressions: Rethinking Women's Movements in the United States," and revisit this quote of "how individuals are socially located in the middle of crosscutting systems of oppression that form mutually constructing features of social organization."

REVOLUTIONARY NARRATIVES: THE SEEDS OF CHANGE: THE PERSON IS POLITICAL

Social Change, Collective Action, and Social Movements

There are two main ways of looking at social change: We can focus either on major shifts of a *revolutionary* kind or on steady *evolutionary* development. A phenomenon related to the former perspective was the media hype surrounding the so-called digital revolution, illustrated by stories about get-rich-quick, dot-com millionaires in Silicon Valley. These enterprising individuals, it was said, had faith in themselves and their ability to succeed, and thereby brought about a revolution. Bill Gates's success story is the most famous example. It was only after the crash in technology shares in 2000 that commentators began to ask whether the reality of social change might be more complex. Before that, in 1999, a typical bullish story about Silicon Valley would have had the same breathless quality as the opening lines of the box titled "Generation Equity." Yet only a short time later this sunny vista was clouded over.

Taken together, the two items in this box raise questions about the nature of social change, especially change referred to as revolutionary. The first is an excerpt from a story that originally appeared in *Wired*—a glamorous story about the digital revolution. Pictured on the cover are five young entrepreneurs dressed in fashionable black, with glowing faces and a "deal with it" pose, framed against a clear blue sky—with no clouds on the horizon. They resemble the crew of *Star Trek*. They believe their mission has "historical implications." This, it is said, is no gold rush or mass mania, unlike many earlier episodes of irrational collective behavior. The media assure them that they are part of something bigger and historic—a revolution.

By 2001, less than two years after the *Wired* magazine story appeared, their dream lay in tatters. As detailed in the box's second item, they were now being informed that they had been victims of a "naïve delusion," a "classic bubble," or an "elaborate con job."

AN INDIVIDUAL OR A SOCIAL STORY?

American dream *The ideology that an individual of low social status and opportunity in the United States can, through hard work and perseverance, climb to the top of the social hierarchy.*

Social revolution *A revolution that involves a fundamental change in social practices (as distinct from a political revolution, which involves the overthrow of one type of political regime by another).*

One possible lesson to be learned from this 2001 follow-up is that we should be wary of media stories of dramatic change brought about by individuals who, at the same time that they are transforming society, are themselves being transformed from "rags to riches." The belief in individual enterprise—the optimistic conviction that the individual is capable of making a difference—is part of the **American dream** (sometimes also referred to as the *American ideology*). But it is counterbalanced for many people by an awareness that, in their own lives, things may not be so simple. Meanwhile, on the larger stage of society and history, bringing about major social change is usually a complex process involving gradual institutional transformations—some the result of technological inventions and individual innovations, others the result of social movements or collective efforts over a long period of time. The question is especially pertinent today: Are we living through a **social revolution,** a transformation of the social order from one type of society to another?

ANALYZING SOCIAL CHANGE

The **evolutionary view of social change** is the one favored by most sociologists. However, sociologists have also recognized that the accumulation of changes may eventually result in a transformation that amounts to a *revolution*—that is, a change from one type of social order to another type. For example, the great theorist of revolutionary change, Karl Marx, believed

THEORY

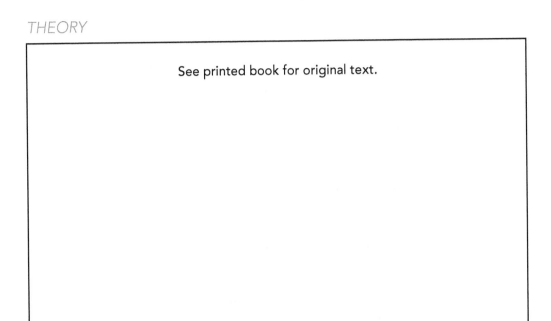

See printed book for original text.

there would eventually be a revolutionary change of the capitalist social order to a socialist society (albeit one that would occur only after capitalism had developed through all its possible stages). He even suggested that in some countries, such as America and En-gland, there would be a peaceful revolution, owing to their particular cultures and institutions (cited in Tucker 1978: 523). But in most countries, Marx argued, revolution could be expected to occur as the result of a final violent struggle by workers to overcome the resistance of the capitalist class, which, in turn, would fight to defend its wealth and power.

Usually, when sociologists talk about a social revolution, they are referring to a phenomenon different from the one that political commentators mean when they describe the overthrow of one type of political regime by another. A *social revolution* involves a fundamental change in social practices. So, when a revolution is described as a change in society as a whole, the word *society* is often included in the identifying phrase—such as *information society*. Some contemporary writers on the theme of social revolution, especially the digital revolution (also known as the *information revolution*), echo their nineteenth-century predecessors in presenting a picture that is a mix of long-term developments and revolutionary

Evolutionary view of social change *A perspective on social change that implies a gradual transformation through a series of stages of increasing complexity (as distinct from the revolutionary view of social change, which assumes that a revolution is necessary for social change to occur).*

change. A typical example is the work of the famous "futurologist" Alvin Toffler, who has written over a dozen best sellers, starting back in 1970 with *Future Shock*. Toffler presents, in a popular form, ideas about stages of social development that can be traced back to the founders of sociology (e.g., Auguste Comte and Herbert Spencer) and have been elaborated by their successors to take account of the complexity of contemporary changes. The central premise is that human history, though complex and contradictory, can be seen to fit a pattern. According to Toffler, this pattern has manifested as three great advances or waves:

- The first wave of transformation began about 10,000 years ago when someone, probably a woman, planted a seed and nurtured its growth. That was the beginning of the *agricultural age*, and its social significance was that people moved away from nomadic wandering and hunting and began to cluster into villages and develop an elaborate culture. Wealth was land.

- The second wave, the *industrial age* or machine age, was based on machine power; commencing in the eighteenth century, it gathered momentum after America's Civil War. People began to leave the peasant culture of farming to work in city factories. This wave culminated in World War II, during which machine-age juggernauts clashed and atomic bombs exploded over Japan. Wealth diversified into three factors of production: land, labor, and capital.

- The third wave, the *information age* or knowledge age, is said to characterize our current era. Based on mind rather than muscle, it is powerfully driven by information technology. Wealth is increasingly contingent on the possession of knowledge/information.

This three-stage model of historical development has a long history. Sociologists in the nineteenth century (including Comte) could not have anticipated the development of the computer, but they did have a futuristic view that encompassed a vision of the increasing importance of scientific knowledge and associated social changes. Contemporary analysts such as Toffler have the advantage of being able to contrast some of the emerging characteristics of the computer age with aspects of the earlier industrial age.

A central characteristic of the industrial age was centralization and **standardization.** At its height, everything was "mass," from mass production to mass destruction. The task of factory workers was to turn out the longest possible line of identical products. This was one point on which there was agreement between the assembly-line capitalist Henry Ford and the leader of communist Russia (then called the U.S.S.R.) Joseph Stalin. The bureaucracy and pyramid power structure of the industrial age had many faults, but at its best it was efficient at turning out large quantities of standardized goods. One drawback was the sameness of the goods. As Henry Ford explained, "They can have a car any color they like, so long as it's black."

The pressures of competition led the giant producers of standardized goods to seek to *differentiate* their products and to satisfy (or create) different tastes. The arrival of computer technology brought about a period of transition in which the massive corporations were able to begin to provide more differentiated products for "niche markets." The large manufacturers of automobiles increased their range of vehicles to satisfy different market segments—sports utility vehicles (SUVs) for families with small children to ferry around, sports cars for affluent young singles, and saloon cars with varying engine sizes and accessories to suit different income levels. Even the humdrum cup of coffee underwent this series of changes. In the 1920s, towns still varied in terms of the kind of coffee they had available, but by the 1970s it was the likes of Maxwell House and McDonald's that made sure you had the same limited choice of coffee everywhere you went. In the 1990s many small coffeehouses sprang up, offering a rich variety of choices to satisfy consumer preferences, with ingredients and combinations that would have seemed exotic only a decade or two previously. Today, you can have industrial-age McDonald's-style standardization combined with information-age product choice simply by walking into one of the thousands of Starbucks coffee shops nationwide (soon to be worldwide). If anything, people are beginning to complain about too much choice—choice overload!

As the coffee example makes clear, it wasn't just cars, furniture, and other household goods that were standardized in the industrial age. Many forms of culture and entertainment were also standardized for sale to mass markets. The Marxist sociologists in the famous Frankfurt Institute, founded before World War II in Germany, were fierce critics of the capitalist "culture industry"—especially that of Hollywood, which they accused of providing standardized culture for the masses. Whether mass culture had the kind of degrading ideological effects on working people that the Frankfurt critics imagined has been disputed. However, mass culture did not vanish with the arrival of the

McDonald's is ubiquitous as an example of standardization with choice. However, critics such as Morgan Spur-lock in *Super Size Me* have pointed out that too much choice can be a problem. (AP Photo)

See printed book for original Art.

Standardization *A characteristic of the industrial age whereby everything was produced en masse, following the same guidelines and design protocol and resulting in identical products.*

information society. Hollywood blockbusters, million-selling popular music recordings, and TV soap opera series are still very much around. But alongside these are many demassified niches. The Internet, for example, boasts thousands of special-interest newsgroups. This is the "plus side" of the current era. On the "negative side," however, it should be noted that the Internet has promoted a surge in hate groups. In March 1998, the *Los Angeles Times* ran an article reporting an all-time high of 474 hate groups in the United States; in just three years, 163 new websites had appeared on the Internet to preach hatred (Serrano 1998).

Inequalities of opportunity are also being reported. Access to the Internet is still markedly unequal among ethnic and income groups in the United States; in 2000, for example, 77 percent of white non-Hispanic children were living in homes with computers, compared with only 43 percent of African-American children and 37 percent of Hispanic children (U.S. Department of Education 2003). Indeed, determining the presence of a computer and the Internet among households is an effective way of measuring the digital divide in the United States. Table 9.1 illustrates this divide as a function of race/Hispanic origin, education, and family income.

The digital divide at the global level can be calculated using measures such as access to information and communications technology (ICT). Table 9.2 lists Digital Access Index values for the twenty highest-ranked and twenty lowest-ranked countries based on five variables: "availability of infrastructure, affordability of access, educational level, quality of ICT services, and Internet usage" (International Telecommunication Union 2003). The original study analyzed a total of 178 economies.

Returning to the "plus side" we find that the information age has witnessed a welcome increase in the number and variety of radio stations, offering music to suit all tastes, from classical to zydeco, and catering to different ethnic groups. In 1980 there were only 67 Spanish-language stations in the United States, but by 2000, according to the Arbitron ratings service, at least 559 of the nation's 12,800 stations were broadcasting in Spanish. Chronicling the long march of Spanish-language radio from Miami and Los Angeles to the rural towns of the Rocky Mountains, the Southeast, and the Great Plains, the *Los Angeles Times* reported: "Every month, it seems, another station gives up its English format—oldies or talk—in favor of what's known in the business as 'regional Mexican.' From one night to the next, the airwaves switch from farm reports and Howard Stern to the oom-pah-pah beat of the *norteña* and the wailing ballads of the *ranchera* and the *corrido*" (Tobar 2000).

Also on the rise, however, are "shock talk" radio programs, in which aggression and intolerance are worrying features. Some media sociologists even argue that the trend toward increasing diversity of radio content has begun to reverse direction. The evidence they cite is the massive consolidation that occurred following deregulation of ownership in 1996, with just a few giant media companies owning hundreds of radio stations. This "huge wave of consolidation," the trade publication *Variety* observed in 1999, "has turned music stations into cash cows that focus on narrow play lists aimed at squeezing the most revenue from the richest demographics" (Stern 1999: 8).

TABLE 9.1 Presence of a Computer and the Internet Among U.S. Households, by Race/Hispanic Origin, Education, and Income, 2001

CHARACTERISTICS	TOTAL HOUSEHOLDS*	PRESENCE OF A COMPUTER		PRESENCE OF THE INTERNET	
		YES PERCENTAGE	NO PERCENTAGE	YES PERCENTAGE	NO PERCENTAGE
Total Households	109,106	56.3	43.7	50.4	49.6
RACE/HISPANIC ORIGIN					
White	90,680	58.6	41.4	52.7	47.3
White not Hispanic	80,734	60.9	39.1	55.2	44.8
Black	13,304	37.3	62.7	31.1	68.9
Asian/Pacific Islander	4,081	72.3	27.7	67.5	32.5
Hispanic (of any race)	10,476	40.0	60.0	32.2	67.8
EDUCATION					
Less than high school graduate	17,463	23.2	76.8	18.0	82.0
High school graduate or GED	33,469	46.4	53.6	39.7	60.3
Some college or associate's degree	29,410	64.5	35.5	57.7	42.3
Bachelor's degree	18,457	78.4	21.6	73.8	26.2
Advanced degree	10,308	82.2	17.8	77.7	22.3
FAMILY INCOME					
Total Families	74,044	64.6	35.4	57.9	42.1
Less than $5,000	1,322	27.9	72.1	20.5	79.5
$5,000–$9,999	2,287	24.6	75.4	18.0	82.0
$10,000–$14,999	3,656	31.6	68.4	23.5	76.5
$15,000–$19,999	3,034	36.0	64.0	24.9	75.1
$20,000–$29,999	8,274	46.2	53.8	36.7	63.3
$30,000–$39,999	7,891	59.3	40.7	50.9	49.1
$40,000–$49,999	6,307	71.5	28.5	63.1	36.9
$50,000–$59,999	6,334	76.3	23.7	68.7	31.3
$60,000–$74,999	6,727	82.7	17.3	76.8	23.2
$75,000 or more	16,472	90.8	9.2	87.0	13.0
Not reported	11,740	53.6	46.4	48.2	51.8

Note: Numbers in thousands.

Source: U.S. Bureau of the Census (2001b: Table 1A).

TABLE 9.2 Access to Information and Communications Technology (ICT), by Country, 2002

HIGHEST ACCESS	DAI*	LOWEST ACCESS	DAI*
Sweden	0.85	Gambia	0.13
Denmark	0.83	Bhutan	0.13
Iceland	0.82	Sudan	0.13
Korea (Rep.)	0.82	Comoros	0.13
Norway	0.79	Côte d'Ivoire	0.13
Netherlands	0.79	Eritrea	0.1
Hong Kong, China	0.79	D.R. Congo	0.12
Finland	0.79	Benin	0.12
Taiwan, China	0.79	Mozambique	0.12
Canada	0.78	Angola	0.11
United States	0.78	Burundi	0.10
United Kingdom	0.77	Guinea	0.10
Switzerland	0.76	Sierra Leone	0.10
Singapore	0.75	Central African Rep.	0.10
Japan	0.75	Ethiopia	0.10
Luxembourg	0.75	Guinea-Bissau	0.10
Austria	0.75	Chad	0.10
Germany	0.74	Mali	0.09
Australia	0.74	Burkina Faso	0.08
Belgium	0.74	Niger	0.04

*On a scale of 0 to 1, where 1 = highest access. Digital Access Index (DAI) values are shown to hundreds of a decimal point. Countries with the same DAI value are ranked by thousands of a decimal point.

Source: International Telecommunication Union (2003).

According to the media watchdogs at the Project for Excellence in Journalism, the degree of consolidation in radio is not only greater than that in other media, such as television, but also more insinuating—in particular, because "technology has made it ever easier to seamlessly splice pieces of local information into a generic broadcast to give the appearance that the programming is local." Accordingly, "radio listeners may not give a second thought to what company might stand behind their local radio station. They may be aware of the presence

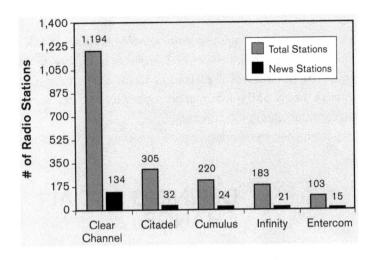

Figure 9.1

Number of Stations Owned by Top Five Companies, 2004

Source: PEJ (2005).

of corporations like Clear Channel or Infinity Broadcasting, but they might not understand how large their presence is. More than that, they might not know what impact the ownership question has on what they listen to" (Project for Excellence in Journalism 2004: 8). In fact, Clear Channel has the largest ownership of radio stations by a wide margin (see Figure 9.1).

The changes that have occurred in the economy and culture of the United States—from the massification and standardization of industrial society to the diversity said to be characteristic of the information society—have certainly not been clear-cut. Some features of the old order exist alongside those of the new, suggesting that the present period may be one of transition. In some areas there may even be reversals of trends, as in the context of radio-content diversity, which we discussed earlier, or in the economic sphere where corporations seek to maintain profits by taking over competitors or reducing the variety of products. Toffler regards such reversals as merely temporary setbacks in the inevitable development of the information society. He is less optimistic, however, about certain other social changes associated with the information society, such as the proliferation of family types that are replacing the standard industrial-age nuclear family, which had a working father and a stay-at-home mother. These new family types include the remarrieds, the adopteds, the blended family, the single-parent family, the same-sex family, the zero-parent family, the family of convenience, and the virtual family. (See also Chapter 7, on marriage and the family.) Toffler expresses concern about the effects of this fracturing of the American family that has occurred in the past thirty years, but it is, after all, in keeping with other recent social changes, especially the demands for greater individual freedom and choice.

Toffler's sweeping view of history, divided into three waves, is reminiscent of the work of nineteenth-century theorists such as Comte, Spencer, and Durkheim, as we will see. Other contemporary sociologists have not been quite so ambitious. When they do talk about *postindustrial society* or the *information age*, they are likely to specify contradictory developments and a limited range of changes. This point is well illustrated by Daniel Bell's theory of postindustrial society and Manuel Castells's theory of the information society (or *network society*, as he now calls it), both of which we consider later in the chapter.

How have sociologists attempted to develop precise accounts of social change?

Social change *The alteration of social structures with respect not only to institutions and actions but also to changes in cultural elements, such as norms, beliefs, and values.*

Cultural lag *The phenomenon whereby cultural elements, such as religious beliefs, change more slowly than structural elements, such as technological innovations. The term cultural lag was coined by William Ogburn.*

DEFINING SOCIAL CHANGE

Admittedly, it may not be very profitable to attempt a precise definition of **social change,** because the term refers to so many different phenomena that such a definition would likely end up being too broad or omitting something important. Nevertheless, we can recommend the usage offered by Wilbert Moore, who defines *social change* as the "significant alteration of social structures" and by *social structures* means "patterns of social action and interaction" (Moore 1967: 3). Moore's definition has the advantage of focusing on observable patterns of social action, such as changes in family and work patterns; however, it gives little specific attention to various cultural elements, such as values, norms, and beliefs, which may not be so easily observable. This is not to say that culture is less relevant to social change than are structures. But it is important to stress that culture should not be seen as a static set of norms, values, and beliefs, contrasted with the more dynamic social structures. Culture is a dynamic dimension of social practices or social actions. Being a member of a culture involves being engaged in a variety of practices that are distinguishable from those of other cultures and other times, ranging from ways of eating to religion and family life (Calhoun 1992: 280). It is true that elements of culture may sometimes lag behind changes in structure, as when religious beliefs and rituals change more slowly than scientific or technological innovations—a phenomenon that sociologist William Ogburn (1964) termed **cultural lag.** But sometimes the opposite is the case, such that cultural changes lead to changes in economic, political, or technological structures. For example, in *The Protestant Ethic and the Spirit of Capitalism* (1904), Max Weber illustrated how changes in religion—specifically, the rise of Calvinism in the sixteenth century—influenced the development of capitalism.

Questions about social change have always been central to sociology. The social thinkers who laid the foundations of sociology in the nineteenth century were concerned about the impact of industrialization and urbanization on social life. They not only faced upheaval in their own societies in Europe and America but also were hearing reports of seemingly "primitive" tribal and clan societies in Africa and the indigenous peoples of America and Australasia. There was talk of cannibalism, polygamy, totemism, and magic.

Increased information and curiosity about less developed "primitive" societies raised questions about the nature of "modernity" and the direction of human development. The early sociological theories of social change focused on the stages of social development over long periods of time and throughout whole societies or even civilizations. In other words, they tended to be macrosocial, historical theories of development. "Modernization" and "progress" were the key motifs common to most of these theories. However, the early theorists diverged over whether to explain these developments in terms of social evolution or social revolution.

Social evolutionary theories viewed social change as advancing gradually through certain basic stages of development, such as from "military society" to "industrial society," and from simple agrarian forms to more complex industrial-urban ones. They were developed in the nineteenth century by some of the first thinkers to refer to themselves as sociologists—Auguste Comte, Herbert Spencer, and Émile Durkheim. In the mid-twentieth century, aspects of this evolutionary view were still to be found in *functionalism*, which regarded social change as the adaptation of a social system to its environment through **differentiation** (specialization of the parts) and increasing structural complexity (Parsons 1951b). For example, the institution of the family became more limited in its functions, and some of its former functions were taken over by institutions in other spheres such as education and the economy. By contrast, *theories of revolutionary change*, such as those deriving from Karl Marx, emphasized increasing *conflict* among different parts of society—particularly different economic groups (classes)—as the funda mental source of social change. The distinction between these two sets of theories can be illustrated in terms of the different images they favored: A typical functionalist image was that of society evolving gradually like the human organism from infancy to maturity, whereas Marx's conflict theory of revolutionary social change led

Differentiation *In the context of development of the modern social system, this process involves the separation of major social functions so that each is the specialized responsibility of an appropriate social institution.*

Metanarratives *All-encompassing, macrosocial theories of development.*

him to prefer metaphors such as the sudden and sometimes violent emergence of the new baby from the womb, preceded by a period of painful labor.

These all-encompassing, macrosocial theories of development—sometimes referred to as **meta-narratives**—began to come under sustained criticism in the second half of the twentieth century. They seemed to be attempting to explain too much—to be claiming to have discovered a kind of universal pattern of development. For example, Comte's social evolutionary theory of human development maintained that all humankind passed through three stages of intellectual development—theological reasoning, metaphysical thought, and positive (scientific) reasoning—and that these corresponded to three stages of social development—primitive military society, an intermediate stage of defensive military organization and a gradual switch of emphasis to production, and finally, modern industrial society.

One early twentieth-century theorist who warned against generalizations of this sort was Max Weber. Although he talked about long-term changes similar to those described by the other theorists, he emphasized the limited and specific historical character of social forms, such as Western capitalism and the modern form of bureaucratic organization. This approach proved attractive to professional sociologists in the second half of the twentieth century, who preferred "bite-sized" or "middle-range" theories (Merton 1949) over the sweeping generalizations that had suited the theorizing appetites of their predecessors.

It was only toward the end of the twentieth century that theories of macrosocial, historical change began to come back into prominence, with references to shifts from industrial to postindustrial society or information society, and from modernity to postmodernity. In contrast to the reception given to the earlier theories, these new theories have been challenged to specify the criteria and empirical evidence against which they can be judged. For example, some sociologists argue that it is misleading to talk about a change from industrial to postindustrial society because many service jobs are devoted to assisting manufacturing, as in the case of administrative staff in a factory. Furthermore, service jobs vary in type, some of which are still basically manual jobs, as is true of many cleaning and catering operations. Other sociologists, such as Manuel Castells (1996), prefer to use *information age* to emphasize the growing importance of information technology in the economy; this term, they say, is not only more specific than *service* but also allows for the fact that manufacturing may still constitute a major part of the economy. *Postmodern*, however, is even less clear-cut, as it is used to refer to a variety of social and cultural changes, not just to postindustrialism. Nevertheless, the theorist remains obligated to try to specify the criteria as clearly as possible. And, indeed, it might be easier to be specific if one links the term *postmodern* to certain changes in culture before going on to speak more generally of postmodern society—especially as *postmodernism* was originally the name of the cultural style that succeeded *modernism*.

INDUSTRIAL SOCIETY

Both Karl Marx and Max Weber viewed modern industrial society as a socioeconomic system in which the *manufacturing firm* was central. For Marx, the factory was important as a prime example of the methods used by capitalists to make a profit out of combining machinery and workers to produce goods for sale; it was a means of concentrating and organizing labor. For Weber, the manufacturing firm typified the modern form of organization, which was highly rational and bureaucratic. The question to consider is: Have the changes implied by such terms as *postindustrial society* or *information society* been so revolutionary that they constitute a break with the modern society analyzed by Marx and Weber?

In addressing this question, let us consider Marx's theory of capitalism, which has been summarized as follows:

- Capitalism is a historically transient form of society—it emerged out of the constraints of a previous form of society (feudalism) and was destined to eventually give way to socialism once it had exhausted all its possibilities.

- It contains a distinctive way of producing goods, a *mode of production* that is (1) built around the production of commodities, (2) where human labor itself is commodified, and (3) where profit is created by the extraction or "exploitation" of surplus value from the workers.

- It is based on a division of ownership of the *means of production*, so that those who own the means of production (factories, machine tools, land, etc.)—the *capitalists*—are separated from those who work in or with them—the *working class*.

- It is a dynamic process, involving (1) technological progress—the incorporation of science [into] the production process in order to constantly develop methods of production through the use of increasingly complex and efficient machinery and (2) increasing the scale of production—to pay for more complex and expensive machinery, more commodities must be produced and sold to generate the profits that the enterprise requires. (Hamilton, 2002: 101, adapted from Bottomore 1985)

It is clear that, for Marx, what defines capitalism is neither the factory nor technology but rather the **social relations of production.** These are the relationships between the main groups engaged in the production of goods for sale—workers and those who supervise them on behalf of the capitalist owners. The factory, on the other hand, simply represented a way of concentrating workers within one space, working for a given period of clock time at a specific rate sufficient to yield a profit for the owner. Profit, in turn, represented the *surplus value* available to the owner once he or she had met all the costs of labor and machinery. From this point of view, the use

Social relations of production *The relationships between the main groups engaged in the production of goods for sale—workers and those who supervise them on behalf of capitalist owners. According to Marx, it is neither the factory nor technology that defines capitalism but rather the emergence of new, problematic social relations of production.*

of computerized information technology does not fundamentally alter the relations between workers and capitalist owners. And thus the introduction of such technology would not in itself indicate the emergence of an information society that could be regarded as a revolutionary change in the socioeconomic structure of capitalist industrial society.

Weber's approach to capitalism differed from Marx's in that he saw the emergence of the capitalist economic system in the West as one element of a wider socioeconomic phenomenon that he called **rationalization.** The process of rationalization entailed the replacement of traditional institutions and values by those based on principles of rational calculation regarding the most efficient means to achieve empirical ends. The process was exemplified in two main areas of modern social life: the *market economy* and the *modern bureaucracy.* The "free" market—unfettered by traditional customs and sentiments—represented an arena in which the formal, technical, calculative rationality of supply and demand operated. And the modern bureaucracy—whose performance could be checked and rechecked against quantifiable criteria—functioned on the basis of explicit, standardized, and calculable rules.

In the light of these two major components of modernity—rationalization and bureaucratization—we can see that Weber would have had no difficulty in regarding information and communications technology (ICT) as simply a continuation of such processes. Indeed, computerized financial data systems are an asset to the kind of accountancy practices that Weber regarded as typical of rationalization; for example, the personal computer (PC) achieved preeminence in the mid-1980s because of its ability to deliver standardized accounting techniques and word processing. ICT has also been a means of extending the technical rationality of bureaucracy by manipulating stored data and distributing them via **networks.** Bureaucrats no longer need to refer to written rules or to interpret them; rather, computers store the rules in application programs and apply them in standardized ways to all cases.

Weber regarded the bureaucratic administration of the state as the epitome of the rationalizing process at the heart of modernity, and computers have become its tools. The early form of the computer, the punch card machine, was invented in 1890 for the specific purpose of making the processing of U.S. Census information more rapid and efficient. Similarly, the Internet had its origins in linking federally funded defense researchers. It appears that ICT will continue to have close links with the formal and technical rationality of both the modern state and commercial organization. Thus, even though the PC offers individuals the promise of expanding human possibilities, computers continue to be used by government and corporations to exercise greater control over individuals. It is this kind of bureaucratic control that Weber described as the "iron cage" of modern society. From a Weberian perspective, then, the emergence of contemporary forms of ICT represents not a revolutionary change in society but simply an extension of rationalization and bureaucratization.

This pessimistic view of the capacity of ICT to transform society—to give individuals greater freedom and control over their lives—contrasts with the more optimistic view of those contemporary "futurologists" who, like Alvin Toffler, believe we are witnessing the dawn of a new, postindustrial society. A more mixed message is presented by the sociologist Daniel Bell.

Rationalization *The process by which traditional institutions and values are replaced by those based on rational calculation regarding the most efficient means to achieve empirical ends. The market economy and modern bureaucracy are examples of this process. According to Max Weber, rationalization is the defining characteristic of modernity.*

Networks *The components of an interconnected system through which social actors are organized toward the attainment of goals. Networks arguably represent the new social structure and organization replacing the hierarchical form exemplified by the welfare state.*

POSTINDUSTRIAL SOCIETY

For Bell, who popularized the concept of *postindustrial society* in the early 1970s, the term signifies an intermediate stage between industrial society and a future form of society, the precise nature of which was still to be established. In his book *The Coming of Post-Industrial Society* (1973), Bell divided society into three spheres: social (or techno-economic) structure, polity (the state and political institutions), and culture. The coming of postindustrial society, he argued, primarily involves changes in social structure, especially in the economy and in areas such as work, science, and technology. Although his focus in the book was directed to these structural changes, he was aware that they had implications for the polity and culture as well.

The main changes involved in the transition to postindustrial society are as follows:

- A shift occurs from the predominance of goods production to that of services. Among the various types of services (including banking and retail, for example), health, education, research, and government service are the ones most important to postindustrial society.

- In the occupational realm, knowledge workers such as those in professional and technical work, especially scientists and technologists, rise to prominence. Assembly-line workers and other manual occupations become less central.

- The type of knowledge central to postindustrial society is theoretical knowledge, in contrast to the empirical knowledge valued in industrial society. In the transition to postindustrial society, science as well as research and development (R&D) work grows exponentially, catalyzed by the codification of theoretical knowledge.

- Given postindustrial society's orientation toward the assessment and control of technology and its impact, there is reason to hope that new forecasting and mapping techniques can be developed, making possible the planned advance of technological change and reduced economic uncertainties.

- Decisionmaking involves the creation of a new intellectual technology to handle the large-scale complexity of postindustrial society, the components of which include information theory, cybernetics, decision theory, game theory, utility theory, and stochastic processes. (Adapted from Bell 1973: 29)

Bell's account resembles some of the earlier grand theories (metanarratives) of social development, inasmuch as it comprises a narrative of change from preindustrial to industrial and finally postindustrial society. At the time he was writing, only the United States had reached the postindustrial stage; Western Europe, the (former) Soviet Union, and Japan had reached the industrial stage; and Asia, Africa, and South America were largely still stuck at the preindustrial stage. Bell drew out a number of distinctions among these three types of society or stages of development. In particular, he claimed that they differed with respect to dominant occupations: In preindustrial society, the central figures were farmers, miners, fishermen, and unskilled workers; in industrial society, they were semiskilled workers and engineers; and in postindustrial society, they are professionals and technical scientists. (One outcome relating to the transition under discussion has been the decline in U.S. manufacturing jobs, which is mapped in Figure 9.2.) The key power groups changed correspondingly: They comprised landowners and members of the military in preindustrial society, industrialists and politicians in industrial society, and scientists and researchers in postindustrial society.

Many criticisms can be made of this grand narrative of development. The most obvious one is that there is little sign that power has shifted from business to scientists. Similarly, although service jobs have increased in number and variety, many of them are routine and relatively unskilled, rather than technically and scientifically advanced. Furthermore, many service jobs are still devoted to servicing manufacturing and production processes—design, marketing, finance, and administration. However, when considering the validity of arguments about the

Figure 9.2

Map of Decline in U.S. Manufacturing Jobs, 1998–2005

Source: U.S. Department of Labor (2005).

coming of postindustrial society, we should note that the thesis was developed on the basis of research carried out in the 1960s. The emergence of new information technologies from the 1980s onward, including the World Wide Web, was still some way off when Bell's *The Coming of Post-Industrial Society* was published and French sociologist Alain Touraine was writing *The Post-Industrial Society* (1971). Nevertheless, Bell can be given credit for forecasting some of the developments, especially in ICT, that led later sociologists to refer to the emergence of an information society. We also need to recognize that Bell did not claim that society had already undergone a revolutionary change; rather, he said it was in transition. Indeed, elements of preindustrial and industrial society were coexisting with emerging postindustrial elements. It could even be argued that some of these elements or stages remain in contradiction or conflict with one another.

The theme of contradiction became more prominent in Bell's later publication, *The Cultural Contradictions of Capitalism* (1976), when he turned his focus from social structural changes to cultural changes. The book is premised on the idea that the three focal realms are governed by contrary axial principles: for the economy, it is efficiency; for the polity, equality; and for

MEDIA MOMENTS

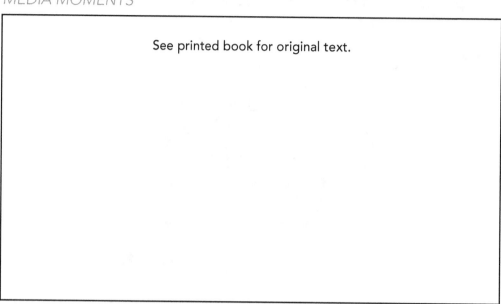

See printed book for original text.

culture, self-realization (or self-gratification) (Bell 1976: xi–xii). Bell's main concern here is with the conflict between the techno-economic and cultural realms: As he put it, the *techno-economic realm* still seemed to be ruled by the old character traits of self-discipline, restraint, and delayed gratification, which were in conflict with the hedonism that seemed to characterize the *cultural realm.* Bell discerned the emergence of a postmodern culture based on consumerism, "concerned with play, fun, display and pleasure" (Bell 1976: 70). He was ahead of his contemporaries in identifying some of the characteristics of the emerging postmodern culture. Among the issues that he mentioned in this connection were the dominance of visual culture, the presence of nonrationality and irrationality, the breakdown of the distinction between high and low culture, and loss of the sense of a unified self.

Among the many scenarios or visions of the future that exist today, some paint a bleak picture while others are enthusiastically optimistic. Most of the people who have encountered the postmodern debate have done so through the cultural dimension, which encompasses the arts, architecture, and film. Consider, for instance, *Blade Runner* (1982), deemed the acme of postmodern movies. A summary is provided in the box titled "Postmodern Futures."

What makes *Blade Runner* postmodern? According to sociologist David Lyon (1999), it contains several postmodern themes:

- "Reality" itself is in question within this movie. The replicants want to be real people, but the proof of "reality" is a photographic image, a constructed identity. One of the debates about media Moments postmodernity is whether it's possible to have verifiable knowledge about society and people (including our own identities). Or are we faced with a mélange of artificial images from television and other media? A more optimistic view is that postmodernity liberates us from definitions of "reality" imposed by authorities, leaving us free to shop around.

- Another theme is that, in the postmodern or postindustrial economy, information/knowledge has replaced industry and labor as the axial organizing principle. According to Tyrell, the corporation featured in the movie, developing knowledge has produced commerce "more human than human," with genetic engineering producing human simulacra (imitations). The replicants exist in a world that has overcome the limitations of time and space, thanks to the information and communications technology (ICT) of the "global village." The traditional and modern structures of space and time have been supplemented or supplanted by "virtual" spaces. The solidity and coherence of once-separate societies, whether nation-states or other territorially bounded communities, are undermined as global communications and relations erode the older sense of time and space. Production is internationalized: An automobile may be designed in one country and manufactured in another, with the company headquarters located in a third. Sociology itself is forced to become more global in its analyses as it seeks some sense of the new patterns formed by flows of people, data, images, and capital.

- A less prominent but still discernible postmodern theme is that of "consumer society," where everything is a spectacle and images are what matter. Some of the most memorable scenes in the movie feature decadent entertainment spectacles with bizarre characters and costumes. For example, Zhora, a female replicant, dies crashing through storefront windows in a seemingly endless arcade. Everything is on offer to be consumed, no matter how strange, and boredom threatens to loom unless new excitements can be presented. One of the few things distinguishing replicants from humans is what they consume—echoing the postmodern theme that "we are what we eat." Otherwise, the difference between reality and simulacra is not obvious in the postmodern world of *Blade Runner*. It is as if America has become Disneyland for real, which is the conclusion of Frenchman Jean Baudrillard (1988), one of the foremost sociologists of postmodernity. According to Baudrillard, the postmodern cultural life of America is now so permeated with media images that it is impossible to distinguish a "real" America from that of Disneyland.

Social and cultural diversity is evident in the streets of the postmodern L.A. of *Blade Runner*, where all ethnic groups are represented. It a truly global city. We get an impression of social fragmentation and cultural pastiche—key themes of postmodernism. These tendencies were already evident in early-modern industrial society. As Karl Marx demonstrated, the meaning behind the constant revolutionizing of production was that "all that is solid melts into air." This process is accentuated in postindustrial, postmodern society, where everything has become

The Taliban regime in Afghanistan continues to resist modernization of that country. (AP Photo/Amir Shah)

See printed book for original Art.

a commodity for sale, including images and identities, and there is a constant pressure to change. In the words of one *Blade Runner* replicant, experience is "washed away in time like tears in rain."

Of course, *Blade Runner* was set in a future time, and sociologists who prefer the term *late modernity* over *postmodernity* (Anthony Giddens is one of them) argue that many of the characteristics of modernity still exist—even in the most advanced global cities of the information age, such as Los Angeles. Alongside the gleaming dream factories of Hollywood and Disneyland, we find Third World people scraping a living and forming what Marx might call an exploited postindustrial proletariat. The Hispanic service workers who clean supermarket floors and tend the homes and gardens of the middle class may even be a vestige of a preindustrial servant class that is now on the increase again after having declined during the industrial phase of modernity. But one could also argue that the term *postmodernity* is useful precisely because it does point to the contradictory tendencies that are appearing, including new localisms and fundamentalisms in response to globalization and rationalization. The Taliban Islamic fundamentalism that dominated Afghanistan until it was overthrown after September 11, 2001, is a recent example of resistance to globalization and rationalization. The Taliban sought to reestablish traditional cultural practices, such as the confinement of women in the home and family, denying them education and employment. It is not alone in reacting in this way. Christian fundamentalists in America, too, are highly suspicious of globalization, opposing bodies such as the United Nations, championing biblical creationist beliefs against the scientific theory of evolution, and attempting to promote traditional family values.

INFORMATION SOCIETY, GLOBALIZATION, AND SOCIAL MOVEMENTS

Some observers of the information society go so far as to insist that it is profoundly changing the very contours of social structure and organization. They claim that, in place of the hierarchical form of social structure and organization typified by the centralized welfare state and the bureaucratic corporation, an older form of organization—that of the *network*—has risen to a new global prominence thanks to the computerization of information, knowledge, and communication (Castells 1996–1998, 2000, 2002).

The danger posed by this new form of organization is that, once programmed to achieve certain goals, it may impose its own logic on its members (human actors). All computer-based systems work on a binary logic: inclusion/exclusion. And "[w]hat is not in the network does not exist from the network's perspective, and thus must be either ignored (if it is not relevant to the network's task) or is eliminated (if it is competing in goals or in performance)" (Castells 2002: 127). Many sociologists would dispute Castells's pessimistic picture of the

Welfare state *A state in which the government takes responsibility for its citizens' well-being. A welfare state typically devotes a significant portion of its expenditures to programs that provide access to resources such as housing, health care, education, and/or employment for its citizens.*

impossibility of bringing about internal change in the interpretation of organizations' goals. That is precisely how reforms occur in many organizations in society as groups and parties battle over the meanings that define the goals and the means to attain them. However, we can see that there is some truth in Castells's analysis wherever computer-based systems are in operation, as in global banking and financial systems, or in economic production systems that are programmed to switch production or sourcing of materials to the cheapest provider. In such cases, there may be a social struggle to assign goals to the network but afterward, members (actors) find themselves having to ply their strategies within the rules of the network. In order to bring about the assignment of different goals to the network, actors may have to challenge the network from the outside and, in fact, destroy it by building an alternative network around alternative values. Another option is to attempt to withdraw from the network and build a defensive, non-network structure (e.g., a "commune") that does not allow connections outside its own set of values. It is because global networks tend to exclude the possibility of changing their goals that there has been a growth of social movements opposing them (e.g., antiglobalization movements) and of "fundamentalist" communal movements seeking to separate themselves from them.

Castells discusses three types of social movements and identities that can be generated in response to the globalization of information flows and networks: *legitimizing*, *resistance*, and *project*. The first type—**legitimizing movements and identities**—is manifest in the mainstream institutions of society. They are generated by or in churches, labor unions, political parties, cooperatives, and civic associations. Such bodies constitute civil society—the part of political activity and influence that lies outside the state but has legitimate access to state power. Once again, Castells is more pessimistic than many other sociologists—in this case, about the possibility that such legitimizing movements and identities will bring about substantial

Legitimizing movements and identities *As described by Manuel Castells, social movements that are generated through institutions of civil society that are outside of the state, yet have legitimate access to state power.*

Resistance movements and identities *As described by Manuel Castells, social movements that are based on the identity of excluded groups (i.e., racial and ethnic minorities) and are the product of resentment toward dominant institutions and alienation from mainstream ideologies.*

transformations in the information society by way of state action. The reason for this pessimism, according to Castells, is that the state itself is weakened by globalization (e.g., global corporations, global capital flows, and global information flows elude state control). Its power is also eroded by the decline of the bureaucratic *welfare state* that grew up in industrial society but is no longer so firmly rooted in the information society. For example, Castells concludes that the nationally based *labor movement* now has little prospect of wielding influence to bring about the rebuilding of a welfare state that would provide all its citizens with standardized forms of social security. In America, the labor movement is weaker than ever before and the growth of a strong welfare state has been opposed by the ideology of individualism, which favors private provision of security benefits (e.g., private health care and pensions). Even in Europe, where the welfare state is more highly valued, the influence of the labor movement has weakened and a shift has occurred toward more private provision of benefits.

In early 2005, the U.S. Department of Labor's Bureau of Labor Statistics issued a press release reporting the most recent data on the decline in labor union membership. These data revealed a reduction in the number of wage and salary workers who were union members from 12.9 percent in 2003 to 12.5 percent in 2004. This proportion had steadily declined from a high of 20.1 percent in 1983, the first year for which comparable union membership-rate data were available.

Highlights from this 2005 press release include the following:

- About 36 percent of government workers were union members in 2004, compared with about 8 percent of workers in private-sector industries.

- Two occupational groups—education, training, and library occupations, on the one hand, and protective-service occupations, on the other—exhibited the highest unionization rates in 2004 (about 37 percent each). Protective-service occupations include firefighters and police officers. Farming, fishing, and forestry occupations (3.1 percent) and sales and related occupations (3.6 percent) had the lowest unionization rates.

- Men were more likely to be union members (13.8 percent) than women (11.1 percent).

- Black workers were more likely to be union members (15.1 percent) than white workers (12.2 percent), Asian workers (11.4 percent), and Hispanic or Latino workers (10.1 percent).

- About 1.6 million wage and salary workers were represented by a union on their main job in 2004, while not being union members themselves.

- In 2004, full-time wage and salary workers who were union members had median usual weekly earnings of $781, compared with a median of $612 for wage and salary workers who were not represented by unions. (U.S. Department of Labor 2005b)

The second type described by Castells comprises **resistance movements and identities.** Familiar among the resistance identities are those grounded in religious fundamentalism, race and ethnicity, queer culture, and other excluded groups. Castells describes resistance movements and the identities they produce as "defensive sociocultural formations"—that is, as products of alienation and resentment in relation to the dominant institutions and ideologies of society. He is pessimistic about the prospect that these movements will be able to bring about institutional changes, as he thinks they have little influence over the centers of state power. Other sociologists, however, have pointed to the successes of some of these groups in securing recognition for themselves and their demands.

The third type is **project movements and identities.** A project identity is formed "when social actors, on the basis of whichever cultural materials are available to them, build a new identity that redefines their position in society and, by so doing, seek the transformation of the overall social structure" (Castells 1997: 8). Castells cites the environmental movement and the women's movement as examples. In contrast to resistance movements, project movements move beyond issues of exclusion by seeking to transform existing institutions or by constructing new ones. For instance, the women's movement projects itself into society at large by undermining male dominance (patriarchy) and reconstructing the family on a new basis of equality, as well as by seeking to

Labor union participation declined in the last part of the twentieth century; however, one of the most powerful unions, the teachers' union, still mobilizes many members in support of state funding for schools, as this Pennsylvania rally shows. (AP Photo)

See printed book for original Art.

Project movements and identities *As described by Manuel Castells, social movements that use available cultural resources to create new identities that redefine one's position in society and try to change the overall social structure. The women's movement and environmental movement are examples of project movements and identities.*

abolish gender distinctions in other major institutions such as work and politics. Castells notes that not all religious fundamentalisms can be ruled out as project identities; some religious communities, he argues, can be said to have transformative potential through their efforts aimed at "remoralizing society, reestablishing godly, eternal values, and embracing the whole world, or at least the whole neighborhood, in a community of believers, thus founding a new society" (Castells 1997: 357).

Social movements have attracted increasing attention from sociologists, especially those who believe we are entering a new stage of social development, such as the information society or network society described by Castells. But what are social movements, and why are they becoming so important?

Mario Diani has defined a social movement as "a network of informal interactions between a plurality of individuals, groups and/or organizations, engaged in a political or cultural conflict, on the basis of a shared collective identity" (1992: 13). Based on this definition, the key characteristics of a social movement can be summarized as follows:

Social movements *Movements whose key characteristics are (1) an informal network of interactions among activist groups, indivi-duals, and organizations; (2) a sense of collective identity; and (3) engagement in political or cultural conflict over social change.*

- It is an *informal network* of interactions among activist groups, individuals, or organizations.

- It is defined by a sense of *collective identity* among participants.

- It is engaged in *political or cultural conflict* over social change.

Diani's definition is useful because it makes a clear distinction between social movements and other temporary episodes of collective behavior, on the one hand, and established political organizations, on the other. Consider, for example, an episode of collective behavior such as a panic caused by a leak of radioactive material from a nuclear

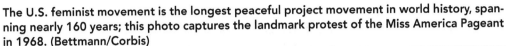

The U.S. feminist movement is the longest peaceful project movement in world history, spanning nearly 160 years; this photo captures the landmark protest of the Miss America Pageant in 1968. (Bettmann/Corbis)

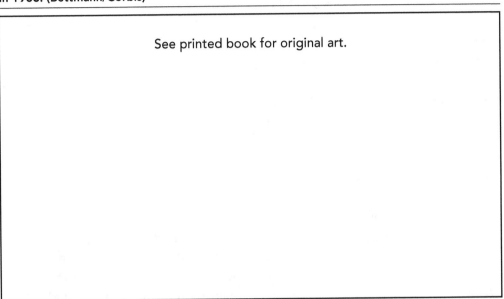

See printed book for original art.

reactor. As a temporary phenomenon it does not in itself bestow an identity, but it may evolve into an environmentalist social movement devoted to closing nuclear power stations or halting their spread. Bear in mind, however, that while a social movement may become organized and even bring together a number of organizations to pursue its objectives, it is broader and more loosely structured through an informal network than the more rigidly structured single organization.

Analysis of social movements was originally included in the study of the broad range of phenomena referred to as **collective behavior.** Sociologist Neil Smelser defined collective behavior as "mobilization on the basis of a belief which redefines social action" (1962: 8). Following is a list, based on his analysis, of the stages through which an episode of collective behavior typically develops:

> **Collective behavior** *As defined by Neil Smelser, mobilization on the basis of a belief that redefines social action.*

- *Structural conduciveness.* Conditions exist that permit or encourage collective behavior to occur, as when a money market creates conditions conducive to a panic about a financial crash.

- *Structural strain.* Uncertainty, conflict, or some other anxiety-producing circumstance is present.

- *Growth and spread of a generalized belief.* A shared belief identifies the source of strain, gives it meaning, and specifies certain appropriate responses.

- *Precipitating factors.* An event triggers an episode of collective behavior, as when a rapid drop in the price of tech stocks leads to a panic selling.

- *Mobilization of participants for action.* Information from or actions by influential figures summon people to act, as when a respected stockbroker's advice is quoted.

- *The operation of social control.* Collective behavior occurs as a result of lack of action by those otherwise capable of controlling the situation and thereby heading off the behavior.

According to Smelser, collective behavior occurs as a result of the passage through these stages in a cumulative progression—what amounts to a *value-added process.*

This approach has been found useful for understanding the emergence of certain forms of collective behavior, such as panics. But because the overall category of collective behavior is very broad, ranging from single events to long-lasting social movements, the study of social movements has given rise to other theories as well. These include resource mobilization theory and new social movements (NSM) theory (Storr 2002).

Resource mobilization theory, as developed by John D. McCarthy and Mayer N. Zald, starts with the question Why do people get involved in social movements? The seemingly obvious answer is that they get involved because they want to bring about social change as a result of their own experiences of disadvantage or oppression. Accordingly, we might expect gay men and lesbians to join a movement for social change because they suffer homophobia or blacks to join an antiracist movement because they suffer racism. McCarthy and Zald (1987) suggest that this is an oversimplification. On the one hand, some people experience oppression but do not join a social movement—and this may be a rational choice on their part. For example, homosexual individuals who do not actively participate in the lesbian and gay movement may have decided that it is not worth "coming out" in public if they risk losing their jobs, and perhaps they hope that homophobia will end at some indefinite point in the future. On the other hand, some people who do join social movements may not have experienced discrimination or disadvantage themselves. Indeed, there are heterosexuals who have been involved in the gay and lesbian movement, just as there are white people who participate in antiracist movements. Why do some people join a social movement and others do not? Or to put the question another way: How do social movements mobilize people to participate?

The key insight of resource mobilization theory is that social movements need resources—money, volunteers, know-how, and so on. The more resources they can mobilize, the more success they will achieve. In short, the main task of a social movement, according to resource mobilization theory, is to increase its pool of available resources. It can do this by persuading individuals to become involved as active members and to place some of their own resources at the disposal of the organization. In its search for resources, a social movement will not necessarily limit itself to those who stand to benefit directly from social change; for instance, a lesbian and gay movement may try to secure participation and resources from sympathetic heterosexuals as well as from gays and lesbians. And since there may be perfectly rational reasons for individual gays and lesbians not to join, it is no less rational for heterosexuals to join. In fact, resource mobilization theory assumes that social movements and individuals always operate on a rational basis and make rational choices. It is thus a form of *rational choice theory*, which signifies "that in acting rationally, an actor is engaging in some kind of optimization. This is sometimes expressed as maximizing utility, sometimes as minimizing cost, sometimes in other ways" (Coleman and Fararo 1992: xi). Resource mobilization theory also tends to treat social movements as if they were companies in search of investors. For instance, McCarthy and Zald (1987) explicitly compare social movements with industries and use terminology from economics to analyze them.

The major problem with resource mobilization theory, however, is that it tends to reduce all sociological analysis to a form of economic analysis. It is not really interested in the aims of social movements—the social changes these movements want to achieve or the protest actions they employ. Consequently, it has little to tell us about the *culture* of specific movements—the kinds of symbols or styles they use and the meanings attached to them. For example, an interesting feature of the gay liberation movement is that its public demonstrations often feature members dressed up in "drag" costumes. This approach might not seem the best way to attract resources, but as a form of political action directed against heterosexual gender norms it is symbolically very expressive.

The other theory introduced above—*new social movements theory*—is more interested in the analysis of culture and meaning in social movements. What is new about NSM theory is not the theory itself but the social movements that have come to the fore—and those social movements are new because, according to many sociologists, the form of society in which they are occurring is new. Indeed, new social movements have emerged in the information society, and they are engaged in struggles over information—they are attempting to bring about social change by influencing the public to see things their way. These are struggles over meanings and identities: The new social movements are more concerned with nonmaterial issues—identity and lifestyle and the inequalities they are subject to—than with economic inequality, as was the case with the older social movements of the industrial age, such as the labor movement (Inglehart 1990).

One of the leading thinkers behind new social movement theory is the Italian sociologist Alberto Melucci. His outline of the key characteristics of the new social movements in the information society includes the following:

- The centrality of *information*. Activists in the information society are centrally concerned with the production and circulation of information and meaning.

- The *self-reflexive form of action*. Because new social movements are struggles about meanings, activists must take account of the meanings generated by their own actions. Actions are primarily viewed as acts of communication; the protest action is a form of message and so is the activist himself or herself.

- The *global dimension*. New social movements are able to make links with global events and issues by using global networks of communication, especially the Internet.

- *Latency and visibility*. There are times when social movement activity is very visible and other times when it seems almost to disappear. Hence sociologists sometimes talk about different "waves" of a social movement—for example, "first-wave feminism" followed by second-wave and even third-wave feminism (editorial, *Feminist Review* 64 [2000]: 1–2). Alberto Melucci maintains, however, that a wave of activism should not be understood as a new arrival of energy, which subsequently disappears; rather, sociologists should focus on the networks of individuals and communities that periodically become visible as "waves" of activism. (Melucci 1995; Storr 2002)

A final point made by Melucci is that the success or failure of a social movement should be judged not solely by its "political" achievements but also in terms of its more subtle cultural results. Since new social movements are concerned with conveying and changing meanings, the very fact that a protest action takes place could be responsible for changing old meanings or creating new ones. The protest can make people aware of power structures and imbalances of power.

Many sociologists who subscribe to the idea that the contemporary societies with the most developed economies have become postindustrial societies or information societies would also accept that the new social movements are expressions of a postmodern culture and lifestyle. Many members of such movements seem to be engaged in constructing a lifestyle from a pastiche of elements, picking and choosing among a number of choices on offer—from dress codes and food consumption codes to sexual identity. This point is borne out if we look at some of the main examples that are given of new social movements: the gay and lesbian movement, the environmental or ecology movement, the women's movement, and so on. It has been said that people do not so much "join" such movements as "live" them. This "picking and mixing" has led to the criticism that involvement in a new social movement is often itself an expression of a postmodern lifestyle.

It's easy to draw too sharp a contrast between old and new social movements. Some of the new social movements are still engaged in a struggle over perceived inequalities, even if they are inequalities of recognition and respect (as in the gay and lesbian movement) or of power and status (as with many movements in behalf of ethnic groups and the women's movement). However, the new social movements are also concerned with lifestyle and identity—that is, with influencing public perceptions of lifestyle options and identities that seem to deviate from established mainstream opinion. But in order to wield this influence, they have to grapple with images in the mass media and the ways in which these "frame" or socially construct the issues. This phenomenon has led sociologists to develop a **frame analysis** of social movements, drawing on the earlier work of Erving Goffman (1974). Frame analysis reveals forms of interpretation that allow individuals or groups "to locate, perceive, identify, and label" events, thereby rendering meaning, organizing experiences, and guiding actions (Goffman 1974: 21). It is an approach that has been used in media studies to analyze the process by which news organizations define and construct a political issue or public controversy. Sociologists who have employed this method suggest that social movements are more likely to succeed in getting their message across if they frame it so as to be aligned with the frames of those receiving the message ("frame alignment") (Snow et al. 1986); if they ensure that the message resonates in a way that transforms the receivers' existing frame (Snow et al. 1986); or if their performance in the dramas surrounding public controversy attracts sympathetic attention to their values and beliefs, drawing on symbolic aspects of the movements' own subculture and that of the wider culture (Alexander 2006).

Frame analysis *A method of determining the ways in which social movements are socially constructed, interpreted, and repre-sented both by actors in the movement itself and by outside influences, such as the mass media.*

One of the newest social movements to attract wide support from young activists in many parts of the more economically developed world is the antiglobalization movement (sometimes referred to as the anticapitalism movement), which combines some of the characteristics of the old social movement struggle on behalf of the disadvantaged against the powerful, on the one hand, with new social movement issues of lifestyle, such as excessive consumerism and protecting the environment, on the other. It also uses many of the symbolically expressive tactics of new social movements in order to catch public attention

Globalization increases the flow of cultural products that shape the frames through which other cultures may view themselves, such as this *Star Wars* poster in Korea. (Reuters/Claro Cortes IV)

See printed book for original Art.

and encourage people to think differently. As suggested earlier, demonstrators who dress in unusual outfits or stage eye-catching stunts may gain media attention, but they also run the risk of being met with derision or even of being reduced to objects of ironical discussion in the newspaper style section. A review in *Extra!* of the media coverage of the Washington, D.C., demonstrations against the International Monetary Fund and the World Bank in April 2000 illustrates the problem, as detailed in the box titled "For Press, Magenta Hair and Nose Rings Defined Protests."

Whatever success is attributable to the styles and symbols of the antiglobalization movement, it has drawn attention to a subject that many people in the poorer parts of the world believe is not sufficiently publicized in more economically developed societies. Within the latter, especially the United States, emphasis tends to be placed on the advantages of worldwide communication through new information technologies, increased international trade, and the free flow of cultural products. The policies of international agencies like the International Monetary Fund (IMF) and the World Bank are intended to assist such developments; the antiglobalization movement seeks to publicize what it regards as their ill effects.

Globalization increases the flow of cultural products that shape the frames through which other cultures may view themselves, such as this *Star Wars* poster in Korea. (Reuters/Claro Cortes IV)

THEORY

See printed book for original text.

GLOBALIZATION

Exactly what is *globalization*? The term has many definitions, but one of the simplest has been offered by David Held: "Globalization may be thought of initially as the widening, deepening and speeding up of worldwide interconnectedness in all aspects of contemporary social life, from the cultural to the criminal, the financial to the spiritual" (Held et al. 1999: 2). This seems a fairly straightforward and uncontroversial proposition. However, it is disputed on a number of grounds.

First, whereas the phrase *worldwide interconnectedness* implies a single world system, the interconnectedness may actually exist only among certain nations and regions. Indeed, evidence indicates that the majority of international trade and communication occurs between neighboring countries (e.g., the United States and Canada) and within regional groups of nations or "trading blocs" (e.g., the European Union, Asia Pacific, and North America) (Hirst and Thompson 1996).

Second, the common assumption that globalization involves a neutral process of increasing "interconnectedness" may disguise the possibility that the flows between connected points are mainly in one direction, or consist of one side dominating the other (i.e., the more economically developed societies dominating the less developed ones). In fact, research demonstrates that use of the Internet is overwhelmingly situated in North America and Europe, and that America exports more television programs than any other country and imports only a tiny amount from other countries (Held et al. 1999: 356–360).

Third, as opponents of globalization in the environmental and anticapitalist movements have argued, the pursuit of profits leads to overexploitation of global resources by the more economically developed societies. This observation does not invalidate the term *globalization*, but it does seem a valid criticism of the effects of certain aspects of globalization, particularly the overexploitation of natural resources such as fossil fuels (oil, coal, and natural gas) and some of the antiregulation policies of international institutions such as the World Trade Organization, the World Bank, and the IMF. On the other hand, the term *globalization* has also been used in the context of increasing environmental degradation. The Western predilections for the motor car and profligate energy use entail a very large release of greenhouse gases into the atmosphere that has significantly contributed to global warming. Some national governments have been reluctant to reach an international agreement to limit the growth in these and other pollutants if doing so jeopardizes their national commercial interests. The U.S. government, for example, withdrew from such an agreement—the Kyoto agreement—in 2002, on the grounds that it might adversely affect profits and jobs in America.

On balance, it is probably safe to say that there is evidence of increasing globalization in the sense of worldwide interconnections on various dimensions—communications, financial transactions, trade, cultural flows, environmental problems, and so on. But these connections are uneven and unequal in their effects. And, in any case, there have been reactions against globalization. On the one hand, national governments and regional blocs have taken action to protect their interests, and on the other, social movements, including not just the antiglobalization movement but also local and religious movements, have arisen to protest globalization.

CONCLUSION

It is time to return to the question posed at the beginning of this chapter: Are we living through a social revolution, a transformation of the social order from one type of society to another? *Wired* magazine's famous five "poster children" were led to believe that they could "make a difference" and play a part in bringing about the digital revolution. Their hopes were dashed, but they still had faith that long-term changes were under way. As one of them said: "Tech is going to be around forever. It was overhyped a couple of years ago when magazines like *Fortune* said the Internet was going to change the world, and it's overhyped now when people say the whole economy is crashing. Who's to say things aren't going to get better next year?" (quoted in Hubler 2001: 2).

We live in a media-saturated culture that is described as postmodern because it has become increasingly difficult to avoid the hype and to judge what is really happening. It is an information society in the sense that we have access to vast quantities of information. The problem, however, is that we may be suffering from information overload. Futurologists have exploited this scenario by joining with the media to provide exciting stories of revolutionary social change, heralding a new type of society or a "new wave"—for example, Toffler's

Third Wave (1980). And sociologists have the task of carefully weighing the evidence and explaining where and to what extent long-term social changes are occurring. Sometimes the use of terms like *information society* can be helpful, by directing attention to significant changes; but they need to be qualified, in the sense of taking account of evidence of inequalities and reversals in these changes. Indeed, social sources of resistance to change as well as social movements influencing the course of change in a different direction can also be subjected to sociological analysis.

EXERCISES

EXERCISE 1

As noted in this chapter, a central question in research on social movements has to do with why people get involved in social movements. Have you ever participated in a social movement?

Why did you decide to join? How did you convince others to get involved? Describe the goals or desired outcome of this social movement. Which of the theories discussed in this chapter best explains its success or failure?

EXERCISE 2

Another important concept discussed in this chapter is *cultural lag*. This term refers to the gap that often exists between cultural practices and technological innovations. The failure of culture to keep up with science is often used to explain social conflict. Do you think that American society suffered cultural lag with the introduction of the Internet? Did the introduction of this technology raise new moral and legal questions?

STUDY QUESTIONS

1   What is the difference between evolutionary and revolutionary social change? Are they mutually exclusive? How is social revolution different from political revolution?

2   What are Alvin Toffler's three "waves" of social development? Briefly describe each of these stages by identifying its dominant form of economic production, its basis of wealth, and its social significance. Which stage are we in now?

3   What is Wilbert Moore's definition of *social change*? What are the advantages and disadvantages of this definition? Why is *social change* so difficult to define?

4   What two types of theories of social change emerged during the nineteenth century? Who are the major theorists associated with each theory? Which one describes development in terms of evolution, and which one in terms of revolution?

5   What events prompted the first attempts to explain social change in the nineteenth century? How were the first theories of social change criticized by sociologists of the twentieth century?

6   How did Karl Marx understand the role of the factory in modern capitalism? How did Max Weber understand the role of the manufacturing firm? Does the information society constitute a radical break from the modern society that these two theorists describe?

7   Name the three social spheres described by Daniel Bell. What is the axial principle of each sphere? According to Bell, what conflict characterized the transition to postmodernism?

8 Briefly describe Manuel Castells's three types of social movements and the corresponding identities generated in response to the globalization of information flows. Which one is he most optimistic about in terms of its ability to bring about substantial changes in the information society?

9 What are the key characteristics of a social movement? What is the difference between social movements and collective behavior?

10 What is the central insight of resource mobi-lization theory? Why is it considered a form of rational choice theory? What is the major problem with resource mobilization theory?

11 What is David Held's definition of *globalization*? What are the main criticisms of this definition and of globalization in general?

FURTHER READING

Eyerman, Ron, and Andrew Jamison. 1998. *Music and Social Movements: Mobilizing Traditions in the Twentieth Century*. New York: Cambridge University Press.

Langman, Lauren. 2005. "From Virtual Public Spheres to Global Justice: A Critical Theory of Internetworked Social Movements." *Sociological Theory* 23, no. 1: 42–74.

McAdam, Doug. 1996. *Comparative Perspectives on Social Movements: Political Opportunities, Mobilizing Structures, and Cultural Framings*. New York: Cambridge University Press.

Project for Excellence in Journalism Report. 2004.

"State of the News Media 2004: An Annual Report on American Journalism." Available online at http://www.stateofthenewsmedia.org/chartland.asp?id=323&ct=col&dir=&sort=&col1_box=1 (accessed July 31, 2005).

———. 2005. "State of the News Media 2005: An Annual Report on American Journalism." Table based on unpublished data from BIAfn MediaAccess Pro, available online at http:// www.biafn.com. Available online at http://www.stateofthenewsmedia.org/2005/chartland.asp?id=360&ct=col&dir=&sort=&col1_box=1&col2_box=1# (accessed January 16, 2006).

Ritzer, George. 2003. *The Globalization of Nothing*. Thousand Oaks, CA: Pine Forge Press.

Snow, David A., and Robert D. Benford. 1988. "Ideology, Frame Resonance, and Participant Mobilization." *International Social Movement Research* 1: 197–217.

Tilly, Charles. 1978. *From Mobilization to Revolution*. New York: McGraw-Hill.

U.S. Department of Labor. 2005. "Union Members Summary." USDL 05-112. Washington, DC: U.S. Bureau of Labor Statistics, Division of Labor Force Statistics. Available online at http://www.bls.gov/news.release/union2.nr0.htm (accessed July 31, 2005).

Webster, Frank. 2002. *Theories of the Information Society*. 2nd ed. Routledge.

The Occupy Wall Street Movement and Its Precursors

On the other side of the world, the outbreak of Occupy Wall Street (OWS) events throughout the United States also caught many people by surprise. The Occupy social movement that began in 2011 was motivated by both the Arab Spring mobilizations and the Indignados movement (introduced in this chapter), and it borrowed many of the strategies and tactics employed by both. Occupy Wall Street would eventually result in a mutation into a variety of different spinoff groups, and while the overall movement has been rather dormant since 2012, whether it will once again blossom is unknown at this point. This chapter highlights a few ways in which recent social movements like OWS can inform resource mobilization theory by showing how the Internet and social media now serve as key resources for social movement actors. It also raises theoretical questions regarding new organizational styles of social movement activity as allowed for through new media and how they help us to update and inform other traditional theories of social movements.

Both OWS and the Indignados movement were enabled by new technologies and displayed a distinct organizational structure that set them apart from previous forms of collective behavior that embrace contentious politics. Traditional social movements tended to rely more on a hierarchical model, professional experts, formal and well-established SMOs, and charismatic leaders, and they provided a clear set of grievances and demands as the cornerstone of their mobilization efforts. OWS and the Indignados relied instead on a more horizontal infrastructure of connectivity that broadened the public sphere as participants and supporters shared grievances through peer-to-peer networks and coordinated political action at the grassroots level through the use of ICTs, the grass-rooting of civil society

Victoria Carty, "The Occupy Wall Street Movement and Its Precursors," *Social Movements and New Technologies*, pp. 125-152. Copyright © 2015 by Taylor & Francis Group. Reprinted with permission.

(Castells 2001). The up-to-the-minute information sharing, organizing, and strategizing through new media facilitated both social movements in challenging their opponents. These two cases also demonstrate that it is now easier, cheaper, and faster for activists to get their message out, quickly reach a critical mass, and mobilize into a formidable political campaign, thus enhancing the explanatory power of theories of new media.

THE INDIGNADOS MOBILIZATION

To put OWS in perspective, we can first examine one of its key precursors, the Indignados movement, which coalesced in response to the global economic crisis that began in Europe and the austerity measures imposed by governments to address the financial fallout. The collective behavior against such measures originated in Spain with the M15 (May 15) movement and eventually became part of a broader, global movement. The organization began two weeks before the Spanish national elections in resistance to both of the two final candidates whom Spanish citizens feared would further the neoliberal agenda (rooted in economic policies that embrace privatization, deregulation, and cuts to social programs) that was currently in place (Amy Goodman 2012). More specific concerns were lack of political accountability among elected officials and their failure to represent citizen concerns, high levels of unemployment, cuts to public services, bank bailouts, and home foreclosures.

SOCIAL MEDIA AS ORGANIZATIONAL PLATFORM

In the spirit of the Tunisian and Egyptian revolutions, organizers of the Indignados movement, under the name Ya Democracia Real, called for an uprising via the #spanishrevolution hashtag on Twitter. Social media and the Internet provided the organizational platform after a few friends met in a local bar and shared their opinions about the dysfunctional political and economic systems in Spain (Baiocchi and Ganuza 2012). Truly grassroots in nature, and representative of what some scholars would refer to as a new social movement in terms of organizational structure (for example Melucci 1996; Giddens 1991), the participants were not affiliated with or supported by any political party or civic organization. As summed up by one of the protesters: "We are not a party. We are not a union. We are not an association. We are people. We want to expel corruption from public life … now, today, maybe something is starting to happen" (Amy Goodman 2012).

Resource mobilization theory can also provide a framework for understanding the development of the Indignados mobilization because it was the networking with other groups and building alliances that helped to launch the movement in both cyberspace and the real world.

For example, Indignados joined forces with Youth Without a Future (Juventud Sin Futuro) to put out calls on Twitter and Facebook for the original and then subsequent protests (Rainsford 2011). Dozens of groups gathered in fifty-eight cities throughout Spain to demonstrate, primarily against the lack of job opportunities. At the time Spain had a 21 percent unemployment rate and a youth unemployment rate of almost 50 percent (Escobar 2011).

This diagnostic framing served as a critique of the 2010 bank bailouts that coincided with cuts in social programs (Snow et al. 1986; Ryan and Gamson 2006). The first M15 protest framed their central concern with the slogan "we are not goods in the hands of politicians and bankers." Later, through frame amplification, the motivational framing expanded to broader issues under the tagline "without work, without home, without pension, without fear" under the umbrella slogan of "Youth without a Future." Signs also read, "If we can't dream, you won't sleep," demarcating the lack of hope among young citizens (Escobar 2011). Framing the problem as a structural one protesters chanted, "It's not a crisis, it's the system" and, in a more humorous tone, "It's not a crisis, I just don't love you anymore" (Burns 2012).

Other participants painted the word GUILTY on bank offices and ministries as they marched, using the tactic of visibly shaming their target. Additionally, though the initial mobilization was very much youth centered, the young activists used frame bridging to resonate with mainstream concerns held among the population at large. These included concerns about austerity measures and the lack of a safety net, increasing rates of unemployment, and a lack of transparency and legitimacy with the political system. This enhanced recruitment efforts and ultimately impacted public opinion in support of the movement, giving it legitimacy on the basis of proven WUNC (Tilly 2004).

Activists promoted several types of disruptive nonviolent tactics as the mobilization efforts progressed. To establish collective identity, activists marched and occupied public spaces for months. According to Ya Democracia Real, about 50,000 demonstrated in Madrid alone on May 15. After the march the activists carried out a sit-in on a busy street and were met with police violence. Twenty-four were arrested following the melee (El Mundo 2011). Another rally took place after the arrests in opposition to the police response, and about twenty remained to camp out in Madrid's main plaza, Puerta del Sol. They stayed overnight but were removed the next day.

Word spread about the occupation through the hashtag #acampadasol, and this fast-paced flow of information led to further political strategizing (Day and Cobos 2012). The following day two hundred people showed up in the square. After the police removed them once again, activists used Twitter and Facebook to call for another occupation the next evening. Two days later almost a thousand Spaniards occupied the plaza, which was followed by a judicial injunction against the encampment (Burns 2012). In retaliation, tens of thousands of Indignados marched in eighty different cities across Spain.

The movement quickly garnered international attention and support. In acts of global solidarity, demonstrations were held in London, Amsterdam, Brussels, Lisbon, and elsewhere. On

May 20 more than 10,000 camped out in Puerta Del Sol. In response to the police aggression intended to deter the protests on the next day, an estimated 20,000 showed up in solidarity (Silva 2012).

The squatters were soon accompanied by other tenters across Spain who gathered in Barcelona, Seville, and thirty other cities throughout the country in local acts of solidarity. The events were live-streamed on Ustream.tv as they unfolded, which served to enhance recruitment efforts (*EFE* 2011). Collective identity was easy to create and sustain, as youth initially made up the core of the contentious activities. However, because of the reality of the European economic crisis that was ravaging the lives Spaniards of all age brackets, the shared grievances provided a platform from which to extend collective identity among broad segments of the population regardless of age cohort.

Cultural theories and theories of new media give us a framework to analyze these events because it was new technology that helped to raise awareness about the mobilization, spread information through peer-to-peer channels, and recruit new members to the cause (Bennett and Iyengar 2008; Van Aelst and Walgrave 2003; Giugni 1998). Yet, similar to the Arab Spring mobilizations, the real difference happened on the streets, through the occupation of public spaces in local communities where activists forged strong ties after the initial weak ties were kindled in cyberspace and through virtual communities (McAdam and Paulsen 1993).

THE INDIGNADOS AS A NEW SOCIAL MOVEMENT

The Indignados mobilization also displayed elements of what some theorists classify as new social movements, operating in an ad hoc fashion and leaderless in nature (Melucci 1996; J. Cohen 1985). The one-day demonstration that the students orchestrated on May 15, which initiated the Indignados movement, quickly and spontaneously transitioned into open-ended sit-ins and a months-long self-governing encampment. This would serve as a template for a new type of communal resistance. Additionally, both the international and national support is representative of Tomlinson's (1999) distantiated identity.

The Indignados movement continued to press on as Spain's economic situation became worse. On February 19, 2012, hundreds of thousands protested across the nation in fifty-seven cities against economic reforms that would decrease workers' bargaining rights and social services. Long-established squatter networks joined forces with members of the M15 movement in protest of the hundreds of thousands of evictions that had taken place across the country beginning in 2011 and ending in 2012 (Burns 2012). This collaboration has led to highly effective "squatting offices" in major cities that coordinate information on empty buildings and offer consultations to people who want to squat. The movement right now is dormant, however, and there has been no visible activity since 2012.

Figure 10.1

A peaceful demonstration of several thousand Indignados in the Plaza Catalunya in Barcelona, the epicenter of the M15 movement.

Despite its now apparent inactivity, 8 million people claimed to have participated in at least one event hosted by the Indignados during the outbreak of activity in the streets (Day and Cobos 2012). As we will see later in the chapter, the Indignados' tactics were borrowed and implemented by occupiers in the United States, including using the Internet and social media tools as an organizational platform to propel the mobilizations and recruit new members across diffuse networks in both the virtual and real world. They also relied heavily on Twitter and Facebook to arrange meetings and facilitate online, and later offline, discussions and meetings to plan strategies. Similar to the Indignados uprising, OWS participants relied heavily on the device of framing to promote their agenda in a way that would resonate with mainstream concerns. Finally, the use of ad hoc civil disobedience through marches, sit-ins, rallies, occupying public spaces by means of tenting, and the relatively leaderless nature of the resistance were essential tactics that the US-based mobilizations emulated, representing what some scholars (in particular Melucci 1996) consider to be new social movements.

THE INDIGNADOS MOVEMENT SPREADS

Ten days after the Madrid protests began, the contagion of unrest spread to Greece. Sparked by similar economic factors as those Spain was experiencing, 80,000 citizens congregated in Athens's main square in June 2012 in opposition to the austerity measures proposed by the government. They waved banners in solidarity with the Indignados of Spain and other European countries (Ouziel 2011). Organizers used Facebook and other social media sites to organize the efforts. The Indignados then traveled to various city squares throughout Mexico to further engage in grassroots organizing. Combining new and old types of media and tactics, as well as cyberactivism and street protest, students collected proposals and suggestions, using blackboards to allow people to write their ideas or proposals, and then posting photos of the suggestions on social network sites and in street exhibitions (Bacon 2011).

In Mexico, they expressed grievances similar to those articulated in the Spanish and Greek outbreaks of collective behavior. Over 7 million young people in Mexico are unemployed, and the country has the third-highest rate of unemployment among fifteen- to twenty-nine-year-olds in member countries of the Organization of Economic Cooperation and Development. The Indignados in Mexico spent two months camping in front of the Mexican Stock Exchange following a forty-two-day hunger strike by university professor Edur Velasco, who set up a tent outside the building on October 11 (Appel 2011). He demanded that the government guarantee greater access to higher education among youth, and a few days later students and other activists joined him in setting up tents. Though there are many recent uprisings over the government's inability to curb the drug cartels, the Indignados movement in Mexico was particularly concerned with political corruption and lack of economic opportunities. It shows that physical forms of protest in real communities are the main driving force in struggles for social change, which are assisted in key ways by new information technologies and media.

MEXICAN SPRING

Then there was the Mexican Spring in preparation for the July 2012 presidential election. The organic uprising began at the elite Iberoamerican University on the day that Pena Nieto, the Institutional Revolutionary Party candidate, was scheduled to speak. After organizing through Facebook and Twitter, 20,000 marched in Mexico City, and thousands demonstrated in six other cities throughout Mexico shouting, "Down with Televisa" and, "This is not a soap opera" (Johnson 2012), in reference to Nieto's wife, who is in a telenovela soap opera on Televisa (Kennis 2012).

Highlighting the significance of the marches and the role social media played in their organization and turnout through horizontal information exchanges among peer networks, one high school student explained, "This is the digital age, and you don't find out about leaders appearing on the television; you hear about it from the Internet and your friends on line" (Kennis 2012). This statement also illustrates the tendency of contemporary social movements to forego vanguards or spokespersons and their often-sporadic nature (Melucci 1996).

One of the biggest demonstrations, consisting of about 10,000 Mexicans, took place outside of the headquarters of Televisa. Cognizant of the significance of the public sphere as an arena to shape common perceptions, the main complaint was the unfair media coverage provided by the two main TV stations, Televisa and TV Azteca. Together, the two stations have a 95 percent Mexican media share, and protesters claimed that both manipulated the information through coverage biased in favor of Nieto. Participants insisted that the mobilization was nonpartisan and targeted only the television monopolies. These concerns, having a free exchange of ideas at the grassroots level without state or market control, are at the crux of certain new social movement theories. Nieto accused students of being dupes of the leftist candidate, Andres Manuel Lopez Obrador. The media labeled the contentious activities a conspiracy. In fact, Televisa reported that "they didn't look like Ibero students," "they are anti-democratic," and "they had to be paid protesters" (Kennis 2012).

Mexico's largest newspaper chain, El Sol, also assisted the state by claiming external infiltrators were behind the disruptions. To counteract these accusations, supporters of the cause put out a call on Facebook pleading for student support. Minutes after the message was posted, a response showed up on the student's screen that had sent the message saying, "We have 131," that 131 students responded to the original student who put out the call (Molina 2012). In a showcase of how quickly challengers can respond to attempts at elite repression given new media platforms, the Indignados posted a YouTube video that displayed the 131 students who participated in the demonstrations flashing their student ID cards. The video had more than a million hits and served as a great recruitment tool to get more students involved in the protest activity.

Students then created the hashtag #YoSoy132 on Twitter that exploded in popularity and led to the creation of a campaign and a social movement called Yo Soy 132, meaning that they surpassed the original number of 131. They also created a website to announce future planned marches. The evening before the election, Yo Soy 132 organized the largest student march since the infamous 1968 student protests advocating for democracy in the Tlatelolco Plaza that resulted in a brutal massacre by the authorities. Online activity spread onto the streets as protesters gathered on July 2 to continue with their demands regarding economic and political corruption and more precisely to rebel against El Sol's allegations that they were outside agitators. To succinctly frame the issue and foster collective identity among challengers, protesters held signs stating, "If there's an imposition, there will be revolution. Isn't that what we said?" (Molina 2012). These are the primary variables that cultural and sociological theorists, such as Ryan and Gamson (2006), point to.

The tech-savvy Mexican youth also employed digital technology to support their cause during their election itself. Prior to the election the Indignados, with the help of mojos, circulated a video that asked citizens to observe the polling stations, record instances of fraud with their video cameras or cellphones, and send them the official Yo Soy 132 e-mail address (Molina 2012). On July 5 the site showed clips revealing people receiving prepaid supermarket cards from the Nieto staff in exchange for their vote, among other violations. The Yo Soy Observer Commission received more than 1,000 reports of irregularities. Thus, new media and the capabilities they offer to hold authorities accountable and expose corruption is something that resource mobilization theory can include in these activists' repertoire of contention.

Additionally, these documented observations challenged the official narrative put forth by the state and the mainstream media. The unrest continued after the election, as much of the population was convinced that it was corrupt, a claim supported by international election observers (Molina 2012). Though Mexico is infamous for electoral fraud, this was the first time citizens organized collectively to fight what has typically been viewed as business as usual.

Mexican agitators engaged in more contentious politics on July 7 when they occupied many public plazas throughout the country and put out a call for international supporters to demonstrate outside of Mexican embassies. In Mexico City more than 90,000 marched to the chant of "No to imposition!" Activists in the Indignados movement also successfully translated their original grievances of the high cost of education and unfair media coverage to broader political issues of corruption and economic injustice at the societal level as the cause gained traction through frame amplification (e.g., Snow et al. 1986). Dignity became the rallying cry. One member of the Yo Soy 132 movement explained, "We should continue organizing and fighting for the country that we want, but first we must regain our dignity, become indignant, and transform this country" (Molina 2012). On July 7 and 8, Yo Soy 132 held a National Summit of Students to strategize for the future.

The main goal was to seek out allies among other SMOs to establish horizontal links, and both work in conjunction with active groups and organize dormant sectors of civil society. These include groups working on issues of human rights, education, social violence, indigenous rights, public health, environmental issues, freedom of speech and equal access to media, gender issues, and cultural issues. Through these efforts they have linked with international groups in more than thirty countries including the UK, Spain, Italy, Canada, China, the United States, Portugal, and Argentina (yosoy132.wordpress.com). This too is symbolic of how new social movements operate—at the grassroots level, without recognizable representatives, and forging alliances with other groups through frame bridging and frame amplification. Yet again, as resource mobilization points out, and though we are witnessing different types of organizational structures and forms of connectivity that digital technology enables, traditional SMOs and forms of organizing are still an important resource for sustained social and political mobilizations.

The Indignados in Europe and Mexico were harbingers of the subsequent Occupy Wall Street movement in the United States. The declining US economic conditions and the shared grievance of a lack of political representation by elected officials helped to spark this social movement. Below we will examine the underlying frustrations that led to the mobilization; the strategies and tactics that activists applied; how they framed their issues, forged collective identity, and created networks of resistance with other allies; and how activists utilized digital tools to initiate and sustain the campaign, as well as the consequences of Occupy Wall Street.

OCCUPY WALL STREET IN THE UNITED STATES

Both the Arab Spring and the Indignados movement sparked revolution across the United States in the fall of 2011. Then–New York mayor Michael Bloomberg anticipated this occurrence because the declining economic conditions in the United States were hitting youth particularly hard: "You have a lot of kids graduating college, can't find jobs. That's what happened in Cairo. That's what happened in Madrid. You don't want those kinds of riots here" (Einhorn and Siemasko 2011). The members of OWS did not riot in the United States, but tens of thousands did orchestrate and maintain ongoing protests, demonstrations, and encampments across the country. Similar to most contemporary social movements, OWS activists organized using digital technologies that allowed them to circumvent professional experts, charismatic leaders, or formal SMOs. Instead, they shared grievances and planning strategies in a horizontal fashion through new media to quickly and cheaply get the word out about their campaign and reach a critical mass.

The OWS social movement was made up of an assortment of activists. Many were young, many had been foreclosed upon, and many were unemployed or underemployed. Though left-leaning, they were not officially associated with any political party yet shared a concern for the current economic and political predicament in the United States. Though they worked cooperatively, the various groups were only loosely connected and had no central leadership or spokesperson. The lack of any central form of leadership or concise diagnostic frame was a strategic tactic because it welcomed inclusivity and participatory democracy and was an enhancement of the public sphere. This, in turn, opened up avenues for alliances with other advocacy groups that would prove critical to the sustainability of Occupy Wall Street in various formats once the tenters were decamped.

Under the rubric of the We Are the 99 Percent campaign, Occupy participants began discussions about the essential nature of the political and economic systems that they participate in and thus help legitimize. The US economic and political climate was ripe for protest at the time. For example, at the start of the 2008 recession, the collective wealth of the richest 1 percent of Americans was greater than that of the 99 percent combined. The United States now has the largest concentration of wealth since 1928 and is the most unequal of any industrialized country. While CEOs' compensation rose 36 percent during 2010, wages stagnated for the rest of the population, and people were losing their homes at alarming rates because of Ponzi schemes carried out by the major banks (Sherter 2011).

In September 2011 the OWS campaign swept across the country with hundreds of occupations in various forms. The first to take place was the occupation of physical spaces including parks, plazas, and public spaces outside of federal buildings. These forms of nonviolent civil disobedience resulted in more than 7,000 arrests in 114 cities as citizens engaged in large-scale disruptive activities that have been absent in this country for decades (OccupyArrests.com). It only took a few months (in some cases weeks), however, for most tenters to be forcibly removed by the police. After the disencampments, participants in OWS found other venues through which they could continue their protest activities.

In many popular accounts OWS is portrayed as a spontaneous, youthful unleashing of collective behavior that seemed to come from nowhere. The reality is somewhat different. The roots of OWS first began in July 2011 when the soon-to-be occupiers (mostly young and with little social movement experience) met with veterans and organizers of the Indignados (Milkman, Lewis, and Luce 2013). Resource mobilization theory (McCarthy and Zald 1973) addresses how both leaders and formal organizations, in addition to media attention, are key requisites for successful and sustained social movement activity, thus giving us a lens through which to evaluate and make sense of the origins of OWS.

A case in point is that it took the large-scale protests against Wisconsin Governor Scott Walker and the events of the Arab Spring to begin the planning of the protests in the United States. Another misconception is that Occupy was born on the Internet (similar assumptions have been made about the Arab Spring, both of which have been dubbed the "Facebook Revolution" by some journalists). This is also false. In the aftermath of these initial meetings with OWS, planners held a conference encouraging people to meet at a park near Wall Street to begin the more formal and broader strategy of mobilization. The encampments were also inspired by the Canadian magazine *Adbusters* when the editors put out a call to occupy Wall Street in their July edition. The ad asked, "WHAT IS OUR ONE DEMAND? #OCCUPYWALLSTREET SEPTEMBER 17. BRING TENT" (Milkman, Lewis, and Luce 2013). The same message was sent to the 900,000 people on its listserv. Taking a cue from Arab Spring, *Adbusters* also sent out an e-mail that read, "America needs its own Tahrir," and on July 4 it tweeted, "Dear Americans, this July 4 dream of insurrection against corporate rule." On August 30 the hacktivist group Anonymous (discussed in Chapter 2), released a video in support of this call, urging its members to "flood lower Manhattan, set up tents, kitchens, peaceful barricades and Occupy Wall Street."

SOCIAL MEDIA FUELS THE FLAMES

A distinguishing characteristic of the Occupy movements that parallels the Indignados and the Arab Spring uprisings was that revolutionary communication tools and mobile techno-logical devices enabled citizens across the United States to break out of their isolation, raise awareness of the issues that concerned them, and take their rage onto the streets in a collective cause. The recognition that they were not alone by sharing their stories through new media, on the streets, and in the camps imbued citizens with a sense of agency. Tumblr.com was instrumental in sparking the protests by publishing the "We are the 99 percent" blog: personal stories of lost jobs, lost homes, crippling debt, and a lack of government support or accountability (Jacobs 2011). This sharing of stories and grievances aided in constructing a sense of collective identity through weak ties that become strong ties (McAdam and Paulsen

Figure 10.2

A young man meditates amid the Occupy Wall Street demonstration near the
New York Stock Exchange on September 21, 2011, in New York City.

1993; Boulainne 2009). Bimber's (2003) accelerated pluralism accounts for the broadening
formats for political discussions, communicative action, and the public sphere in general.
Theories of the Internet, therefore, are pertinent to an analysis of this outbreak of collective
behavior.

The "We are the 99 Percent" slogan summarized the main motivational frame and further
helped to solidify collective identity among participants in the movement. This framing technique also made reference to the sheer numbers of those affected by the growing inequality, thus
dramatizing the cause. Additionally, the OWS movement's use of framing was unique because
participants did not make specific demands but wanted collectively, through dialogue and debate, to create an alternative to the current economic and political systems. Some of the signs
that reflected this sentiment, again relying on the tactic of clever framing (while injecting humor),
were "Wake Up From the American Dream. Create a Livable American Reality," "Lost my Job
Found an Occupation," and "Dear Capitalism, It's not You it's Us. Just Kidding, It's You" (occupy-

wallstreet.org). These injustice frames are something that constructionist theories promote as being effective in drawing in new recruits, creating sympathy for a cause and swaying public opinion, and ultimately creating social change).

OWS was also characterized by a yearning for new ways of living by establishing novel types of relationships and ways of interacting, which is emphasized by certain schools of thought in new social movement theory (e.g., Johnston 1994). For example, general assemblies were held in the spirit of what this new system might look like. The assemblies were open to the public with the intention of giving everyone a voice in the decision-making process (Jennifer Preston 2011b). The goal was to foster genuine communicative action, or in Habermas's terms, "ideal speech situations," and to open the public sphere to individuals oftentimes excluded. There were other concrete forms of creating community as well: basic needs like food, shelter, medical care, sanitation, security, education, and culture were handled by working groups, copying the organizational structure of the Indignados encampments in Spain and Tahrir Square in Egypt, as well as the earlier occupation of the State Capitol in Madison, Wisconsin. By borrowing these tactics, OWS demonstrated that social movements tend to build on strategies that have proven successful in the past and that this replication provides an important resource for social movement actors.

2.0 TECHNOLOGY SUSTAINS OCCUPY

Digital technology was a driving force behind the OWS campaign because the shared stories provided citizens with a sociological imagination—an understanding that their personal problems were rooted in social issues and structural flaws in the economic and political systems. In addition to Tumblr there were dozens of wikis and web pages where citizens could further engage in the discussions and planning of Occupy Wall Street.

Three of the most popular websites were howToOccupy.org, take thesquare.net, and especially OccupyWallst.org, which raised thousands of dollars from dozens of groups and hundreds of individuals and provided food, shelter, and gas mask protection to occupiers (Jennifer Preston 2011b). While ICTs are clearly changing some aspects of collective behavior and contentious politics, which resource mobilization theory now must take into account, traditional resources are still relevant. To organize the various protests, activists also used Meetup.com and Foursquare, two location services that people can download and use on their cellular devices to track schedules of marches, location changes, and alternative routes (Glantz 2011).

Online activity quickly translated into interest, motivation, and street activity. On September 17 about 1,000 people gathered to occupy the financial district in New York City. One week later they undertook an unpermitted march that began at Zuccotti Park (renamed Liberty Plaza by the occupiers), and the number of participants soared to more than 2,500 as marchers made their way through the streets of Lower Manhattan (Moynihan 2011). Riot police met the demonstrators, and, in the first incident of police violence, a commander was filmed pepper-spraying in the face women standing on a public sidewalk after being "kettled" along with many others (the term kettled refers to ordering protesters to disperse but using orange nets to capture small groups of demonstrators in isolated spaces with no escape route).

The video of these women falling to the ground and screaming in pain went viral, promoting anger and triggering sympathy and support for the activists. Thus, the aggression used by the police authorities backfired and gave the mobilization a boost in terms of recruitment, sympathy, media coverage, and shaming the target of resistance. At the end of the assembly, a total of eighty protesters had been arrested (Moynihan 2012). In yet another instance the public, on-the-ground mobilization efforts of activists in circulating these images was key.

The next major event occurred on October 1 when 700 activists were arrested on the Brooklyn Bridge for blocking traffic (Pilkington 2011). This resulted in a class-action lawsuit against the New York Police Department, and after the mass arrest several major labor movements endorsed the occupiers. Service Employees International Union organizers and healthcare workers' Local 1199 in Manhattan, for example, not only marched and camped out with the occupiers in the park but also delivered blankets, ponchos, food, and water to help them sustain the encampment. This fit well with one of the most common signs that were visible throughout Zuccotti Park which read, "Compassion is our new currency," a good example of how the successful framing of issues can foster and nurture collective identity and propel social movement activity. The assistance of formal organizations in terms of resources and strategic alliances most strongly emphasized by resource mobilization theory and to a lesser extent by political process theory.

Another example of compassion under the umbrella of solidarity in action was when a call for pizza went out and $2,600.00 worth arrived in less than an hour. Wisconsin's state house was supplied with pizza in a similar fashion, including some paid for and dispatched by Egyptian revolutionaries (Solnit 2012). These cross-national and international networks of support could not have happened without digital media, which underscores the importance of cross-fertilization among organizational supporters as a key resource for timely social movements.

THE ROLE OF TRADITIONAL, ALTERNATIVE, AND SOCIAL MEDIA

On November 16 police moved in and cleared Zuccotti Park. Acknowledging the importance of media coverage and its critical role in the public sphere and civil society in exposing wrongdoing by the authorities, police attempted to make filming of the event difficult if not impossible through physical obstruction and "frozen zones." In this way they prevented even credentialed journalists from entering the area (Julia Preston 2012b) under the guise of security (for their own personal safety). However, activists got around police obstacles by live-streaming the events from their cell phones, and a live chat window ran alongside the video player of both

Livestream and Upstream which allowed users to comment on events as they unfolded (Stelter 2011). The Occupystream.com site also provided links to real-time online streams following OWS and protests abroad. There were more than seven hundred Occupy-related channels, 70 percent of the live-streaming content was created on mobile phones, and 89 percent of it viewed on mobile phones (Jennifer Preston 2011a). Thus, through novel technological devices activists circumvented the dominant institutions to voice their concerns and organize their agenda in an example of Mann's (2000) interstitial locations. This is a critical component of new social movements and is what Habermas (1993, 1989) would consider an invaluable asset in ordinary citizens' attempt to regain control over the public sphere and aspects of communicative action. It is also demonstrative of Melucci's (1996) intermediate public space through which individuals can politicize issues through dialogue outside of the influence of authorities. It is also indicative of Castells's (2001) grassrooting of civil society. Therefore, theories of new media provide a good lens for understanding and analyzing the developments of Occupy Wall Street.

Additionally, throughout the encampments New York City organizers continuously updated Livestream news in the form of videos and photos onto the Twitter account, #OccupyWallST, with more than 90,000 followers and liked by more than 300,000 Facebook users worldwide (Saba 2011). There were also more than one hundred accounts on Twitter pertaining to Occupy Wall Street with tens of thousands of followers that collaborated under the hashtag #OWS. The main account, @occupywallstnyc had more than 100,000 followers (Kelley 2011).

#Occupy and #occupywallstreet hashtags organized events through websites such as Occupytogether.com. YouTube also helped to keep the Occupy Wall Street movement sustainable. There were 1.7 million You-Tube videos tagged with the key word "occupy" in YouTube's news and politics section that were viewed 72 million times (Berkowitz 2011). There were also more than four hundred Facebook pages for Occupy and 2.7 million fans around the world (Jennifer Preston 2011a). Protester Craig Juedlman posted a photo of his bruised face on Facebook containing the message, "just got punched in the face like 5 times by NYPD … guess they saw my earlier post" (Berkowitz 2011). Similar to the Arab Spring, the brutality exercised by the authorities only provoked more activists to join the protests out of a sense of compassion and empathy under the rubric of Jasper and Polletta's (2001) perceived shared status, or feeling of collective identity, thus once again giving relevance to cultural theories to make sense of how the events of OWS transpired.

In one of the cleverest challenges to police attempts to suppress leaks, activist Tim Pool acquired a Parrot AR drone, which can be purchased (cheaply) on Amazon.com, that he named the "occucopter" (Sharkey and Knuckey 2011). It is controlled with an iPhone and has an onboard camera, which Pool modified to stream live video to the Internet. This increased support for the social movement actors because the police and other authorities had a more difficult time manipulating the narrative to discredit the dissenters in yet another example of how new technology is expanding Habermas's idea of the public sphere and of participatory democracy.

Protests and acts of civil disobedience continued on December 17 outside of the World Financial Center, whose owner, Brookfield Property, also owns Zuccotti Park. On New Years' Eve OWS called for Occupy 2012 in an attempt to retake Zuccotti Park. What began peacefully turned into a mêlée when protesters breached the park's barricades and police arrested several people. On the six-month anniversary of the first occupation, on March 17, police arrested dozens more in Zuccotti after hundreds gathered following a march (Moynihan 2012).

The police, it turns out, have not completely escaped accountability. For example, in April 2013 Michael Premo, a longtime housing activist was found innocent of charges of assaulting a police officer because of the work of a mojo. Premo was arrested in 2011 when he, with other members of OWS, tried to occupy a vacant lot in lower Manhattan. When police prevented them from doing so, they began a march and were subsequently kettled. The video taken by the amateur journalist clearly showed the officer tackling Premo as he tried to get up after falling down during the skirmish (Kane 2013).

Thus, while resource mobilization usually acknowledges the role of the media in terms of gaining access to mainstream media, mojos turn this dynamic on its head. Access to, and utilization of, new digital tools gives contemporary activists leverage that social movement organizers and participants did not have in the past. This is one of the ways in which theories that account for the role of new media can nicely supplement resource mobilization theory in understanding OWS.

THE AGENDA DIVERSIFIES

As the movement developed, OWS participants shifted their priorities from forming outdoor, self-sustaining communities and holding general assemblies to focus on more concrete issues such as the housing crisis, lack of regulation of the financial system, and the sharp increase in student debt (discussed in the depth in the next chapter). One spin-off group, Occupy Our Homes, for example, has occupied homes of families facing eviction, hoping to get media attention by humanizing and dramatizing the evictions. It has had numerous successes in warding off foreclosures and evictions throughout New York City (Anderson 2011).

Another subgroup, Occupy Wall Street New York, has also held what they label "move your money relays." In March 2012 activists began escorting people from Bank of America branches, where members closed out their accounts and transferred their money into community banks and local credit unions. Supporters of the cause created a website called FTheBanks.org, which provided instructions for transferring money, as well as information regarding when collective efforts to do so were taking place. On another front, the Fight BAC (Bank of America campaign) went nationwide after being advertised on the alternative news provider *AlterNet.org*. During "Move Your Money," or "Bank Transfer Day," activists helped more than 40,000 Americans remove their money from large banks, and more than 65,000 citizens switched to credit unions in October alone (Maharawal 2012). Religious groups moved $55 million out of the Bank of America by November 2012, and a San Francisco interfaith group moved $10 million from Wells Fargo in observance of Lent.

OCCUPY OAKLAND

Occupy Oakland was the most violent of all the encampments. The first clash between activists and police occurred on October 15 and gained international attention when an eighty-four-year-old retired schoolteacher was pepper-sprayed at the encampment at Frank Ogawa Plaza and the image went viral over YouTube. Five of the participants were arrested for camping violations (Ash 2012). After police cleared the camp, many of those who were ejected planned a street march for later that afternoon in protest of the closure. When approximately 30,000 protesters tried to re-establish the encampment, another confrontation resulted. This massive and spontaneous show of support was made possible by information sharing through the Internet.

Two days later several videos circulated showing a protester being punched in the face at the follow-up demonstration by a deputy inspector. Once again the police attempted to clear the area, only to have demonstrators come out in even larger numbers, thus setting in motion a cycle of protest, violence, and retaliation through bigger and bigger demonstrations. Outrage only escalated when Iraq marine veteran Scott Olsen was badly injured after being hit by a projectile dispersed by the police (Ash 2012). The peer-to-peer distribution of information helped build collective identity and frame the grievances in a way that would disgrace certain members of the police force.

For example, the Occupyoakland.com website consistently and thoroughly provided details about the events as they unraveled. One thread, regarding the raid on the park read: "this morning at 5 am over 500 police in riot gear from cities all over central CA brutally attacked the Occupy Oakland encampment … the police attacked the peaceful protest with flash grenades, tear gas and rubber bullets after moving in with armored vehicles" (Seltzer 2011). Dramatizing the events in an attempt to sway public opinion is a main concern of political mediation theory (Soule and King 2006).

Allies across national borders also developed, made possible by digital technology. For example, in a display of international solidarity and collective identity, Egyptian activists held a march from Tahrir square to the US Embassy in Cairo to show support for the Occupy Wall Street actors. Within the United States protesters marched in Manhattan, for instance, chanting, "New York is Oakland, Oakland is New York" in solidarity (Nir and Flegenheimer 2012).

Calls to regroup after the raid went out over Twitter immediately, as did a call to e-mail the office of the mayor with complaints. A few weeks later, on November 2, more than 5,000 people watched the Oakland Police Department raid during a one-day general strike that activists held, thanks to mojos distributing the images virally (Romney 2012). More than 10,000 protesters shut down the port (which is the fifth busiest in the United States). One resource that enhanced the efforts of the insurgents was the organizational support that helped build and sustain the infrastructure of the movement. Prior to the strike Occupy Oakland began networking with one of the strongest trade unions, the International Longshoreman and Warehouse Union, which became a key ally and helped with recruitment efforts (Romney 2012). Working in conjunction with allies and formal organizations of course is one of the important variables that enhances political struggle according to resource mobilization theory.

Following the raid the Occupy Oakland website encouraged activists to fight back stating, "Reconvene today at 4pm at the Oakland Library on 14 and Madison" (Romney 2012). That evening there was a second confrontation following a rally at the Oakland Public Library. The battle continued on December 12 in a second general strike, fortifying collective identity. Thousands of OWS protesters blocked access to several major West Coast ports from San Diego to Anchorage in synchronized demonstrations. This brought work to a standstill in Oakland, California, Longview, Washington, and Portland, Oregon (Romney 2012). A diagnostic frame on one sign read, "Sorry for any inconvenience while we fix our democracy."

City Hall was shut down a few days after the general strike when two dozen Occupy Oakland protesters tried to storm the building. Members of Occupy Oakland's interfaith coalition had called for protesters to take over the mayor's and city administrators' offices after police arrested twelve in Frank Ogawa Plaza the day before in an attempt at another encampment (Gwynne 2012). On January 28, four hundred people were arrested once again outside of City Hall after police engaged in a mass kettling maneuver. In fact, they were waiting in riot gear before the activists arrived, declaring they were alerted by media sites that described the actions as "antipolice." This exemplifies how digital technology can be both detrimental as well as helpful to activists' mobilizing strategies, as Hindman (2007) warns.

There are other examples that demonstrate how the authorities are also quite savvy in using new technology in counteractions to contentious politics. Members of the Oakland Police Department, for example, collected photos of occupiers at demonstrations and sought out those individuals at subsequent protests, specifically protesters with prior arrests. In one instance on January 4, an Occupy Oakland media committee photographer, Adam Katz, was singled out by the police. He had been arrested while filming the raid of the disencampments and charged with obstruction of justice. He contended, "Officers who knew my name, and knew that I took pictures, deliberately went after me and arrested me under completely false pretenses." In another occurrence, during a January 15 general assembly in the

Figure 10.3

During Occupy Oakland, information shared online helped to build collective identity and frame grievances to disgrace certain members of the police force. © Steve Rhodes/Demotix/Corbis.

plaza, police approached an occupier and showed him his photo in a book they had and informed him that they knew he was on probation (Cagle 2012).

OCCUPY EVENTS IN OTHER CITIES

While the mass arrests in New York and Oakland received most of the media attention, in large part because of the violence that occurred, other actions took place from coast to coast across the United States that received less notice. All in all, more than 1,600 cities were occupied during Occupy Wall Street (Barsoumian 2011). Occupy Los Angeles was one of the most peaceful of the occupy movements and among the least disruptive disencampments. In fact, the mayor initially welcomed the encampment outside of City Hall and on a rainy day handed out ponchos to the campers, and the Los Angeles City Council adopted a resolution in support of the movement (Wilson 2011). Police looked on passively until the camp was cleared in April, purportedly because of health and safety concerns, as declared by the city. Though the camp was cleared, the initial receptivity afforded activists time and space to raise awareness, gain visibility and media attention, and debate issues both informally among campers and more formally in the general assembly meetings.

In July 2012 activists pushed the boundaries of more traditional tactics and regathered to hold a "Chalk Walk" in direct response to people being charged with felony vandalism for writing political messages on sidewalks (much of this outside of major banks). In the "free chalk for free speech" event, organizers handed out chalk to passersby, warning them that they may be arrested for writing on the sidewalk (Ebright, Castelan, and White 2012). This tactic can be viewed as a way to augment the public sphere that allows for free expression of political ideas and sentiments—literally "free." Many made chalk drawings and were arrested, and police used tear gas, rubber bullets, and batons to disperse the crowd, in some ways recalling the regimes in the Arab Spring countries that tried to block the Internet and social media to stifle free speech, which was viewed as a threat to the status quo.

INTERNATIONAL SOLIDARITY FACILITATED BY DIGITAL PLATFORMS

After the tent evictions across the United States, the Coalition for the Political Rights of Mexicans Abroad, which is part of the Indignados movement, sent a letter of support to OWS activists under attack. It declared, "We greet your movement because your struggle against the suppression of human rights and against social and economic injustice has been a fundamental part of our struggle, that of the Mexican people who cross borders and the millions of Mexican migrants who live in the United States" (Bacon 2012). In an effort to bolster future transnational collaborative efforts in the Occupy struggle there has been much online activity to try to establish a shared, yet loose, agenda. Recently, an international assembly consisting of members of Occupy groups on all six continents released a declaration of intent. The meeting was held online and included thousands more over e-mail. The statement emphasized that it is both a work in progress and that it represents a global movement. It was distributed publicly for more input and suggestions (*AlterNet* 2012).

Alvaro Rodriguez of the Indignados movement in Spain and one of the drafters of the statement elaborates:

> This is the beginning of a new global process of bringing the opinions of many people around the world together. It represents the beginnings of a form of global democracy in its infancy which is direct and participatory—of the people, by the people, and for the people. While the statement does not represent the position of local and city assemblies, the next

step is to present it to assemblies around the world for consideration, discussion and revisions, as part of a dialogue of the "Global Spring" movements taking place across six continents. ... The process of writing the statement was consensus based, open to all, and regularly announced on our international communication platforms, that are also open to all (e.g. the "squares" mailing list, the weekly global roundtables and the "international" Face-book group).

In a statement printed in the *Guardian* on October 25 and circulated in cyberspace, one Egyptian activist wrote,

To all of those across the world currently occupying parks, squares and other spaces, your comrades in Cairo are watching you in solidarity. Having received so much advice from you about transitioning to democracy, we thought it's our turn to pass on some advice ... As the interests of government increasingly cater to the interest and comforts of private, transnational capital, our cities and homes have become progressively more abstract and violent places, subject to the casual ravages of the next economic development or urban renewal scheme. An entire generation across the globe has grown up realizing, rationally and emotionally that we have no future in the current order of things."(*Guardian* 2011)

This international collaboration, which is leading to a sense of collective identity that crosses borders, is possible only through the use of new media tools, especially considering how quickly and efficiently it was being organized in a decentralized fashion. This gives us notice of the relevance of theories of new media in affecting social change. This cross-national sense of solidarity also gives support to theories of new social movements (Giddens 1991; Tomlinson 1999; Johnston 1994).

CONCLUSION

Although it is a bit difficult to generalize across the various Occupy events and settings, and although the political and theoretical ramifications are yet to be sorted out, there are some notable achievements secured by OWS as a social movement. In addition to the global fermenting of organizational networking, the movement has altered the media and political narrative about economic inequality in the United States. A Pew Research Center survey of 2,048 adults, for instance, found that 66 percent of Americans now believe there are "very

---

_____ THEORY TOOLKIT _____

THEORY TOOL KIT TO UNDERSTAND OCCUPY WALL STREET

We can apply a few of the theories discussed in Chapter 1 to the emergence and evolution of Occupy Wall Street:

- **Political mediation theory.** The OWS social movement, though now dormant, showed the relevance of political mediation theory by altering the conversation about and impacting public opinion on class inequality in the United States.

- **Theories of new media.** These theories are also relevant to understanding how ICTs helped to influence the mainstream media to cover the story and therefore raise awareness about the grievances of the occupiers. New media is transforming contentious politics, as evidenced in OWS's peer-to-peer online sharing of images and video captured by mojos of the often violent reaction by the authorities, which helped the OWS participants to sustain their cause, at least for a while. Incorporating these theories of new media with culturally oriented theories of social movements shows how collective identity can emerge in cyberspace and result in the spillover effect on the streets.

- **New social movement theories.** Certain aspects of these theories are also important in making sense of the OWS encampments. These encampments were decentralized and leaderless organizational structures that operated in a more horizontal fashion in terms of power sharing and decision making, made up of citizens attempting to have a stronger voice in determining how the political, economic, and social spheres should function.

---

strong" or "strong" conflicts between the rich and poor, a 19 percent increase from 2009. Thirty percent say there are "very strong conflicts" between poor people and rich people—double the proportion that offered that view in July of 2009 (_Common Dreams_ 2011).

This shift in attitude is partially a consequence of the media coverage that OWS activists secured. For example, the word "protest" appeared in newspapers and online exponentially more in 2011 than at any other time (Power 2011). A LexisNexis search showed that US newspapers published 409 stories with the word "inequality" in October 2010. In October 2011 it swelled to 2,269. In October 2010 there were 452 stories that covered issues of greed, as opposed to 2,285 in 2011 (Heuvel 2012). Also in October the Nexis news-media database registered almost 500 mentions of "inequality" each week; the week before OWS started there were only 91, and there was a seven-fold increase in Google searches for the term "99 percent" between September and October (Stelter 2011).

Other analyses by Pew Research Center's Project for Excellence in Journalism found that the Occupy Wall Street movement accounted for 10 percent of national news coverage in the week of October 9 and 10 percent of the mainstream media's news coverage in the week of October 10 to 16 (Pew Research Center 2011). In November _Time_ magazine ran a cover story entitled

"What Ever Happened to Upward Mobility?" (Foroohar 2011). In January the *New York Times* ran a piece on mobility and inequality in today's America as well as a front-page story entitled "Harder for Americans to Rise from the Lower Rungs" (Blackwell 2012).

In addition to other factors and resources, ICTs helped to influence this shift in the national narrative and propelled the mainstream media to cover these issues, which until the OWS uprising had ignored for the most part. It was the online organizing and information sharing that got people onto the streets, which increased the visibility of the encampments. Supporters of OWS garnered the attention of the mainstream press, swayed public opinion in their favor, and increased momentum because mojos distributed the episodes of unprovoked violence by the authorities against nonviolent protesters. Though at first mainstream media either ignored or trivialized the mobilization, the spillover effect onto the streets facilitated by ICTs forced mainstream journalists to report on the happenings and take OWS, and the grievances of the participants, seriously.

The events of OWS show that online activity not only informs individuals about certain events but also motivates people into action in certain circumstances and thus serves as a hybrid of online and offline participation in political causes. Therefore, theories of new media are well suited to comprehend OWS because they suggest that collective identity can be established, at least originally, through weak ties in cyberspace and can lead to activity in the real world to forge a stronger sense of collective identity in tangible community settings.

This analysis can also help to update resource mobilization theory by taking into account the new digital tools that activists have in their current repertoire of contention. It expands the ways we can envision political openings as discussed by the political process model. Furthermore, the ambitions and formations of the encampments fit within the contours of theories of new social movements, which focus on democratizing new areas of social life and allowing for marginalized voices to be heard through horizontal chains of communication. The communities that were created and maintained (albeit short lived) in the occupation of public spaces were intentionally designed for this—to allow for dialogue and to foster new ideas about how to reclaim citizens' role in political, economic, and social life.

DISCUSSION QUESTIONS

1 In what ways did the Arab Spring, the Indignados, the Mexican Spring, and the Wisconsin battle lead to Occupy Wall Street? Do some research and update what is happening now for each of these cases. What theories best apply to recent developments? Do you agree that leaderless social movements are a good strategy for activists to employ? Make a case for and against this new development with specific examples not addressed in this book.

2 What role did mojos play in sustaining the causes that this chapter describes? Summarize how they are playing critical roles in other social movements through your own independent research.

3 How was the emergence of OWS misrepresented in some popular accounts? Compare and contrast how the media distorted outbreaks of contentious politics in this situation to other social movements.

4 Track further mutations of OWS. What is going on now in your local community in terms of Occupy events, issues, or discussions?

The Role of Social Movements

S ocial movements have a major impact on our world. Often for better and sometimes for worse, movements vent frustration, express dissent, articulate grievances, organize groups, establish identities, mobilize resources, institute reform, transform politics, create culture, provoke revolutions, exercise power, change society, and more. Although movements are among the most important topics in sociology, the discipline paid little attention to them until recent decades.

Movements are especially important for critical sociology. People drawn to its analysis of problems are often frustrated by its lack of solutions. Whether critical sociology should prescribe solutions is debatable. What it can do is describe how ordinary people have used movements to solve problems and study the circumstances under which they have succeeded. For these reasons, movements deserve a central place in both mainstream and critical sociology.

SOCIOLOGY AND SOCIAL MOVEMENTS: SIBLINGS OF MODERNITY

Sociology began with modernity and the Enlightenment's promotion of science and reason to understand the world. The analysis of modernity has always been at the core of sociological inquiry. Modernity made sociology possible by advocating a scientific approach to all things, including social things. The modernizing world also gave sociology a wealth of social things to interpret.

The most basic premise of the sociological perspective is that the world is a social construction. Enlightenment-inspired sociology did not see society as God given, naturally ordered, or biologically determined. It was rather a social product resulting from the conscious intentions of people as well as the unintended and unanticipated consequences of those actions. If society is a social construction, then sociology has a lot of explaining to do. The broadest questions involve how and why one kind of social order gets created rather than another.

Sociology is thus a child of modernity, but modernity has many children and sociology has many siblings. One of its closest siblings is the social movement. Their common ancestor is the premise that the world is a social construction. Without that premise, there would be no sociology, because there would be nothing to explain in sociological terms. And without that premise, there would be no social movements, because society would appear beyond human intervention. Sociology and social movements are thus closely linked by the common premise that the world is a social construction (Buechler 2000).

The claim that social movements are distinctly modern might sound odd, because people have challenged authority throughout history. By the same token, there have always been social thinkers who pondered the world around them. But just as sociology became a distinct discipline only in the modern era, collective action only became the social movement in the same era.

The ways we refer to this period have unfortunate side effects. Terms like *modernization*, *development*, and *rationalization* imply a smooth, gradual process of change with a clear direction. In reality, "modernization" was experienced by most people as chaotic, unpredictable, and deeply threatening to traditional ways of life.

The disruptions created by modernization were pervasive. Economically, the transition from feudalism to capitalism and then industrialization fundamentally changed people's connections to land and livelihood. The fancy word is *proletarianization*, which means the transformation of rural peasants who survived through subsistence agriculture into urban workers who had to sell their labor. Alongside proletarianization, rapid urbanization and overcrowding created new conflicts.

Politically, modernization brought a new political organization known as the nation-state. The boundaries of newly formed nations were contested and ultimately established through political and military conflicts. The resulting governments used centralized political power to privatize property, impose taxes, conscript citizens, and coercively control problematic populations.

The speed and extent of these changes demonstrated that society was a social construction because one society was dismantled and another was created right before people's eyes. These changes also provoked collective resistance. Some actions—bread riots, peasant uprisings, and conscription protests—defended traditional ways of life against intrusions by market capitalism and state power. Other actions—labor movements, urban rebellions, slave revolts—challenged arrangements that harmed ordinary people. Still other actions—independence struggles, suffrage movements, and democratization efforts—sought a political voice for ordinary citizens.

Through such actions, the modern social movement was invented. The "idea of conscious collective action having the capacity to change society as a whole came only with the era of enlightenment" (Neidhardt and Rucht 1991, 449). Put differently, "social movements are genuinely modern phenomena. Only in modern society have social movements played a constitutive role in social development" (Eder 1993, 108). Modern social movements are self-conscious about constructing society. They are advocates for how society should be organized. They engage in deliberate efforts to promote a certain kind of future.

Consider the role of ideology in the modern age. Ideologies envision how society should be organized; they can provide legitimacy to existing authority or challenge it through opposing visions and social movements. Whether advocating liberalism, conservatism, socialism, anarchism, authoritarianism, or communism, the flowering of ideologies only occurs when society is seen as a social construction and people are seen as having the capacity to reconstruct it through social movements.

These circumstances facilitated "the birth of what we now call the social movement—the sustained, organized challenge to existing authority in the name of a deprived, excluded or wronged population" (Tilly 1995, 144). Emerging in Great Britain and elsewhere in Europe by the 1790s, the social movement was a new way for ordinary people to make claims by repeatedly intervening in national affairs through coordinated, large-scale action. Previous forms of collective action were defensive and localized, involving revenge or resistance. The modern social movement greatly expanded the tactics ordinary people used to pursue their interests.

This new repertoire of contention was cosmopolitan rather than parochial, meaning it was not confined to one community but rather oriented to multiple centers of power. The new repertoire was modular rather than particular, meaning that new forms of protest could be adapted to many different causes. And it was autonomous, because it allowed movement leaders to communicate directly with national centers of power. This new repertoire of contention also fostered special purpose organizations for pursuing group interests by articulating a national agenda and promoting mass mobilization to support it (Tarrow 1994; Tilly 1995).

The rise of social movements was thus intertwined with modernity itself. The growth of cities, expansion of literacy, and democratization of culture were crucial to the flow of ideas that motivated people to act collectively. The rise of the national state was also crucial, because it provided the target of grievances and the repository of resources for social movement challenges.

As siblings of modernity, sociology and social movements both saw society as a social construction. Whereas sociology sought to explain it, social movements tried to change it. The connections became even closer, as movements challenged the very society that sociology sought to understand, thereby provoking new understandings.

The link was already there in sociology's response to modernization. Many of sociology's core ideas reasserted the conservative worldview that was undermined by the Enlightenment and its political challenges. These included the ideas that society is an organic unity, that it antedates the individual, that it consists of interdependent parts, that social customs and institutions are positively functional, that small groups are essential to social order, and that status and hierarchy are also essential to social order (Zeitlin 1987, 47–48).

Some of sociology's central insights were thus provoked by social movement challenges to existing social order. The pattern continued. Capitalism was criticized by radical thinkers and opposed by socialist movements. Sociology was enriched by these conflicts, as some of the best work done by classical theorists like Weber and Durkheim emerged through a debate with "Marx's ghost" about the correct diagnosis for modern social ills.

The pattern replayed again. By the 1950s, mainstream sociology had settled into a static functionalist approach that denied conflict and ignored change. The social movements of the next decade—and the world they created—demolished these assumptions. This activism established movements themselves as a legitimate focus of sociological analysis. Moreover, these movements transformed the sociological study of power, conflict, race, gender, sexuality, ecology, and globalization.

In all these ways, sociology and social movements continue to have a close relationship. Their common premise that the world is a social construction has inspired social movements to remake the world while enriching sociology's efforts to explain how social worlds get constructed, deconstructed, and reconstructed.

UNDERSTANDING SOCIAL MOVEMENTS

For much of its history, sociology ignored its social movement sibling. When acknowledged, movements were often seen as the black sheep of the family, and people who engaged in them were sometimes viewed as disreputable and deviant.

Marx had offered a more promising start with his analysis of working-class formation. What he showed was that solidarity *within* classes was intimately tied to conflict *between* them. Over time, such solidarity should promote collective identity, class consciousness, and political action. This logic should fit any chronic group conflict; we should expect "group formation" in all such cases. These are the logical result of social conflict and the rational expression of group interests.

Durkheim provided an alternative view. He was concerned about social integration, because it provides social control and normative regulation. When integration undergoes strain or breakdown, control is weakened or destroyed. This fosters anomie, as people lose their social bearings and cultural guidelines. This in turn promotes spontaneous, unstructured, and potentially dangerous collective behavior. For Durkheim, collective behavior is less an expression of group interests than a sign of social breakdown.

Sociology followed Durkheim's lead, and the collective behavior approach prevailed for much of the twentieth century. The general idea is that social stress, strain, or breakdown sparks psychological discontent or anxiety in individuals, who respond with collective behavior, ranging from panics, crazes, and crowds to social movements. Such behavior tends to be formless, unpatterned, and unpredictable; its noninstitutionalized quality separates collective from conventional behavior.

These assumptions spawned several versions of collective behavior theory. The symbolic interactionist approach focused on circular reaction, contagion, and excitability as provoking social unrest (Blumer 1951). The structural-functionalist approach outlined a stage model of collective behavior as "short-circuiting" normal channels of social action (Smelser 1962). A social-psychological version identified relative deprivation as the catalyst that spurred people into collective behavior (Geschwender 1968).

These variants all see collective behavior as spontaneous, unstructured, and sometimes irrational or deviant. Grouping social movements with panics, crazes, and fads obscured the politics, the organization, the rationality, and the longevity of at least some social movements (Buechler 2011, ch. 4, 6).

A major shift occurred after the social movements of the 1960s. The civil rights movement was critical, but it was also the catalyst for student, antiwar, ethnic, feminist, environmental, and gay and lesbian movements. Such movements were hard to explain through the logic of collective behavior theory. As a result, sociologists developed paradigms that reversed many collective behavior premises.

These newer approaches saw social movements as a form of political struggle (McCarthy and Zald 1973, 1977; Oberschall 1973; Tilly 1978). In contrast to the collective behavior tradition, movements were seen as normal, rational, institutionally rooted political challenges by aggrieved groups. These approaches redefined collective action from an example of deviance and disorganization to a topic for political and organizational sociology.

In keeping with this logic, people are seen as joining movements based on conscious decisions rather than spontaneous impulses. Individuals are seen as rational actors who join movements when the potential benefits outweigh the anticipated costs. The emphasis on rational calculation meant that grievances were not enough; movements only emerge when resources become available that allow groups to act on their grievances.

This general logic spawned two related paradigms. Resource mobilization theory proposed an entrepreneurial model of activism that equated movements with small businesses trying to survive in a competitive environment (McCarthy and Zald 1973, 1977). This model explicitly downplayed grievances and emphasized resources. When groups can accumulate resources—money, people, organization, commitment, communication, and the like—movements follow. The role of leaders is especially important; they are like entrepreneurs who gather the resources needed to launch movements.

Political process theory sees a world divided between political insiders and outsiders. The insiders have routine, low-cost access to decision making, so they don't have to resort to social movements to achieve their objectives. Political outsiders without institutional power must create movements to achieve their objectives. This requires groups to identify collective interests, create effective organization, and mobilize available resources. When this state of readiness finds opportunities to act, movements emerge (Tilly 1978).

Both emphasize resources, but resource mobilization theory stresses movement leaders and top-down strategies, whereas political process theory emphasizes mass support and bottom-up strategies. The latter also stresses "cognitive liberation" whereby people come to believe that change is possible and that their action will make a difference. Finally, opportunity remains crucial. It arises whenever the power gap between elites and movements is reduced. If movements act when their opportunities are greatest, they are most likely to succeed (McAdam 1982).

These theories fundamentally reoriented the study of social movements. Where collective behavior theory equated movements with fads, panics, crazes, and riots, the resource mobilization and political process paradigms saw them as serious, organized, political struggles (Buechler 2011, ch. 7, 8). Before long, however, these new theories also attracted critics.

Some said they went too far in dismissing grievances. They argued that grievances must be socially constructed through "framing," which imparts meaning to elements within a frame and sets them apart from what is outside the frame. Framing thus assigns meanings to movement claims. Framing underscores how social interaction is essential to transform objectively existing conditions into subjectively meaningful grievances.

Grievances are framed in several ways (Snow and Benford 1988). Diagnostic framing identifies a problem and assigns blame or causality, so the movement has a target for its actions. Prognostic framing suggests solutions and remedies, including tactics and strategies that are likely to work against the opposition. Together, these frames create movement sympathizers. Recruiting them requires motivational framing or a "call to arms" and a rationale for action (Benford 1993). Successful framing thus translates vague dissatisfactions into well-defined grievances and compels people to join a movement to act on them.

Movements also engage in several types of frame alignment to recruit people (Snow et al. 1986). Frame bridging happens when movements publicize their views and recruit those who already agree with them. Frame amplification appeals to values and beliefs in the general population and links them to movement issues; in this way, people's preexisting values entice them into the movement. Frame extension enlarges an initial frame to include issues important to potential recruits, making the movement a logical response to preexisting concerns. Finally, frame transformation creates new values, beliefs, and meanings to recruit people. In these ways, movements actively work to identify, create, and connect people's beliefs with grievances and participation.

The framing approach also describes "master frames" that broadly define grievances in terms of oppression, injustice, or exploitation and solutions in terms of liberation, fairness, or equity (Snow and Benford 1992). Their generality allows master frames to be adopted by many movements. Because of this, master frames often accompany cycles of protest that include many aggrieved groups. Thus, the 1960s protest cycle had master frames of emancipation or liberation that began with the civil rights movement and became organizing frames for many other movements.

The social constructionist approach does not deny the importance of resources, but argues that they are not enough. Movements also involve grievances, participants, and identities that must be framed to promote participation. Without such framing, movements are unlikely to emerge or to succeed (Buechler 2011, ch. 9).

Alongside resource mobilization, political process, and framing approaches, a fourth contemporary approach is new social movement theory (Cohen 1985; Klandermans 1991; Klandermans and Tarrow 1988; Larana, Johnston, and Gus-field 1994; Pichardo 1997). This European import identifies links between certain kinds of societies and particular types of movements. Thus, industrial societies promoted an "old" movement on behalf of working-class interests. With the coming of postindustrial society, new social movements displace the labor movement, just as postindustrial society has displaced industrial society.

New social movements respond to specific conditions of contemporary society. These include markets and bureaucracies that breed alienation, anomie, and dehumanization. New social movements, by contrast, provide personal, meaningful, human-scale relationships for participants. In addition, whereas the old labor movement revolved around materialist demands, new social movements often have postmaterialist goals. They are less about economic gain and more about winning recognition, acceptance, and participation for previously excluded groups.

Issues of identity are central in new social movements. In a postindustrial society, collective identity becomes more fluid and changeable across different situations and groups of people. This means that collective identities are often constructed through movement activity. In fact, the major accomplishment of such a movement might be to nurture a collective identity that gains newfound recognition and acceptance. This is why (in contrast to the old class movements) new social movements might be organized around race, ethnicity, nationality, gender, age, sexual orientation, or religion.

New social movements also emphasize cultural aspects of social life. They promote symbols and identities that foster acceptance and legitimation for previously marginalized groups. Some new social movements thereby resemble subcultures or countercultures that carve out alternative social worlds alongside mainstream society. As a result, participants in new social movements see close connections between movement goals and everyday life, and the politics of new social movements are often expressed in routine decisions and actions. For new social movements, "the personal is political," and personal life becomes a major site of movement activism (Buechler 2011, ch. 10).

At the close of the twentieth century, then, sociology had developed several contemporary paradigms for analyzing social movements that transcended the problematic assumptions of the older collective behavior approach. This prompted vibrant and productive debates between these paradigms and fostered various proposals for synthesizing them (Buechler 2011, ch. 11). Most importantly, the black sheep of social movements found new acceptance by its established sibling of sociology, making it easier to see their common premise that society is a social construction.

While some worked on synthesizing these approaches, others proposed yet another paradigm shift from the analysis of social movements to the dynamics of contention (McAdam, Tarrow, and Tilly 2001; Tilly and Tarrow 2007). These advocates argued that even the newer approaches were too structural and static as well as too movement-centric, thereby divorcing the study of movements from closely related phenomena. The dynamics-of-contention model was intended to transcend these limitations.

Rather than focusing on background factors, static variables, or movement histories, the dynamics-of-contention approach proposed a more relational focus on mechanisms and processes at the heart of contentious episodes. Through paired comparisons of seemingly divergent contentious episodes, they sought to show how "similar causal mechanisms and processes appear in quite dissimilar varieties of contentious politics . . . and appear in episodes producing massively different general outcomes" (McAdam, Tarrow, and Tilly 2001, 87).

This approach is narrower than previous social movement theory because it focuses on contentious episodes to the exclusion of other elements of social movements. It is broader than previous movement theory because it includes a wide range of contentious politics, from riots, strikes, revolts, and rebellions to revolutions and democratization struggles. The contentious dynamics paradigm thus seeks to put movements in their place alongside other forms of collective action and to recognize the similarities across these forms (Buechler 2011, ch. 12).

In sharp contrast to the dynamics-of-contention paradigm, a more diffuse but conceptually coherent "culturalist" approach to social movements appeared as well. Its proponents did not advocate a "cultural paradigm" in contrast to a "structural" one but rather argued that cultural elements are inevitably fused with and constitutive of so-called structural factors. Put differently, this approach underscored the inevitable cultural underpinnings of all social action, including social movement action.

Three components of culture are especially relevant: "cognitive beliefs, emotional responses, and moral evaluations . . . are inseparable, and together these motivate, rationalize and channel political action" (Jasper 1997, 12). Protest, in turn, rests on four irreducible dimensions of resources, strategies, culture, and biography. When they coalesce, these elements give rise to derivative levels of political structure, social networks, or formal organization. The inclusion of cultural, strategic, and biographical factors alongside resources emphasizes the "artfulness of protest." Rather than a deterministic outcome of abstract mechanisms and processes, protest is the artful creation of self-reflexive agents (Jasper 1997).

This approach also fostered a new appreciation of the multiple roles of emotion in social activism (Goodwin, Jasper, and Polletta 2001). With this recognition, emotions went full circle from being viewed negatively in the collective behavior tradition to being banished from recent theories to being restored to an important, but not pejorative, role in the study of movements (Goodwin, Jasper, and Polletta 2000). Indeed, almost every aspect of movement mobilization—from grievances to motivation to identity to framing—rests on an emotional foundation that had been explicitly rejected in previous models of the "rational actor" in social activism (Buechler 2011, ch. 12).

Sociology has thus developed many useful approaches for understanding movements. The collective behavior tradition analyzes spontaneity, contagion, and group dynamics. Resource mobilization theory underscores resources, organization, and entrepreneurial leadership. Political process theory emphasizes mobilization, opportunity, and indigenous support. Social constructionism reveals how grievances must be framed as meaningful if movements are to arise. New social movement theory illuminates struggles around collective identities, cultural politics, and everyday life. The dynamics-of-contention paradigm reveals both similarities and differences in highly disparate and diverse episodes of contention. And finally, a "culturalist" emphasis restores an appreciation of the foundational roles of meaning, cognition, and emotion in all aspects of social activism. These approaches collectively illuminate how social movements have pursued their goals and shaped the modern world in the process.

Despite the richness of contemporary social movement theory, there is at least one major gap in this work. Whereas much of the most important work of the 1970s and 1980s analyzed how capitalism shaped movement grievances and dynamics, this focus on capitalism has largely disappeared from more recent theoretical approaches. Given the ever-expanding penetration of capitalism around the globe (not to mention the severity of recent capitalist crises), this lacuna is deeply ironic. It also hampers our ability to fully analyze some of the most important movements of our time. A strong case can be made that "it is time to bring capitalism back into social movement studies" (Hetland and Goodwin 2013, 102).

SOCIAL MOVEMENTS AND PROGRESSIVE POLITICS

The study of social movements reveals many lessons. For critical sociology, the most important is the link between social movements and progressive politics. Such politics empower ordinary people and narrow the gap between them and elites who otherwise dominate political decision making. Struggles for emancipation, liberation, or justice are examples. Campaigns to gain, extend, or preserve civil, social, political, or economic rights are other examples. They contrast sharply with reactionary politics that strengthen elites at the expense of ordinary people. They also contrast with normal, institutional politics whose distribution of power heavily favors elites.

The most important lesson here is that progressive politics have always been driven by social movements. Progressive politics can also include political parties (or wings of political parties), activist subcultures, labor unions, nonprofit enterprises, community organizations, and even some elite individuals or institutions. But what drives them are social movements. When progressive change occurs, it is largely a result of social movements.

This does not mean that all social movements are progressive. Some movements support reactionary politics. The Ku Klux Klan, neo-Nazi organizations, and anti-immigrant groups are ugly movements promoting hatred, discrimination, and injustice. So we must keep our logic clear. Not all social movements are progressive. But progressive politics are always rooted in social movements.

This link is evident both analytically and historically. Analytically, society is an arena of conflict in which elite individuals and organizations pursue their interests. In a few cases, this benefits everyone. More often, however, pursuit of elite interests serves them at the expense of ordinary people and their interests.

Elites control the political arena. This means that normal, institutional politics exercised through major parties, campaigns, and elections mainly serve elite interests. The issues in institutional politics typically involve differences among elites; this is why the "choices" offered in elections are not much of a choice at all. The institutional organization of society and politics leaves little room for popular interests.

This is what links social movements and progressive politics. Movements are almost a prerequisite for getting the interests of ordinary people into the political process. A fundamental way this occurs is through the exercise of disruptive power (Piven 2006). In everyday life, people are embedded in multiple networks of social cooperation. When they deliberately withhold their cooperation, the resulting disruption of those networks creates power for otherwise-powerless people. Strikes, boycotts, occupations, and civil disobedience are all examples of such disruptive power in action.

Disruption thus derives its leverage from the breakdown of institutionally regulated cooperation. It occurs when people violate rules, demand non-negotiable concessions, or use unconventional or illegal forms of collective action to their advantage. It can win immediate concessions, but it can also alter the dynamics of electoral politics to favor popular interests and gain standing for groups and interests previously excluded from the polity.

By working under, over, around, and sometimes through normal channels, social movements have been the most effective way to achieve progressive change. When such change happens, it is because ordinary people have used collective action to pursue social equality, overcome political inertia, and achieve progressive goals.

The link between social movements and progressive politics is also evident historically—and right from the beginning in the United States. Firmly rooted in the Enlightenment, the American Revolution was a form of progressive politics that overthrew British domination and created a new nation. The Revolution also inspired important statements of progressive politics in the Declaration of Independence, the Bill of Rights, and the Constitution itself. The British rulers of the American colonies largely opposed this effort, and it eventually required not just a movement but also a war to achieve the progressive agenda of the American Revolution.

At the same time, these events revealed the complexity of movements, politics, and change. The Revolution was a cross-class movement that temporarily united wealthy, middling, and poor colonists against a common, external oppressor. But even as it was unfolding, elites were crafting a form of government that would preserve their wealth, defend their property, and entrench their power. Once the common enemy was defeated, preexisting class cleavages resurfaced and entrenched a new elite that pursued their interests in the new nation (Zinn 1980).

Many elite interests were tied to Southern plantation agriculture and the slave labor that made it profitable. Although the planter class was powerful and racist justifications of slavery were ubiquitous, slave resistance was also common. By the early nineteenth century, a powerful abolitionist movement added its voice to the progressive cause of ending slavery and extending political rights to African Americans. Many abolitionist arguments were based on rhetoric and rights established by the progressive politics of the American Revolution itself. By extending the definitions of "humans" and "people" to slaves and former slaves, powerful ideological challenges to the ownership of people as property were articulated.

Like the American Revolution, the Civil War was a complex conflict of group interests. In many respects, it was another battle between competing elites (Northern industrialists vs. Southern planters) to see who would control the country. So although it is too simplistic to say that the Civil War was fought to free the slaves, the North could not have won it without freeing the slaves. The Civil War thus provided the abolitionist movement with the opportunity to achieve perhaps the greatest victory for progressive politics in US history: the abolition of slavery and the extension of civil, political, and social rights to newly freed slaves.

Whereas abolitionists challenged chattel slavery, the labor movement challenged "wage slavery." In a culture that prized independence, autonomy, and self-sufficiency, "free laborers" fiercely resisted wage labor, just as slaves resisted their subordination. Although "wage slavery" persisted, this campaign initiated a labor movement that would defend the dignity of labor and the livelihood of workers for decades to come.

Whereas abolitionism attacked slavery and labor opposed capitalism, the women's rights movement challenged male domination. Many women gravitated to women's rights after participating in antislavery work. Abolitionism provided its own provocations by treating women as second-class citizens within the movement. Such unequal treatment convinced many female abolitionists that they needed a movement of their own. It emerged at the Seneca Falls

Convention of 1848, one among a series of women's rights conventions that met up to the eve of the Civil War.

One of the founding documents of this movement was a Declaration of Sentiments and Principles deliberately modeled on the Declaration of Independence. Where the latter document referred to the British or King George as the oppressor of the colonies, the former referred to men as the oppressors of women. Once again, the progressive political rhetoric of the American Revolution was strategically used to make powerful arguments on behalf of a previously excluded category of people. The progressive politics of the women's rights movement were evident in its agenda and its alliances with abolitionism and labor (Buechler 1986).

After the Civil War, normalcy returned in the North. After Reconstruction, white supremacy returned in the South. But new groups advanced progressive politics in the last quarter of the nineteenth century. The Knights of Labor revived the labor movement and defended the status and living standards of workers. Farmers organized to protect their livelihood in a system increasingly dominated by railroads and middlemen.

Farmer's alliances were eventually undermined by an old problem for social movements: they often were cross-class organizations dominated by larger farmers who advanced their distinct interests at the expense of smaller farmers and ordinary citizens (Schwartz 1976). Such populist movements posed other dangers. Their political frustrations could be misdirected, and scapegoating sometimes diverted these movements from their real targets. But at their best, the populist movements of the late nineteenth century advanced progressive politics by seeking greater equality and better lives for ordinary Americans.

At the dawn of the twentieth century, these politics were advanced in cities by the Progressive movement. In response to the corporate excesses and governmental corruption of the Gilded Age, the Progressive movement sought to regulate corporations, dismantle monopolies, reform government, promote education, naturalize immigrants, and mediate class conflict through rational, scientific, and democratic decision making. Corporate capitalism also provoked more radical challenges. In Western states, the International Workers of the World ("Wobblies") sought to organize "one big union" to advance the cause of labor. In many cities, states, and even at the federal level, the Socialist Party offered progressive solutions to the economic and social problems confronting working people.

The Progressive era also revived women's efforts to win the vote. They could only succeed by amending the US Constitution. To do so, the movement sought the broadest possible support, recruiting rural, working, immigrant, and elite women with customized arguments about why they needed the vote. The movement developed new strategies to gain public support from men as well as women. It built on state successes and kept relentless pressure on Congress and the executive branch. It broadened its tactics to include intensive lobbying, militant demonstrations, civil disobedience, and hunger strikes. Victory finally came in 1920, culminating eighty years of social movement activism and progressive politics that dramatically expanded the boundaries of citizenship in the United States (Buechler 1986).

Within a decade, the stock market crash plunged the country into the Great Depression. Progressive forces responded, as the mainstream labor movement became more diverse and militant. Unemployed workers organized and pressured the government to provide work or some form of relief in the absence of work. The Communist Party was especially effective in organizing African American workers, who had historically been shunned by the labor movement. With newfound militancy in a time of economic crisis, these movements won the right to organize unions and established the eight-hour workday. The labor movement then became a major force when wartime production reinvigorated the economy and brought the relative prosperity of the 1950s.

The progressive social movements of the 1930s also played an important role in shaping the New Deal. Some actions were temporary but important, like public works programs that put people to work when the market could not. Other responses were more lasting and fundamental. They include, most obviously, the Social Security system and unemployment compensation insurance that provide economic support for broad segments of the population. The New Deal showed that government could be responsive to ordinary citizens, but it also showed that progressive social movements were needed to ensure that it met such obligations.

Progressive politics then revived the neglected issue of race relations with the civil rights movement. After the abolitionist movement had helped to end slavery, racism took new forms with Jim Crow laws, legal and de facto segregation, and white supremacy. The civil rights movement emerged in the 1950s in the Southern United States to challenge the most egregious forms of segregation and discrimination by seeking integration. Pursuit of this modest goal produced a racist backlash, which led to federal intervention to maintain civil order. Once again, a progressive movement was required to provoke the government into protecting the fundamental rights of citizens (McAdam 1982; Morris 1984).

The civil rights movement ended legal segregation, challenged racial discrimination, reduced terrorist violence against blacks, and advanced voting and other civil rights for racial minorities. These reforms inspired the Great Society programs of the Kennedy and Johnson administrations, including new federal antipoverty efforts and the establishment of Medicare. Once again, progressive social change occurred only in the wake of a powerful social movement.

The civil rights movement also spawned a new cycle of progressive movements in the 1960s and 1970s. As the movement came north and developed more militant strategies of black power, other racial and ethnic movements borrowed this master frame on behalf of migrants, farmworkers, Latino/a groups, and Native Americans. Race-conscious movements also injected new militancy into a labor movement that had become bureaucratic and top-heavy during the complacent 1950s.

The new left also took inspiration from the civil rights movement as it promoted participatory democracy. Many student activists had participated in the civil rights movement, and they took its lessons back to campuses and communities to broaden citizenship and political participation across class, race, and generational lines. This also meant defending free speech to cultivate more participatory solutions to social problems (Hayden 2013).

As US military involvement in Southeast Asia escalated, these movements were fertile ground for antiwar activism. Politicized students found a new target in the war, and the draft in particular. Government repression of dissent illustrated just how limited democracy really was. The antiwar movement contributed to changing US policy in Southeast Asia by dividing elites between "hawks" and "doves" and undermining support for the war. The movement also radicalized a generation of activists who took up other political causes (Gitlin 1993).

Alongside the civil rights, new left, and antiwar movements, there was a parallel and intersecting counterculture. Exemplifying a new social movement, this counterculture challenged mainstream values of authority, materialism, consumerism, competition, and success. By encouraging young people to "tune in, turn on, and drop out," the counterculture sparked critical analysis of the dominant culture (Roszak 1969).

Among the most important movements to emerge out of this cycle of protest was second-wave feminism. Recruiting professional and college women, the women's rights and women's liberation wings became a mass movement by the early 1970s. The movement overturned many public forms of sex segregation and gender discrimination, while revealing the more subtle politics behind supposedly private issues like sexuality, the body, and personal life. It is difficult to overstate the impact of contemporary feminism. Its simultaneous relevance to personal, public, political, cultural, private, global, spiritual, economic, and psychological issues speaks volumes about the role of gender in the social order (Buechler 1990; Ferree and Hess 2000; Reger 2012).

The modern environmental movement also emerged out of this cycle of protest. Although it had predecessors in older conservation and preservation efforts, the environmental movement of the 1970s brought a qualitative shift in how people saw their relationship to the natural world. It is striking that large majorities of people now readily identify themselves as supporters of environmental causes. Although institutional practices and personal behaviors still deviate from these proclaimed values, this movement created an important foundation for future gains.

The "long decade" of the 1960s was one of the heights of progressive politics in US history; as such, it could not be sustained indefinitely. Among its legacies, however, were new cultures of protest that nurtured progressive activism through the turn of the century. Among the movements that drew upon this legacy were peace and justice movements against intervention in Central America; anti-nuclear activism; third-wave feminism; anti-apartheid struggles; anti-sweatshop campaigns; activism around HIV/AIDS; resistance to the 1991 Gulf War; animal rights campaigns; mobilization for reproductive rights; gay, lesbian, and queer movements; anti-globalization activism and protests; renewed antiwar activism around the 2003 US invasion of Iraq; and reinvigorated environmental activism around climate change.

TEA PARTIERS AND OCCUPIERS

An indirect testimony to the impact of progressive movements is the conservative reaction they provoke. Thus, since the 1970s, the already constricted continuum of mainstream politics has narrowed even further, as "liberal" became an epithet and center-right policies prevailed even under Democratic administrations. These institutional shifts have been accompanied by conservative, right-wing, and libertarian movements blending top-down institutional resources with bottom-up populist resentment. If nothing else, this underscores how not all social movements are progressive and how movement repertoires can be harnessed to serve reactionary ends.

These tendencies were dramatically exemplified by the emergence of the Tea Party in the aftermath of the 2007 economic crash and 2008 presidential election. A now-famous rant by CNBC reporter Rick Santelli in February of 2009 about federal assistance to homeowners facing foreclosure triggered what quickly became the most publicized right-wing movement in decades. The Tea Party had a dramatic impact on the 2010 and 2012 election cycles as Republican candidates moved further to the right and appealed to this more extreme base; the strategy succeeded for a number of candidates, particularly in the House elections of 2010.

While some have argued that the Tea Party is nothing more than a top-down, "astroturf" vehicle for reinvigorating traditional Republican policies (DiMaggio 2011), a more nuanced analysis suggests that the Tea Party emerged out of a perfect storm of top-down financial sponsorship, bottom-up populist anger, and relentless right-wing media promotion (Skocpol and Williamson 2012). Thus, the Santelli rant on cable television crystallized populist conservative discontent with the Obama administration, government in general, and anyone perceived as receiving undeserved assistance. The budding movement then quickly attracted major financial backing from wealthy billionaires and conservative political action committees while right-wing cable-television and radio coverage created a self-fulfilling prophecy, turning the movement into a potent electoral force.

Despite its impact on two electoral cycles, the Tea Party may prove fragile and short-lived. In the first place, the very factors that created short-term success may not be sustainable for the long term. In retrospect, it appears that wealthy donors and media promoters functioned as "national usurpers" who "created the misleading perception that the Tea Party was a coordinated national movement, not a crazy-quilt of independent local organizations" (Dreier 2012, 758). Libertarian leanings and deep suspicion of establishment politics within the Tea Party will make sustained organizing a major challenge for such fiercely independent local organizations.

Second, there are also significant cleavages within the movement. One is evident between a populist base seeking to preserve its Medicare and Social Security benefits and elite efforts to dismantle such programs. When Tea Party darling Paul Ryan proposed a budget that would phase out Medicare's guaranteed coverage for seniors, his "proposed healthcare voucher system fell flat among grassroots Tea Partiers, and the GOP moved away from the specifics of this plan" (Fetner 2012, 764). Another internal divide pits social conservatives seeking to fight culture wars against a libertarian wing willing to "live and let live."

Third, despite the depth and passion of Tea Party support, the views of rank-and-file members and affiliated politicians "fall far outside the mainstream of American political culture and belief on most issues" (Dreier 2012, 760). This suggests a widening gap between a party seeking to win elections and a movement insisting on ideological purity; the inability of Mitt Romney to bridge this gap in the 2012 presidential election illustrates this quandary. In the end, the forces dividing and marginalizing the movement may well prove stronger than those that united it from 2009 through the 2012 electoral campaign.

While the Tea Party was grabbing headlines, a more authentically populist movement burst on the scene in Zuccotti Park in lower Manhattan in September 2011 in the form of Occupy Wall Street (OWS). "Many pundits and journalists considered the Occupy movement to be the left-wing counterpart to the Tea Party" (Dreier 2012, 761), but it was always a false parallel. OWS "lacked the money, media contacts and national support network that boosted the Tea Party's influence" (Dreier 2012, 761). Without those resources, it seemed OWS had little more than alternative media and grassroots organizing to launch a movement.

On closer inspection, however, it had more than that. "Unlike any other movement on the American left in at least three-quarters of a century, this movement began with a majority base of support. It was surrounded by sympathy. What it stood for—economic justice and curbs on the wealthy—was popular" (Gitlin 2012, 33). The general public not only supported progressive economic reforms; they also had a more favorable impression of OWS than the Tea Party by a 54 to 27 percent margin (Dreier 2012, 761).

Like the New Left that arose during Kennedy's Democratic administration and was inspired by the civil rights movement, OWS arose during Obama's Democratic administration and was inspired by both national and global activism (Hayden 2013). However, whereas it took the movements of the 1960s three years to "change the conversation," OWS did so in a mere three weeks (Gitlin 2012, 5).

OWS was distinctive in blending social media with face-to-face community. It followed a "virgeo" principle that blended a virtual community of online, global input with a geographically bounded, on-the-ground conversation (Kim 2011, 15). Even as activists used social media in a mundane, taken-for-granted way, they struggled with how unequal access to such media limited some people's participation (Nielsen 2013). Even more intriguing, for all the reliance on electronic media, the top source of information for most activists remained word-of-mouth communications (Gamson and Sifry 2013).

OWS was also distinctive in merging consensus-based activism with a strong critique of social and economic inequality, thus blending the leading characteristics of "new" and "old" social movements (Leach 2013). With a deep suspicion of centralized, bureaucratic structures and a profound cynicism about mainstream politics, OWS insisted on being autonomous, horizontal, collectivist, leaderless, and structureless to the greatest possible extent. These traits allowed OWS to be as inclusive of everyone in the "99%" as any movement in recent history.

These commitments also allowed OWS to harness infectious energy in its striking strategy of encampments in public spaces. These occupiers have been described as earnest, energetic, frivolous, original, mysterious, intense, surprising, and inventive, and their actions were infused with sweetness, affection, and gaiety (Gitlin 2012, xiv, 64). The inclusive, participatory nature of OWS elicited tremendous emotional energy that was sustained through mantras, rituals, symbols, and imagery. The high ritual density and collective effervescence (Collins 2001) of ongoing encampments and round-the-clock activism led many to experience OWS as a euphoric, transcendent, spiritual experience as well as a political statement about social and economic justice.

The spirit of inclusiveness was woven throughout the culture and practices of OWS. Deprived of the use of public address systems, the people's "mic" required everyone to repeat a speaker's words from the front of the stage to the back of the gathering. The use of general assemblies, working groups, and spokescouncils was consciously designed to maximize participation and consensus-based decision making. In general assemblies, the "progressive stack" ensured that groups traditionally marginalized in both society and movements would have privileged access to the stage and the right to be heard (Maharawal 2013).

The care with which these practices were devised and maintained suggests that there was considerable "structure" in the form of norms, rules, and regulations that maximized participation. The same commitments led to OWS's infamous reluctance to make conventional "demands." To do so was seen as granting too much legitimacy to authorities (as being able to grant demands), as well as raising the dangers of divisiveness within and co-optation from outside the movement. Even without conventional demands, "it ought to have been obvious what the movement stood for" (Gitlin 2012, 108). Virtually every march, slogan, placard, and rally hammered home the themes of corporate greed, economic inequality, and government complicity.

With the demise of the encampments that had sprung up around the country in the fall of 2011, OWS lost much of its distinctive character. Its members and working groups remain active, however, in numerous communities, and some have suggested that local, national, and global anti-debt struggles could be the catalyst for ongoing, long-term activism (Taylor 2012; Graeber 2012). In pondering the inevitable limitations and eventual fate of OWS, one participant recommends that we treat it less as a specimen to be endlessly dissected and more as an indicator of bigger patterns and "a name fixed to a flashpoint" (Smucker 2013).

In a similar spirit, a longtime observer of progressive politics notes that movements are not just explosive mass protest and that they ebb and flow as multi-pronged, long-term struggles. OWS may thus be seen as one expression of a long-delayed national and global economic struggle that has taken and will continue to take various forms in diverse locales. From this perspective, "the question is not 'where is Occupy going?' but rather can and how will people find ways to redistribute power and wealth in democratic directions?" (Flacks 2013, 204)

While OWS exemplifies the links between social movements and progressive politics, the Tea Party reminds us that this requires some caveats. Not all movements are progressive. Not all movements succeed. Movements sometimes create new problems. And even with success, progressive victories are often overturned by reactionary forces. Having acknowledged all this, the basic conclusion still stands. Every major progressive social change in the United States has been driven by social movements that have made the world a better place for millions of ordinary people. Critical sociologists often see the glass as half empty, but the only reason it is half full is because of social movements seeking more just and equitable worlds.

THE GLOBAL SCENE

The recent increase in social movement activity has not been confined to the United States. Diverse movements have emerged in many regions and their participants have identified with other activists and campaigns in far-flung places. Occupy Wall Street itself took inspiration from the prior domestic revolt in Wisconsin as well as the Egyptian uprising and the broader Arab Spring. Egyptian activists quickly acknowledged the link by donating money to buy pizzas for Occupy Wall Street activists.

Recent movements around the globe include North African and Middle Eastern rebellions against autocratic governments, student protests for more accessible public education in Chile and Quebec, Greek protests against austerity policies, Tel Aviv encampments for social justice, and the revolt of the *indignados* (indignant people) in Spain demanding more participatory democracy. While each movement responded to specific, local conditions, these uprisings "have had much in common not only in their form but in substance" (Flacks 2013, 204). While it would be premature to see this as a cohesive global movement, the undeniable connections across these campaigns signify a new era of globally self-reflexive activism.

Of all these uprisings, the Arab Spring is perhaps the most noteworthy if only for its unlikely locale and unpredictable timing. The self-immolation of a Tunisian man to protest police corruption is widely credited with sparking nationwide protests that undermined a long-standing police state in Tunisia and destabilized similar states in Bahrain and Yemen. These protests then spread throughout the Arab world, leading to significant regime change in Tunisia, Libya, and Egypt.

Because of its regional significance, complex politics, and ongoing turmoil, the Egyptian case has received the most attention. Many commentators have emphasized the role of communications technology and social media in facilitating protest. However, at least one ethnographic account by a participant observer downplays the role of social media in favor of other factors. Amy Holmes (2012) finds a better explanation of the Egyptian uprising in its revolutionary coalition of lower and middle classes. This coalition allowed protesters to create liberated zones and popular security organizations that were not cowed by state violence. When combined with economically crippling strikes, the movement brought down a widely unpopular autocratic ruler.

The demise of Mubarak, however, was only the first act in what has become at least a three-act drama. The first deposed the "dead hand" of Mubarak's regime; the second displaced the "deadheads" of Mohamed Tantawi's interim government; the third overturned the "dead end" of the increasingly autocratic government of Mohamed Morsi and the Muslim Brotherhood (Friedman 2013). While Friedman's journalistic take on events is somewhat glib, he underscores how Egyptian activism has redirected the country's government on three separate occasions since 2011.

From a more analytical perspective, these events had several novel elements. The movements themselves represent new experiments in nations that historically lacked civil liberties and political freedoms and that have socially and geographically segmented populations (Tilly and Wood 2013, 111–112). In addition, these movements drew upon international connections and social media to amplify growing dissatisfactions and mobilize populations for protest. The movement's success demonstrated that "even youth in cities in Egypt had integrated sufficiently into worldwide circuits of power and communication that their authoritarian rulers couldn't effectively control the domestic and international political activities of their citizens" (Tilly and Wood 2013, 112).

These novel elements were interwoven with more familiar features. The activism itself invoked a conventional repertoire of contention that predates social media, including nonviolent civil disobedience, mass gatherings in public places, symbolic colors, banners and chants, and the like. While social media helped activate this repertoire, its results were also familiar. The early protests in Egypt and elsewhere created a powerful sense of euphoria and a strong bandwagon effect. In social psychological terms, the most significant result was a profound "cognitive liberation" (McAdam 1982) as millions of people realized that an unjust, illegitimate social order could be changed and that their participation could help change it for the better.

Familiar patterns also appeared in the bigger picture of these protests and their aftermath. The Egyptian and Libyan cases reaffirm the truism that when there is a common enemy, coalitions of strange bedfellows can be very effective in deposing unpopular leaders. Upon doing so, previous divisions and schisms re-emerge, trigger prolonged conflict, and hinder efforts to establish stable new regimes. Thus, "there are many examples of broad coalitions coming together to oust dictators but relatively few of them stayed together and agreed on what the new regime should look like. Opposition movements tend to lose steam, falling prey to internal squabbles and the resurgent forces of the old regime" (Berman 2013).

This process applies most obviously to temporary alliances of social classes, political parties, and religious sects, but also includes more basic categorical inequalities like gender. Thus, while women were prominent in the early days of the Egyptian uprising, they were explicitly targeted by military repression and have subsequently been marginalized in the ongoing struggles over the future of the country (Fahmy 2013).

The Egyptian case also reminds us that regime stability is often as dependent on external support as it is on internal legitimation. Just as prior US support for Mubarak was crucial to his tenure, the withdrawal of that support contributed to his downfall. Finally, revolutions rarely succeed if the police, army, and state security forces are not divided or neutral, and the Egyptian military has played a crucial role in Mubarak's downfall as well as all the subsequent political maneuvering that has followed (Cockburn 2012).

While the relative successes of the Arab Spring command attention, it is worth remembering that most movements in the region have not succeeded. In some cases, rulers have strengthened their regimes through a soft path of co-optation. In others, they have stepped up repressive measures and solidified autocratic control. And in still others like Syria, conflict has turned into a brutal and seemingly intractable civil war. Thus, while much of the region enjoyed at least a brief Arab Spring, some nations did not and many are now facing an Arab Winter (Kurzman 2013).

There is a final familiar pattern to be noted. Social movements often seem to appear out of nowhere; a classic case is the civil rights movement that emerged in the southern United States. In a similar way, the Arab Spring was neither predicted nor anticipated, even by knowledgeable observers. Indeed, in a special issue of the journal *Mobilization* (devoted to social movement studies), Charles Kurzman (2012) concedes that prediction (and even causal explanation) may be beyond the capacity of current social science and that we should focus on understanding the lived experience of activists rather than explaining the causal antecedents of their activism.

The "predictable unpredictability" of uprisings like the Arab Spring may have its own explanation, however. The key resides in "'preference falsification,' that is, the fact that people may not reveal publicly their private preferences, whether out of fear or shame" (Goodwin 2011). If researchers don't know people's underlying sentiments and people themselves don't know other people's sentiments, then nobody knows when a "slight shift in this distribution . . . may be sufficient to produce a 'revolutionary bandwagon' in which more and more people take to the streets, encouraged by the relative safety and anonymity of large crowds" (Timur Kuran, cited in Goodwin 2011, 453).

Rather than abandoning attempts at explanation, it would seem prudent to study both the subjective experiences of activists as well as the broader, contextual factors surrounding that activism. As we look beyond the specific—and dramatic—cases of social movements in the twenty-first century, we find no shortage of theoretical efforts to comprehend their causes, dynamics, and trajectories.

THEORIZING GLOBAL ACTIVISM

The recent increase in social movement activity around the globe has led many US observers to speak in terms of "global" or "transnational" social movements (Della Porta and Tarrow 2005; Smith and Johnston 2002). Such terms merit closer scrutiny. They sometimes reflect a US-centric bias in which activism occurring anywhere else in the world is automatically labeled in this way. At the very least, we need to distinguish three types of activism.

First, there are local, regional, or national movements that are responding to equally local, regional, or national grievances. The process of diffusion and speed of new communications technologies can nonetheless make such movements appear more interlinked than they often are. Second, there are movements that respond locally or nationally to the negative effects of broader globalization processes originating beyond their borders. And finally, there are movements that explicitly target neoliberal globalization and its leading institutions and seek to build genuinely transnational coalitions in the struggle against these forces.

This complex continuum of movements has prompted two schools of thought about the "globalization" of social movements. For lack of better terms, they can be called the skeptics and the systematizers.

The skeptics argue that even in the twenty-first century, most activism still relies on national organizational forms and that battles over globalization do not dominate the social movement scene. One of the hallmarks of "global activism" is social media, but this also requires a more nuanced interpretation. While new communications technologies can obviously facilitate mobilization, they also make movements vulnerable to problems of control, commitment, and repression, and they actually heighten inequalities between those with access to such technology and those without. We thus need to avoid "technological determinism" by recognizing the double-edged nature of social media as well as their similarities with previous innovations in how movements communicate their messages (Tilly and Wood 2013).

While there has been an undeniable internationalization of claimants and objects of claims and greater international backing for various campaigns, this does not constitute a "global uprising." For the skeptics, movements in New York, Greece, Spain, Chile, Quebec, and elsewhere are less a coordinated movement than separate protests benefiting from a rapid diffusion of tactics and repertoires of contention. Participants may be increasingly aware of similar campaigns in other places, but they are still primarily fighting battles against their respective national states (Tilly and Wood 2013).

The same interactional factors that have contributed to the intensity of these distinct movements in their respective times and locales may pose inherent obstacles to an equally rich transnational activism. It is highly doubtful whether the face-to-face, interpersonal networks that have proven so vital to localized protests can be replicated for transnational activism; "even with . . . [favorable] structural preconditions, the transaction costs of linking the indigenous groups of a variety of countries into integrated transnational networks would be difficult for any social movement to overcome" (Tarrow 1998, 235).

Such complexities suggest that the frequency and impact of transnational movements are overstated. Many so-called transnational movements involve either temporary campaigns or transnational *issue* networks without the corresponding transnational *social* networks required for full-fledged movements. If genuinely transnational movements require both transnational social networks and sustained campaigns, they are less common than casual use of the term implies (Tarrow 1998; see also Della Porta and Kriesi 1999 and Tarrow 2012). Thus, a close examination of transnational processes in human rights campaigns reveals that some involve domestic actors internalizing international issues, others involve the externalization of domestic issues, and still others create insider/outsider coalitions around domestic issues, but only a handful of cases amount to genuinely transnational movements (Tarrow 2012).

In a similar vein, claims of global citizens in a global civil society should be treated with caution. The activists in most transnational activism are "rooted cosmopolitans" who retain a sense of place and a national identity while also mobilizing national resources for transnational activities (Tarrow 2012). Their campaigns, moreover, are typically focused on specific issues rather than globalization per se. Consider human rights activism once again; its target is not globalization but rather the authoritarian states that are the most grievous offenders against human rights.

The skeptics' case concludes that "none of these processes has radically shifted the global balance from domestic to international politics or created anything resembling a 'global social movement' and all of them worked within international institutions and domestic power structures" (Tarrow 2012, 212). While the skeptics are well aware of the growth in international, transnational, and global organizations and processes, they remain reluctant to accept the "strong globalization thesis" when it comes to social movement activism.

In contrast to the skeptics, the systematizers see the globalization of activism as a logical response to the globalization of so many other processes, including the global political economy itself. Just as new social movement theory argued that contemporary social structures call forth different types of movements than older social structures, the globalization of capital accumulation and political policy formulation has provoked correspondingly global movement challenges. If the rise of nation-states provided the target and the resources for national social movements in the past, the rise of transnational bodies is now playing the same catalytic role in the emergence of transnational movements.

These theorists also emphasize that globalization is not an entirely new phenomenon, but rather an acceleration of tendencies within the world economic system that have been present for centuries. This implies that despite the buzz, transnational movements are not new. World system theorists are particularly interested in anti-systemic movements, and the hypothesis that "for at least several hundred years there have been successive waves of movements that have attacked and destabilized the capitalist world-economy, its hegemonic powers, and dominant geocultures, and yet, at the same time, have come to provide legitimacy and the foundation for a new ordering of accumulation and political rule on a world scale" (Martin 2008, 1).

Antisystemic movement waves can be dated from at least the "long eighteenth century" (1750–1850), when a remarkable range of transformative movements sought to "defend the possibility of social life outside the clutches of capitalism" (Agartan, Choi, and Hunyh 2008, 47). Historical accounts of this period reveal a "startling transnational and transoceanic connection among local movements, something that is often held to be possible only in today's age of globalization" (Agartan, Choi, and Hunyh 2008, 47).

Such activity became full-fledged antisystemic movements between 1848 and 1917. As labor, anarchist, antislavery, and anticolonial movements challenged the imperatives of the world-capitalist system, they paradoxically strengthened state structures by "pulling antisystemic resistance within safer bounds for the ongoing operations of historical capitalism" (Bush 2008, 51). At the same time, such challenges prompted transformations in regimes of accumulation, as when effective national labor movements inadvertently pushed domestic capital to seek cheaper labor abroad.

In the next broad period, from 1917 to 1968, formerly antisystemic challengers assumed or at least shared state power and thereby lost their antisystemic character. As labor and social democratic forces entered the system they formerly challenged, "antisystemic struggle was taken up by radical nationalists in the colonial world" (Bush and Morris 2008, 84). By the end of this period, formerly antisystemic forces were wielding state power to wage wars against national liberation movements, stoking not only anticolonial movements but also a new wave of antisystemic resistance in the form of student, antiwar, and New Left movements in the core and subsequent popular uprisings in the Soviet bloc and the "Third World."

In the most recent historical period, from 1968 to the present, the expansion and penetration of the capitalist mode of production has proceeded along vectors of culture, consumption, subjectivity, and identity. "These developments have in turn reawakened identities and localized groups based on common interest, religion, ethnicity, or 'tribe' . . . while the ideological forces inherent in socialism, nationalism, and communism have weakened" (Kalouche and Mielants 2008, 164).

While traditional socialist, nationalist, or communist challenges to capitalism may have lost much of their ideological coherence, current global activism still retains an anticapitalist dimension. The core of the conflict involves contested versions of globalization. On one side is a neoliberal vision of a globalized world organized around market principles. Its proponents include (some) national governmental bodies, transnational corporations, global financial institutions, currency speculators, and commercial media outlets. On the other side is a vision of democratic globalism built on participation from below. Its proponents include civil society groups; local, national, and transnational movement organizations; elements of progressive political parties; and independent media organizations (Smith 2008, 6ff).

Like previous conflicts within the world system, this one was triggered by a systemic crisis. In this case, it was the decline of US hegemony that began in the 1970s and accelerated through the end of the twentieth century. The elite response was to push for more extreme neoliberal economic policies and austerity programs in an effort to restore profitability. As institutions lost their ability to provide benefits to key groups, they also lost legitimacy, thereby provoking escalating conflict within particular nations and across the world system.

Seen through this lens, many seemingly national movements and conflicts (which may not qualify as "global" or "transnational" for the skeptics) are really responses to the effects of world system dynamics. Discussing protests in Greece, Spain, France, and the Middle East, Jackie Smith and Diane Wiest note that although "these protests focus largely on national government targets, the ultimate cause of their grievances lies in the policies of global and regional financial institutions, and thus in the long term the protests are likely to strengthen movements for changes in the larger world-system" (2012, 6).

If the crisis and the response of austerity have provided the grievances, the rise of a dense network of international bodies and organizations has provided new resources, networks, and opportunities for movement mobilization. While, as the skeptics have noted, most of these organizations are not movements themselves, they provide an institutional outlet for movement initiatives. Thus, since the founding of the United Nations, "antisystemic movements have been inextricably linked to global institutional process, not marginal to them" (Smith and Wiest 2012, 12). Close analysis of "observations of organizing patterns over recent decades suggests that the interactions between movement actors and global institutions have enhanced the capacities for transnational organizing and strengthened the antisystemic potential of movements" (Smith and Wiest 2012, 12).

The same global institutions that provide networks and opportunities can also pose the danger of co-optation. Antisystemic movements have thus also made a conscious effort to "focus on spaces defined by movements and largely autonomous from interstate politics and agendas" (Smith and Wiest 2012, 9) to prevent their issues from being absorbed or preempted by dominant group politics. At their most successful, they have deployed an insider/outsider strategy that provides them with real leverage and avoids the twin dangers of co-optation and marginalization.

Much of the leverage of antisystemic movements, in turn, derives from a reduced ability of states to rely on coercive power. In an ironic twist, neoliberal globalization itself has promoted a certain deterritorialization of sovereignty that "has weakened the role of force and coercion in world politics and strengthened the importance of a complex, emerging, and contested global moral order and an arena of civil world politics" (Chase-Dunn and Curran 2012, 483).

Alongside an (admittedly debatable) reduction in the coercive power of states, a growing discourse on human rights has given a new legitimacy to the normative claims of antisystemic movements. "The expansion and greater institutionalization of international human rights norms, as well as the articulation of enhanced understandings of the global environment as a commons whose survival depends on global cooperation, have undermined traditional bases of state authority" (Smith and Wiest 2012, 13).

Based on a conjunction of systemic crisis, enhanced movement capacities, reduced coercive state power, and the increasing power of normative claims, Smith and Wiest paint a relatively optimistic picture of the potential of antisystemic movements. They also suggest a middle ground in the "skeptics vs. systematizers debate" by acknowledging that many movements do not consciously frame their struggles in antisystemic or antiglobalization terms (as the skeptics have emphasized). Even so, the impact of their activism has often been to obstruct and challenge many of the policies of the top-down version of globalization that is the source of their grievances in the first place.

Mainstream ideology about globalization proclaims there is no alternative. These movements have, in fact, proposed several alternative principles for restructuring a globalizing world (Derber 2002; Starr 2000). Despite variations, they share one thing. Every vision of "globalization from below" calls for more participatory decision making than the reigning form of top-down, neoliberal globalization. Put somewhat differently, such movements are a major force for the democratization of globalization, and we will return to this theme in the next chapter.

Thus, the link between progressive politics and social movements examined earlier in this chapter is also evident on the global scene. If and when a more just, egalitarian form of globalization emerges, it will be largely owing to social movements challenging autocratic globalization.

What It Means to Be a Citizen

Choosing to be accountable *for the whole, creating a context of hospitality and collective possibility, acting to bring the gifts of those on the margin into the center— these are some of the ways we begin to create a community of citizens. To reclaim our citizenship is to be accountable, and this comes from the inversion of what is cause and what is effect. When we are open to thinking along the lines that citizens create leaders, that children create parents, and that the audience creates the performance, we create the conditions for widespread accountability and the commitment that emerges from it. This inversion may not be the whole truth, but it is useful.*

• • •

If what holds the possibility of an alternative future for our community is our capacity to fully come into being as a citizen, then we have to talk about this word *citizen*. Our definition here is that a citizen is one who is willing to be accountable for and committed to the well-being of the whole. That whole can be a city block, a community, a nation, the earth. A citizen is one who produces the future, someone who does not wait, beg, or dream for the future.

The antithesis of being a citizen is the choice to be a consumer or a client, an idea that John McKnight again has been so instructive about. Consumers give power away. They believe that their own needs can be best satisfied by the actions of others—whether those others are elected officials, top management, social service providers, or the shopping mall. Consumers also allow others to define their needs. If leaders and service providers are guilty of labeling or projecting onto others the "needs" to justify their own style of leadership or service that they provide, consumers collude with them by accepting others' definition of their needs. This provider-consumer transaction is the breeding ground for entitlement, and it is unfriendly to our definition of citizen and the power inherent in that definition.

THE MEANING OF CITIZENSHIP

The conventional definition of citizenship is concerned with the act of voting and taking a vow to uphold the constitution and laws of a country. This is narrow and limiting. Too many organizations that are committed to sustaining democracy in the world and at home have this constrained view of citizenship. Citizenship is not about voting, or even about having a vote. To construe the essence of citizenship primarily as the right to vote reduces its power—as if voting ensures a democracy. It is certainly a feature of democracy, but as Fareed Zakaria points out in his book *The Future of Freedom*, the right to vote does not guarantee a civil society, or in our terms a restorative one.

When we think of citizens as just voters, we reduce them to being consumers of elected officials and leaders. We see this most vividly at election time, when candidates become products, issues become the message, and the campaign is a marketing and distribution system for the selling of the candidate. Great campaign managers are great marketers and product managers. Voters become target markets, demographics, whose most important role is to meet in focus groups to respond to the nuances of message. This is the power of the consumer, which is no power at all.

Through this lens, we can understand why so many people do not vote. They do not believe their action can impact the future. It is partly a self-chosen stance and partly an expression of the helplessness that grows out of a retributive world. This way of thinking is not an excuse not to vote, but it does say that our work is to build the capacity of citizens to be accountable and to become creators of community.

• • •

We can see most clearly how we marginalize the real meaning of *citizen* when the word becomes politicized as part of the retributive debate. We argue over undocumented workers, immigration, and the rights of ex-felons—and even their children. We politicize the issue of English as the official language and building a new wall on the Rio Grande that we will have to tear down someday.

Citizenship as the willingness to build community gets displaced by isolationism in any form. It is not by accident that the loudest activists for finding and deporting undocumented workers are some of the leaders of the fear, oversight, safety, and security agenda. They are the key beneficiaries of the retributive society. If we want community, we have to be unwilling to allow citizenship to be co-opted in this way.

The idea of what it means to be a citizen is too important and needs to be taken back to its more profound value. Citizenship is a state of being. It is a choice for activism and care. A citizen is one who is willing to do the following:

- Hold oneself accountable for the well-being of the larger collective of which we are a part.

- Choose to own and exercise power rather than defer or delegate it to others.

- Enter into a collective possibility that gives hospitable and restorative community its own sense of being.

- Acknowledge that community grows out of the possibility of citizens. Community is built not by specialized expertise, or great leadership, or improved services; it is built by great citizens.

- Attend to the gifts and capacities of all others, and act to bring the gifts of those on the margin into the center.

THE INVERSION OF CAUSE

To create communities where citizens reclaim their power, we need to shift our beliefs about who is in charge and where power resides. We need to invert our thinking about what is cause and what is effect. This is what has the capacity to confront our entitlement and dependency.

Being powerful means that my experience, my discovery, even my pleasure are mine to create. This view has us see how audiences create performances, children create parents, students create teachers, and citizens create leaders.

The chicken is the egg's way of reproducing itself.

Peter Koestenbaum

It is not that this shift of cause is necessarily true, but it gives us power. In every case it puts choice into our own hands instead of having us wait for the transformation of others to give us the future we desire. If our intention is to create the possibility of an alternative future, then we need a future formed by our own hands. A handcrafted future.

Inverting our thinking does not change the world, but it creates a condition where the shift in the world becomes possible. The shift is the inversion in our thinking. The step from thinking of ourselves as effect to thinking of ourselves as cause is the act of inversion that creates a culture of citizen accountability. This is the point upon which accountability revolves.

A note: The cause-and-effect, Cartesian clockwork view of the world not only overstated the mechanical nature of the world, but it also put cause at the wrong end of the equation. Double indemnity.

This inversion challenges conventional wisdom that believes there is one right way. And by "inversion" I mean a real inversion: 180 degrees, not 179 degrees. This is not time for compromise or balance. Inverting our thinking about cause and effect gives support to really challenge "the way things work." This is not to say that this way of thinking is 100 percent accurate 100 percent of the time, but it can give added power to our way of being in community. The question to begin to reclaim our power as citizens is, "If you believed this to be true, in what ways would that make a difference, or change your actions?"

This means that the possibility of an alternative future centers on the question, "Have we chosen the present or has it been handed to us?" The default culture would have us believe that the past creates the future, that a change in individuals causes a change in organizations and community, and that people in authority create people in a subordinate position. That we are determined by everything aside from free will. That culture, history, genetics, organizations, and society drive our actions and our way of being.

All this is true, but the opposite is also true.

The shift toward citizenship is to take the stance that we are the creators of our world as well as the products of it. Free will trumps genetics, culture, and parental upbringing.

THE UTILITY OF THIS INVERSION

The first inversion I ran into years ago was the thought that the inmates run the prison. I was skeptical until I worked with some corrections people, who said there is truth in this. Here are some implications of switching our thinking this way:

Inversion: The audience creates the performance.

Implications: Redesign the audience experience. Stop putting so much energy in the talent and message of those on stage. Limit PowerPoint presentations to four slides. Peter Brook immersed the stage in the center of the audience; John Cage held concerts where the rumbling, coughing sounds of the audience *were the show.* When we meet, make it possible for the audience to be engaged with one another. Every auditorium, almost every church, almost every conference room and classroom would be redesigned. Chairs would be mobile; the audience would have sight of one another and know that no matter what occurred onstage, they would not be alone.

Inversion: The subordinate creates the boss.

Implications: Learning, development, and goal setting are in the hands of the subordinate. We would stop doing surveys about how people feel about their bosses, the results of which no one knows what to do with anyway. The attention would turn from the boss to peers, which is the relationship that produces the work.

Inversion: The child creates the parent.

Implications: Parents could sleep through the night. The conversation and industry of inculcating values and forcing consequences onto kids would quiet down. We would focus on the gifts, teachings, and blessings of the young instead of seeing them as problems to be managed. We would listen to them instead of instructing and teaching them again and again. This would allow parents to relax their jaws and index fingers, a secondary health benefit.

Inversion: The citizen creates its leaders.

Implications: Our dependency and disappointment about leaders would go down. The media would have to change their thinking about lead stories. What citizens are doing to improve their community would no longer be human-interest stories but actual news. The cost of elections would be reduced by 90 percent, for the question of whom we elect would be less critical. Candidates for elected office could be poor.

Above all, our leaders would be conveners, not role models and containers for our projections. More on this later.

Inversion: A room and a building are created by the way they are occupied.

Implications: We would be intentional about how we show up. We would spend time designing how we sit in the room, and not be mere consumers of the way the room was intended to be used, or dependent on what the custodians or last group using the room had in mind.

We would redesign the physical space around us—rooms, hallways, reception areas—in a way that affirmed community, so that it had a welcoming feeling and gave the sense that you had come to the right place. Most of all, what we inherited would be a serious subject of discussion.

Inversion: The student creates the teacher and the learning.

Implications: Education would be designed more for learning than for teaching. (This already occurs in many places under the heading of individualized learning. Montessori education has forever operated along these lines.) The social contract in the classroom would be renegotiated toward a partnership between teacher and student. Students would set goals for themselves and be responsible for the learning of other students. Simple ideas, powerful ideas, still rare in practice.

Inversion: Youth create adults.

Implications: Adultism would be confronted. Adults would decide to get interested in the experience of youth instead of always instructing them. When there were meetings and conferences about youth, the voices of youth would be central to the conversation. Youth would become a possibility, not a problem. If we really believed this, we would move our belief in the next generation from lip service to pervasive practice.

Inversion: The listening creates the speaker.

Implications: Listening would be considered an action step. For most of us, listening is just waiting until we get a chance to speak. There might even be a period of silence between statements, and this silence would be experienced as part of the conversation, not dead space. We would also learn what speaking into the listening of the room means. Once again, we would treat the listening as more important than the speaking.

You get the point—the list could go on. In each case, when we invert our thinking, the focus of attention and effort gets redirected.

The power in each of these shifts is that it confronts us with our own freedom. It is out of this freedom, which all of us have ways of escaping, that authentic accountability is born. I will be accountable for only that which I have had a hand in creating, my life and community included.

The inversion of cause refocuses my attention from that person in authority—leader, performer, parent, warden—to that person who together with others also holds the real power. Not to overdo this perspective, for leader, performer, parent, warden are critical partners in community; it's just that they are not the primary or sole proprietors we have construed them to be. We will never eliminate our need for great leaders and people on the stage; we just cannot afford to put all our experience and future in their hands.

• • •

There is no need to argue about this idea of inversion, only to play with its utility. It may not be true, but it is useful in the way it gives us power to evoke the kind of citizen we have defined as crucial to a true community.

Anyone who works in the civic arena has a certain cynicism about citizens. For example, they talk about how hard it is to get parents involved in their child's school. How few people show up at council and board meetings unless they are angry. How such a small number of people are really active in their community. There is truth to this view; it is not just cynicism, it is pretty accurate observation. What restores community is to believe that we play a role in constructing this condition. It is not in the nature of people to be apathetic, entitled, and complainers.

To state the issue simply, as long as we see leader as cause, we will produce passive, entitled citizens. We will put our attention, our training, and our resources wherever we think cause resides. When we see citizen as cause, then this will shift our attention and our wealth, and the energy and creativity that go with it.

This way of thinking takes back our projections and labeling of "others." Plus it counters the expectation that authority figures are essential and central—which not only disempowers students, citizens, audience, but also is a weight too heavy for leaders to carry.

This shift in thinking about cause and effect creates the conditions for a shift in context. The larger import in this line of thinking is that in each case, choice and destiny replace accident and fate. No small thing.

A WORD ABOUT ENTITLEMENT AND ACCOUNTABILITY

One cost of the retributive conversation is that it breeds entitlement. Entitlement is essentially the conversation, "What's in it for me?" It expresses a scarcity mentality, and the economist tells us that only what is scarce has value. Entitlement is the outcome of a patriarchal culture, which I have discussed too often in other books. But for this discussion, I'll simply say that if we create a context of fear, fault, and retribution, then we will focus on protecting ourselves, which plants the seed of entitlement.

The cost of entitlement is that it is an escape from accountability and soft on commitment. It gets in the way of authentic citizenship.

What is interesting is that the existing public conversation claims to be tough on accountability, but the language of accountability that occurs in a retributive context is code for "control." High-control systems are unbearably soft on accountability. They keep screaming for tighter controls, new laws, and bigger systems, but in the scream, they expose their weakness.

The weakness in the dominant view of accountability is that it thinks people can be *held* accountable. That we can force people to be accountable. Despite the fact that it sells easily, it is an illusion to believe that retribution, incentives, legislation, new standards, and tough consequences will cause accountability.

This illusion is what creates entitlement—and worse, it drives us apart; it does not bring us together. It turns neighbor against neighbor. It denies that we are our brother's keeper. Every colonial and autocratic regime rises to power by turning citizens against each other.

To see our conventional thinking about accountability at work, notice the conversations that dominate our meetings and gatherings. We spend time talking about people not in the room. If not that, our gatherings are designed to sell, change, persuade, and influence others, as if their change will help us reach our goals. These conversations do not produce power; they consume it.

ACCOUNTABILITY, COMMITMENT, AND THE USE OF FORCE

Commitment and accountability are forever paired, for they do not exist without each other. Accountability is the willingness to care for the well-being of the whole; commitment is the willingness to make a promise with no expectation of return.

The economist would say this smacks of altruism, and so be it. What community requires is a promise devoid of barter and not conditional on another's action. Without that, we are constantly in the position of reacting to the choices of others. Which means that our commitment is conditional. This is barter, not commitment.

The cost of constantly reacting to the choices of others is increased cynicism and helplessness. The ultimate cost of cynicism and helplessness is that we resort to the use of force. In this way the barter mentality that dominates our culture helps create a proliferation of force. Not necessarily violence, but the belief that for anything to change, we must mandate or use coercion.

The use of force is an end product of retribution, which rejects altruism and a promise made for its own sake. It rejects the idea that virtue is its own reward.

Commitment is the antithesis of entitlement and barter. Unconditional commitment with no thought to "What's in it for me?" is the emotional and relational essence of community. It is what some call integrity; others, "honoring your word."

Commitment is to choose a path for its own sake. This is the essence of power. Mother Teresa got this. When asked why she worked with people one at a time rather than caring more about having impact on a larger scale, she replied, "I was called by faith, not by results." If you want to argue with Mother Teresa, be my guest.

SUPPLEMENTARY QUESTIONS FOR ANALYSIS AND LECTURE DISCUSSION

What we do in our private lives has meaning and is deeply impactful to the larger community around us. Betty Friedan feminist activist and scholar that the personal was political. Our lives have meaning and we can make a difference in forging the seeds of transformation. Social change is inspired by individuals who dare to make a difference and form a collective activism that transform society. The Arab Spring, the Occupy Movement, the Women's march and protests, the Black Lives Matter Movement all were inspired by individuals that felt and urgency to impact change in their lives. These individuals created a movement that some argue has had a significant impact on the political realm. That being stated, what is the difference between a moment and a movement. When our consciousness is awakened and we begin to engage the public sphere, does this formulate the seeds of change and lay the foundation for transformation that ignites a moment of change or a social justice movement for political, social and economic transformation? Based on the readings in the last section of the text, Revolutionary Narratives – The Seeds of Change, provide an analysis on this section of reading. Think about two other related concepts from this last section of readings included in this anthology as you analyze the content. What does it mean to be a citizen in civil society and what is our responsibility to humanity in ensuring equity and justice for all?

CPSIA information can be obtained
at www.ICGtesting.com
Printed in the USA
FSHW022118050820
72728FS

RETIRING RIGHT

PLANNING FOR A SUCCESSFUL RETIREMENT

LAWRENCE J. KAPLAN

Avery Publishing Group
Garden City Park, New York

ABOUT THE AUTHOR

Lawrence J. Kaplan is an authority in the field of personal financial management and retirement planning. He received his M.A. and Ph.D. in economics from Columbia University. He has served as professor of Economics at John Jay College of the City University of New York for the past twenty years and has served as an officer of a Welfare Fund that administers the benefits programs for over 15,000 New York City employees.

Dr. Kaplan is the author of six books in the field of economics and personal finance. Following his own advice, he retired from teaching but continues to lecture extensively to groups, organizations, and colleges. Dr. Kaplan resides with his wife Jeanne in Manhasset, New York.

Cover Design: William Gonzalez and Rudy Shur
In-House Editor: Linda Comac
Typesetter: Bonnie Freid
Printer: Paragon Press, Honesdale, PA

Library of Congress Cataloging-in-Publication Data

Kaplan, Lawrence J.
    Retiring right : planning for your successful retirement / by
Lawrence J. Kaplan.
      p. cm.
    Includes bibliographical references and index.
    ISBN 0-89529-607-1 (pbk.)
    1. Retirement—United States—Planning. 2. Retirement income-
-United States—Planning. I. Title.
HQ1063.2.U6K37 1996
646.7'9—dc20   95-568
                                              CIP